POLITICAL
(IN)JUSTICE

PITT LATIN AMERICAN SERIES

George Reid Andrews, General Editor

Catherine M. Conaghan, Associate Editor

POLITICAL (IN)JUSTICE

AUTHORITARIANISM AND THE RULE OF LAW

IN BRAZIL, CHILE, AND ARGENTINA

Anthony W. Pereira

UNIVERSITY OF PITTSBURGH PRESS

Published by the University of Pittsburgh Press, Pittsburgh, Pa., 15260

Copyright © 2005, University of Pittsburgh Press

Manufactured in the United States of America

Printed on acid-free paper

10 9 8 7 6 5 4 3 2 1

Library of Congress Cataloging-in-Publication Data

Pereira, Anthony W.
  Political (in)justice : authoritarianism and the rule of law in Brazil, Chile, and
Argentina / Anthony W. Pereira.
      p. cm. — (Pitt Latin American series)
  Includes bibliographical references and index.
  ISBN 0-8229-5885-6 (pbk. : alk. paper)
  1. Rule of law—Brazil. 2. Authoritarianism—Brazil. 3. Rule of law—Chile.
4. Authoritarianism—Chile. 5. Rule of law—Argentina. 6. Authoritarianism—
Argentina. I. Title. II. Series.
  KH552.P47 2005
  340'.11—dc22
                              2005011120

To my daughter Bela and my son Bevan—

may you fight to make your world

a more just one than this.

Contents

List of Illustrations   ix

Acknowledgments   xi

Abbreviations   xv

Chapter 1: Repression, Legality, and Authoritarian Regimes   1

Chapter 2: National Security Legality in Brazil and
the Southern Cone in Comparative Perspective   16

Chapter 3: The Evolution of National Security Legality
in Brazil and the Southern Cone   37

Chapter 4: Political Trials in Brazil: The Continuation of
a Conservative Tradition   63

Chapter 5: "Wartime" Legality and Radical Adaptation in Chile   90

Chapter 6: Antilegalism in Argentina   117

Chapter 7: Defense Lawyers in Brazil's Military Courts:
Redefining Free Speech, Subversion, Terrorism, and Crime   140

Chapter 8: Transitional Justice and the Legacies of Authoritarian Legality   159

Chapter 9: The Sword and the Robe: Military-Judicial Relations
in Authoritarian and Democratic Regimes   173

Chapter 10: The Puzzle of Authoritarian Legality   191

Appendix 1: A Note on Sources and Data   201

Appendix 2: Interviews   204

Notes   209

Works Cited   237

Index   253

Illustrations

Figures

Figure 1.1: Variation in legal approaches to repression   5

Figure 9.1: Variation in legal approaches to repression: Argentina, Brazil, Chile, and other cases   176

Maps

Map 1: South America: Argentina, Brazil, Chile   17

Map 2: Location of political trials in military courts, Brazil 1964–1979   64

Map 3: Location of some of the most active military courts, Chile 1973–1978   91

Map 4: Argentina, 1971–1983   118

Tables

Table 2.1: Lethal violence by state forces and other indices of political repression in Argentina, Brazil, and Chile, 1964–1990   21

Table 2.2: Features of authoritarian legality in Brazil, Chile, and Argentina   23

Table 2.3: Comparison of courts analyzed in this book   24

Table 4.1: Acquittal rates in national security trials in regional military courts by location of court, Brazil, 1964–1979   79

Table 4.2: Average sentences in national security trials in regional military courts by location of court, Brazil, 1964–1979   80

Table 4.3: Acquittal rates in national security trials in regional military courts by year of alleged crime, Brazil, 1964–1979   81

Table 4.4: Acquittal rates in national security trials in regional military courts by professional background of defendant, Brazil, 1964–1979   83

Table 4.5: Acquittal rates in national security trials in regional military
courts by charge, Brazil, 1964–1979   84

Table 4.6: Sentences of those convicted in national security trials in
regional military courts, Brazil, 1964–1979   85

Table 5.1: Acquittal rates in national security trials in regional military
courts by location of court, Chile, 1973–1978   109

Table 5.2: Sentences of those convicted in national security trials in
regional military courts, Chile, 1973–1978   112

Table 8.1: A comparison of outcomes in transitional justice: Argentina,
Chile, and Brazil   160

Acknowledgments

This book began as a small part of a doctoral dissertation, defended in 1991 in the Government Department at Harvard University, with the title *Regime Change without Democratization: Sugar Workers' Unions in Pernambuco, Northeast Brazil, 1961–1989*. In chapter 5 of that dissertation, I attempted to assess the impact of political repression on rural trade unions under Brazil's military regime and to understand how trade unionists were prosecuted for crimes against national security in military courts for activities, such as leading strikes and demonstrations, that had been perfectly legal at the time they were conducted. This chapter was left out of the subsequent book based on my dissertation, *The End of the Peasantry: The Emergence of the Rural Labor Movement in Northeast Brazil, 1961–1988* (University of Pittsburgh Press, 1997), mainly because I felt that the issue deserved more extensive treatment in a separate research project.

As that research project developed, I discovered that political trials of the kind that went on in military courts under Brazil's authoritarian regime of 1964–1985 occurred throughout the southern cone in the 1970s, as repressive military regimes attempted to purge society of "subversion" and to reshape social and political attitudes one defendant at a time. However, I soon realized that the procedures in these trials, the relationship of the trials to the repressive apparatus, and each regime's effort to legalize repression varied dramatically across countries. My research led me to try to explain this variation and to look at two military regimes whose legal approach to repression differed substantially from the Brazilian: those of Chile (1973–1990) and Argentina (1976–1983). I concluded that a historical-institutional analysis of the relations between specific organizations within the state, especially the military and the judiciary, best explained the different outcomes observed.

My journey has been a very long one. The making of this book stretched over such an extended period that it would be impossible to thank everyone who helped along the way. However, since the contributions of so many people were important, I will try my best to acknowledge as many of them as possible here. As is usual in such acknowledgments, I free all who are mentioned from any responsibility for errors of fact or judgment that may exist in the work.

First, I thank my mother and father, Mavis and Herbert Perry, for their unstinting interest in and encouragement of this and my other projects over the years. My sister, Lynne Perry, contributed her talent as a graphic artist to produce the maps for this book and the sketch for the cover. She also passed on to me her enthusiasm for and knowledge of the Brazilian playwright and theatrical provocateur Augusto Boal. My brother, Michael Perry, was a constant source of encouragement, sound advice, loony diversions, and paraphernalia from London's West Ham United football club.

The institutions where I worked while researching and writing this book have certainly shaped its contents. The Graduate Faculty of New School University, where I spent most of the 1990s, provided me with an exciting environment in which to learn the crafts of academic teaching, advising, and writing. I was lucky enough to learn from superb practitioners of those crafts such as Andrew Arato, Diane Davis (now at the Massachusetts Institute of Technology), and Charles Tilly (now at Columbia University).

At the Fletcher School of Law and Diplomacy at Tufts University, I was helped immeasurably by professors such as Eileen Babbit, Sugata Bose (now at Harvard), Andrew Hess, Laurent Jacques, William Moomaw, Jeswald Salacuse, Richard Schultz, Scott Thompson, and Paul Vaaler, as well as skillful administrators such as Deborah Nutter and then dean John Galvin.

My current institution, Tulane University, has provided me with a host of opportunities for exploring interesting and important research questions. The Political Science Department and the Stone Center for Latin American Studies constitute an ideal mixture of colleagues with knowledge of the theories, methods, and substantive debates of my discipline and area-studies specialists who have studied in almost every region of every country in Latin America and the Caribbean. This happy marriage between political science and area studies is a rarity on U.S. college campuses, where bitter divorce between the two fields is far more common.

I owe enormous debts of gratitude not only to the institutions that provided the infrastructural support for this project, but also to my funders. The Fulbright Commission awarded a grant in 1994–1995 that allowed me to return to the archives that had been the primary source of chapter 5 of my dissertation so many years ago, the Nunca Mais archives at the São Paulo State University in

Campinas (UNICAMP), Brazil. I subsequently received much-appreciated financial assistance from the Albert Einstein Institution, the John D. and Catherine T. MacArthur Foundation, the Fletcher School of Law and Diplomacy, the Roger Thayer Stone Center for Latin American Studies, and my own Political Science Department at Tulane University. In the summer of 2003, Harvard University's David Rockefeller Center for Latin American Studies awarded me a library fellowship that was invaluable in finishing this book, while the Weatherhead Center for International Affairs gave me the use of an office. Jorge Domínguez also organized a seminar where a summary of this book was commented on and questioned.

For reading and commenting on early versions of parts of the work presented here, I thank Andrew Arato, Amy Chazkel, Oliver Dinius, Sarah Dix, Jonathan Hartlyn, Magda Hinojosa, Mala Htun, Roger Karapin, Peter Kingstone, Steve Levitsky, Paul Lewis, Nancy Maveety, Diego Miranda, Pablo Policzer, Timothy Powers, Cathy Schneider, Miguel Schor, Kenneth Serbin, Hillel Soifer, Charles Tilly and the members of his proseminar at the Graduate Faculty of New School University, and anonymous reviewers of *Latin American Research Review*, *Comparative Political Studies*, and *The Luso-Brazilian Review*. Nathan MacBrien of the University of Pittsburgh Press was a thoughtful and perceptive editorial mentor of the project, and the two anonymous reviewers who read the manuscript in its entirety were enormously conscientious, knowledgeable, and gently skeptical with their comments. Leonardo Avritzer provided excellent feedback on parts of the manuscript, as did Lisa Hilbink and Mark Ungar. Brian Loveman generously shared his abundant knowledge of Latin American military justice systems with me. My graduate students Corinne Boudreaux, Blaz Gutierrez, Charles Heath, Krystin Krause, Amisha Sharma, Trevor Top, Leigh Tudor, and Nomi Weiss-Laxer made perceptive critiques of a draft of chapter 7. In addition, Diane Davis, Jorge Domínguez, and Frances Hagopian provided me with valuable support and advice many times during the writing of this book.

In Brazil, I was helped by Sergio Adorno, Lucia Avelar, David Fleischer, Marco Aurelio Garcia, Terry Groth and Loussia Mousse Felix, Michael Hall and Marilena Chaui, Beatriz Kushner, João Roberto Martins Filho, Lúcio Oliveira, Paulo Sergio Pinheiro, Marcelo Ridenti, Marco Aurélio Vannucchi Leme de Mattos, and many others. My various collaborations with my friend and colleague Jorge Zaverucha have also given me valuable insights into Brazilian politics that have influenced the writing of this book.

Carlos Acuña, Robert Barros, Catalina Smulovitz, Enrique Peruzotti,

Isodoro Cheretsky, Victoria Murillo, and José Maria Ghio were helpful in Argentina. In Chile, Alexander Wilde and Louis Bickford, then both at the Ford Foundation, were generous guides to my research. Elizabeth Lira was a valuable interlocutor, and Lucia Valenzuela served as a guide to the archive of the Vicaría de la Solidaridad. I should also mention those who helped me conduct initial research in Uruguay, a wonderful country that I was ultimately unable to include as a case in this book: Danny and Tina Schoorl, Ellen Lutz, Congressman Felipe Michelini, Colonel Dr. Daniel Artecona, Dr. Ricardo C. Pérez Manrique, Dr. Germán Amondarain, and Jonas Bergstein. The students where I have taught over the years have helped me immeasurably, but my able and industrious research assistants deserve a special mention: Anne Dirsa and Irma León at Harvard University, Colin Naughton and Eva Parker at New School University, Lauro Locks and Juan Velez at the Fletcher School of Law and Diplomacy, and Heather Goodell, Krystin Krause, Stephanie Macik, Astrid Reim, and Steve Sloan at Tulane University.

To my wife, Rita, I give thanks for her gentle love, stoic patience, rock-solid support, and hopeful encouragement. To our two little "Bs", Bela and Bevan, who have interrupted the writing of this book by demanding trips to the park, soccer games, snacks, videos, and a host of other very welcome distractions, I offer an eternal hug and kiss. *Eu te amo.*

Abbreviations

AI-1, -2, -5	Ato Institucional 1, 2, 5	First, Second, and Fifth Institutional Acts (Brazil)
ALN	Ação Libertadora Nacional	National Liberationist Action (Brazil)
APDH	Asamblea Permanente por los Derechos Humanos	Permanent Assembly for Human Rights (Argentina)
ARENA	Aliança Renovadora Nacional	National Alliance for Renewal (Brazil)
BNM	Brasil: Nunca Mais	Brazil: Never Again
CBAs	Comitês Brasileiros pela Anistia	Brazilian Amnesty Committees
CELS	Centro de Estudios Legales y Sociales	Center for Legal and Social Studies (Argentina)
CJM	Circunscrição Judiciária Militar	Military Court District (Brazil)
CJP	Comissão de Justiça e Paz	Justice and Peace Commission (Brazil)
CNBB	Conferência Nacional dos Bispos do Brasil	National Conference of Brazilian Bishops
CODI	Comando Operacional de Defesa Interna	Operational Command for Internal Defense (Brazil)
CONADEP	Comisión Nacional sobre la Desaparición de Personas	National Commission on the Disappearance of Persons (Argentina)
DEOPS	Departamento Estadual de Ordem Político e Social	state political police (Brazil)
DGS	Direção Geral de Segurança	General Directorate of Security (Portugal)
DINA	Dirección de Inteligencia Nacional	National Intelligence Directorate (Chile)
DOI	Departamento de Operações Internas	Department of Internal Operations (Brazil)
DOPS	Departamento de Ordem Político e Social	political police (Brazil)
ERP	Ejército Revolucionário del Pueblo	Revolutionary People's Army (Argentina)
ESG	Escola Superior de Guerra	Superior War College (Brazil)
ESMA	Escuela Superior de Mecánica de la Armada	Navy Mechanics School (Argentina)

FEB	Força Expedicionária Brasileira	Brazilian Expeditonary Force
IACHR		Inter-American Commission on Human Rights
IPES	Instituto de Pesquisa e Estudos Sociais	Institute of Research and Social Studies (Brazil)
IPM	Inquérito Policial-Militar	Police-Military Inquiry (Brazil)
LADH	Liga Argentina por los Derechos del Hombre	Argentine League for the Rights of Man
MDB	Movimento Democrático Brasileiro	Brazilian Democratic Movement
MIR	Movimiento de Izquierda Revolucionario	Movement of the Revolutionary Left (Chile)
OAB	Ordem dos Advogados do Brasil	Brazilian Bar Association
OKW	Oberkommando der Wehrmacht	Armed Forces High Command (Germany)
PCB	Partido Comunista Brasileiro	Brazilian Communist Party
PCBR	Partido Comunista Brasileiro Revolucionário	Brazilian Revolutionary Communist Party
PDS	Partido Democrático Social	Democratic Social Party (Brazil)
PEN	Poder Ejecutivo Nacional	National Executive Power (Argentina)
PIDE	Policia Internacional de Defesa do Estado	International Police for the Defense of the State (Portugal)
PRT	Partido Revolucionário dos Trabalhadores	Revolutionary Workers' Party (Brazil)
PT	Partido dos Trabalhadores	Workers' Party (Brazil)
PTB	Partido Trabalhista Brasileiro	Brazilian Labor Party
PVDE	Policia de Defesa Política e Social	Police for Political and Social Defense (Portugal)
SERPAJ	Servicio Paz y Justicia	Peace and Justice Service (Argentina)
SNI	Serviço Nacional de Inteligência	National Intelligence Service (Brazil)
STF	Supremo Tribunal Federal	Federal Supreme Court (Brazil)
STM	Superior Tribunal Militar	Superior Military Court (Brazil)
TCPs	Tribunais Criminais Plenários	Plenary Criminal Courts (Portugal)
Triple A	Alianza Anticommunista Argentina	Anticommunist Alliance of Argentina
TSN	Tribunal de Segurança Nacional	National Security Court (Brazil)
UDN	União Democrático Nacional	National Democratic Union (Brazil)
UP	Unidad Popular	Popular Unity (Chile)
VGH	Volksgerichtshof	People's Court (Germany)
WVHA	Wirtschafts und Verwaltungshauptant	Economic and Administrative Main Office (of the SS) (Germany)

POLITICAL
(IN)JUSTICE

1

Repression, Legality, and Authoritarian Regimes

ON APRIL 5, 1971, Vinicius Oliveira Brandt sat in a military court in São Paulo to testify on his own behalf.[1] Oliveira Brandt, a young sociology student, was charged with membership in an illegal organization, the Revolutionary Workers' Party (Partido Revolucionário dos Trabalhadores, or PRT), and of organizing the armed robbery of a supermarket. Oliveira Brandt told the court that he had been arrested in São Paulo on September 30 of 1970 and immediately taken to a military-police intelligence facility (known as Departamento de Operações Internas, Department of Internal Operations or DOI). There he was stripped, placed naked on a *pau de arara* (parrot's perch, a beam from which the victim was hung upside down), beaten and given electric shocks. Brandt testified that "the shocks were applied all over the body, especially the genital organs, ears, and mouth," and that after this he was taken down from the parrot's perch and seated in what his torturers called the "dragons' throne," where he was again given electric shocks. His torturers also burned him with cigarettes and lit paper. This first torture session lasted from 7:30 at night until 10:00 the next morning. After a one-hour break another torture session started and lasted all afternoon. At one point, according to Oliveira Brandt, he was threatened with death.

On September 30, 1971, the military court convicted Oliveira Brandt and sentenced him to five years in prison. The court, consisting of one civilian judge trained in the law, plus four active-duty military officers without legal training who served on the bench for three months, gave the defendant the maximum sentence and deprived him of his political rights for ten years.[2] The evidence against him was practically nonexistent. In the twenty-six-page court decision (signed by all the judges), the civilian judge wrote that Oliveira Brandt was "highly dangerous" and a "political delinquent." The judge proclaimed that "the trial proceeded with all the guarantees of humane and democratic laws" while the defendant had made "a profession of faith of a true political delinquent, at the service of international communism."[3] The judge suggested that the defendant was paranoid, sick, and perverse, and had made up his allegations of torture. He also did not explicitly acknowledge a telegram demanding humane treatment and judicial guarantees for Oliveira Brandt from a group of French professors including Roland Barthes, Roger Bastide, Pierre Bourdieu, Michel Foucault, Claude Lefort, Emmanuel Le Roy Ladurie, Serge Moscovici, Nicos Poulantzas, and Alain Touraine. Oliveira Brandt had studied in Paris at the Sorbonne, and because his detention was public knowledge, professors at his former institution had tried to come to his aid.[4]

Oliveira Brandt's lawyer, Idebal Piveta, immediately appealed the verdict. Over a year later, on October 27, 1972, the Superior Military Court (Superior Tribunal Militar, or STM), the appeals court in the military justice system made up of ten active-duty, senior military officers and five civilians, ruled on Oliveira Brandt's appeal. It upheld Oliveira Brandt's conviction but lowered his sentence from five to three years. Defense lawyer Piveta then made yet another appeal, this time as far as it could go—to the civilian Supreme Court, made up of eleven civilian judges. On March 26, 1974, the Supreme Court upheld Oliveira Brandt's conviction. The decision contains a detailed discussion of the defendant's Marxist political views, but no discussion of the charge that he was a member of the PRT nor the lack of evidence for that charge. There was also no discussion of his allegations of torture. Oliveira Brandt was eventually released from prison after serving his three-year term, and he later became a university professor in his home state of Minas Gerais.

Oliveira Brandt's case is representative of a particular type of authoritarian legality. However, the authoritarian legalities of other military regimes in Latin America were often quite different from that of Brazil. While Oliveira Brandt was serving time in prison, political "criminals" were also being prosecuted on the other side of the Andes in Chile. On September 19, 1973, eight days after the start of a military coup that toppled the government of Salvador Allende, seven military officers serving temporarily on a "wartime" military court (*consejo de guerra*) in Antofagasta, northern Chile, issued a sentence in the case of Jorge Bolaños and Carlos Perez. Bolaños and Perez, members of the Socialist Party, were accused of fabricating and distributing homemade grenades, engaging in "subversive indoctrination" of others, trying to infiltrate the police and armed forces, and hiding a cache of weapons. The military court considered the defendants to be "highly dangerous to the security of the armed forces and police, public order, and social peace, due to their intellectual condition and level of cultural preparation," and declared that Bolaños and Perez constituted "a permanent risk to human lives that is necessary to impede at whatever cost" (Arzobispado de Santiago 1989–1991, 1990, Tomo 2, Vol. 1, Rol 347–73, 98–100). The court proceedings were not public, and no French professors sent a telegram on behalf of Bolaños and Perez. The judges sentenced the defendants to death.[5]

Lawyers who later analyzed Bolaños and Perez's case argued that because the alleged crimes had been committed before the military coup and the declaration of a state of siege, the military court was retroactively imposing a wartime penalty on peacetime crimes, violating the 1925 constitution. This did not matter to the military commander of the region, who had the defendants executed by firing squad the next day, in the early morning of September 20, 1973.

Less than three years later, a different kind of execution took place in the River Plate region of South America. Monica Mignone was a twenty-four-year-old medical student in Buenos Aires, Argentina, in May 1976.[6] A military coup d'etat had occurred on March 24 of that year, and the new military junta was carrying out severe political repression. Monica's father, Emilio, was an educator and longtime Peronist activist, and Monica, who lived with her parents, donated some of her limited spare time to a clinic for the poor in one of Buenos Aires' less privileged neighborhoods. Perhaps this alone was what displeased members of the security forces, or perhaps she was apprehended because she was a young and attractive woman. Whatever their motives, plainclothes security agents kidnapped Monica in her home at 5:00 a.m. on the morning of May 14, 1976, and she was never seen again.[7]

The cases of Vinicius Oliveira Brandt, Jorge Bolaños and Carlos Perez, and Monica Mignone are broadly representative of three very different ways of institutionalizing political repression under military rule. The first represents the greatest degree of civilian-military cooperation, the slowest and most public proceedings, and the widest latitude for defendants and their supporters in civil society to maneuver within the system. The Brazilian military regime used peacetime military courts to prosecute political dissidents and opponents without ever suspending the constitution. Torture was widespread but disappearances were rare, and trials in military courts involved civilian participation on the bench and at the bar and left some room for the defense of the accused. Courts issued death sentences in only four instances, and these were never carried out because they were reversed on appeal. In the case of Oliveira Brandt, a suspected member of a revolutionary organization was tortured and then tried in a military court, and his lawyer appealed the case all the way to the civilian Supreme Court, as was possible during the entire period of military rule in Brazil. Lacking evidence, the military court still sentenced the defendant to five years in prison, in part because of his declaration of his oppositional political ideas. In the appeals process, which took almost three years, the conviction was upheld, but the sentence was reduced.

The second case represents a highly autonomous and punitive military court system. The Chilean military regime, created nine years after its Brazilian counterpart, was draconian in comparison to Brazil. The Chilean military suspended the constitution, declared a state of siege, and executed hundreds of people without trial. Torture was common, and most prosecutions that did take place occurred in "wartime" military courts, insulated from the civilian judiciary, for the first five years of the regime. The defendants faced rapid verdicts and sentences, including the death penalty. In the case of Bolaños and Perez, a military court hastily sentenced and executed two political activists whose alleged crimes were not subject to the death penalty at the time they were committed. The defendants had few procedural rights and no effective right of appeal. The Chilean Supreme Court refused to review any military court verdicts, including this one.

The third case was part of a "dirty war."[8] The Argentine institutional matrix, instituted three years after the Chilean coup, was the most drastic of all. In it, courts were largely uninvolved in the repressive system, except to deny writs of habeas corpus and serve as a cover for state terror.[9] Security personnel instead picked up a defenseless person at her home, took her to a secret detention center, interrogated and tortured her, and then "disappeared" her without explanation or record, part of a repressive strategy that had become almost entirely extrajudicial. The ability of victims to maneuver within such a system was very small, and family members were not even given the consolation of the right to grieve over the body of the victim. In institutional terms, the Argentine regime was the most innovative and the most daring of all three military dictatorships. It was the only one of the three that accomplished the rare political feat of creating something truly new.[10]

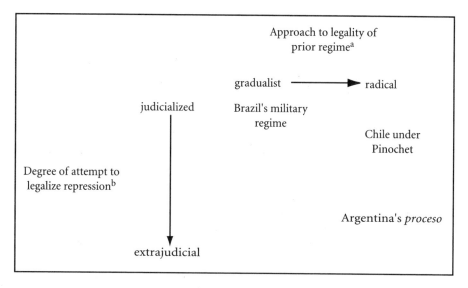

Figure 1.1: Variation in legal approaches to repression

[a]Measured by the ratio of the number of political prisoners prosecuted by the courts to the number killed extrajudicially.

[b]Based on a qualitative assessment of the degree to which the legal system under military rule was different from the legal system prior to military rule, as seen in constitutional changes, institutional acts, decrees, and laws issued by military rulers.

Although all of the regimes that created these institutional complexes were broadly similar, their legal strategies vis-à-vis opponents and dissidents were markedly different. Figure 1.1 highlights two aspects of this difference. The regimes varied in the degree to which their authoritarian legality broke with preauthoritarian legal forms, as well as in the extent to which the treatment of political prisoners was regulated by law (what I call the judicialization of repression).

Authoritarian Legality

To date, few studies of authoritarian regimes have focused on their application of the law.[11] Most studies of authoritarianism assume that regimes that come to power by force cannot rely on the law to maintain control of society or to legitimize themselves; their unconstitutional origins are seen as making such an effort contradictory and impossible. A recent survey of authoritarian regimes in the twentieth century, for example, devotes no attention to legal manipulation, political trials, or the relationship of repression to the legal system; indeed, it does not even list "law" in its index![12] Yet a cursory glance at actual authoritarian regimes should lead to a questioning of this lacuna and the assumption that seems to underlie it. In fact, authoritarian regimes use the law and courts to bolster their rule all the time, in ways that a simplistic distinction between de facto and constitutional (or de jure) regimes obscures. In particular, many regimes resort to trials of their political opponents and the legal foundations and procedures of these trials vary enormously. In 1975, the political scientist Juan Linz wrote, "Unfortunately, we have no comparative analysis of political trials under different types of political system to capture the different styles of the proceedings . . ." (224). His complaint is still valid today.

There are several reasons to care about political trials and differences between types of authoritarian legality. First, the decision to use trials and not sheer force in dealing with regime opponents can—under certain circumstances—make a difference to the overall pattern of repression by an authoritarian regime. In the words of Otto Kirchheimer, political trials can be a "saving grace" of repression that, due to the "very character and procedural hurdles of the judicial system, together with the limits to the powerholders' ability to exercise total control by informal devices, often make the actual administration of a policy of repression fall short of the original blueprint" (1961, 422).[13] When rulers of a state are concerned about legal procedures—even when they manipulate those procedures in their own interest—defense lawyers then may have opportunities to monitor the safety of their clients, and this can save lives (see Shklar 1964, 1–2). Admittedly, trials sometimes lead to executions, as the case of Bolaños and Perez in Chile in 1973 makes clear. Nevertheless, they require adherence to formal procedures that can sometimes mitigate the worst effects of repression.

A second reason for studying political trials and the legal strategies and politics surrounding them is for the insights into authoritarian regimes that this study can produce. Despite the initial tendency to see the military regimes of Brazil and the southern cone as part of a single category of "bureaucratic authoritarian" regime,[14] considerable scholarly effort has been made in recent years to analyze the significant differences between them. For example, Schamis (1991) and Remmer (1989) have shown the important differences in economic policy among these regimes. Linz and Stepan (1996) have argued that variations in five different aspects of authoritarian regimes influence the nature of their subsequent transitions to democratic rule. Similarly, Arceneaux (2001) claims that institutional differences within the military regimes of Brazil and the southern cone influenced each regime's control over the transition, and hence the nature of post-transition democracies. And Feitlowitz shows how the most recent of Argentina's military regimes used rhetoric that drew on the language of Argentine ultraconservative movements and previous regimes (1998, esp. chap. 1). Numerous other studies have provided similar insights, slowly unpacking a generic "bureaucratic-authoritarian" regime type into a more nuanced array of subtypes.

Studying national security legality and political trials can contribute to this effort. Each regime examined here struggled with the legality of its repression and attempted to "frame" at least part of that repression with a scaffolding of laws and legal procedures. Using courts to try political opponents was an effort to gain greater legitimacy but one purchased at the cost of a certain loss of control over the outcome of individual trials. Analyzing how each regime managed this trade-off provides an important insight into its politics and in particular the historical conflict that each was trying to recast or overcome. Political trials record the struggle of the regime to maintain its dominance at a practical and symbolic level; to articulate its core values; and to refute the beliefs of perceived opponents, ranging from those who had risked their lives to take up arms against the established order to others who made apparently innocuous statements construed by someone as subversive. Examining a regime's alleged enemies and how it treated them can therefore reveal much about the motives and aspirations of the regime's leaders.[15]

The third reason for studying authoritarian legality and political trials is that they allow us to construct a more detailed picture of exactly how the law was manipulated, distorted, and abused—or maintained unchanged—under authoritarianism. Such a project is important in an era in which the lack of a strong rule of law in many new democracies is widely recognized as a serious problem (e.g., Holston and Caldeira 1998; Prillaman 2000; Ungar 2002; Linz and Stepan 1996; Méndez, O'Donnell, and Pinheiro 1999; O'Donnell 1999). Furthermore, the distinction between authoritarian and "semi-authoritarian" or "illiberally democratic" regimes also usually hinges on the functioning (or malfunctioning) of the rule of law (see, e.g., Zakaria 1997, 2003, esp. chap. 3; Ottaway 2003). Some scholars also argue that states of emergency or exception are becoming more and more common in established democracies, blurring the distinction between authoritarian and democratic regimes.[16]

An important insight to be gained by examining political trials in Brazil and the southern cone is that none of these regimes was able to completely re-cast the law to fit its perceived national security interests. Judges in the political trials struggled to reconcile newer national security conceptions of law with older liberal notions, and sometimes—surprisingly—upheld the latter at the expense of the former, at least in Brazil.[17]

Just as there was much legal continuity from democracy to authoritarian-ism, however, the transitions to democracy in the 1980s did not entirely dis-mantle the repressive legal apparatus that had been constructed under military rule. For example, the verdicts of the political trials in Brazil and Chile were never repudiated by the state, even after the transitions to democracy. Some of the laws on which the trials were based—and the institutions that prosecuted and tried political defendants—still exist. Looking at the trials helps us to un-derstand exactly what has and has not changed in the legal sphere as a result of democratization in Brazil and the southern cone, and to identify those vestiges of authoritarian legality that still exist there.

Finally, the historical record allows us to give voice to actors whose pas-sions, convictions, and deeds have been largely forgotten in the post–Cold War world.[18] It might well be thought that political trials in Brazil and the southern cone involved only hardened revolutionaries on one side, and committed de-fenders of the national security state on the other. Yet most of the defendants in the political trials of Brazil and the southern cone were not prosecuted for armed actions against the government. Far more frequently, they were charged with crimes of association or opinion, and their views about the regime and its opposition were often considerably more complex, ambiguous, and varied than might be supposed. Similarly, prosecutors and judges in the military courts some-times disagreed with hard-line interpretations of the national security laws and conceded to defense lawyers' arguments that their clients had a right to disagree with the official pronouncements of military rulers.[19] Indeed, hard-liners in these regimes sometimes distrusted members of the judiciary as much as they did the "subversives" that they were fighting.

Political trials and the framework of authoritarian legality in which they were conducted in Brazil and the southern cone thus deserve the attention of social scientists not just because ample documentation about them exists, but because they can help us answer important questions about the politics of au-thoritarian rule, the relationship between law and repression, the role of political trials in authoritarianism, and the views and actions of specific historical actors.

The Argument

The military regimes of Brazil, Chile, and Argentina are good candidates for comparison. They were founded in opposition to left-populist movements that had much in common and they were strongly connected by historical epoch, geographic proximity, common external influences, and roughly equivalent internal dynamics. The three cases are also comparable in terms of level of economic development, position in the global economic system, and cultural traditions of authoritarian rule. They thus allow for structured, focused narratives that control for several factors and explore particular explanations of the differing authoritarian legalities of the regimes.[20]

It might be thought that the regimes' various legal strategies can be accounted for simply by the strength of the opposition faced by each. The Brazilian coup was preemptive and the military's opposition very weak; the Chilean coup was a "rollback" coup,[21] but armed opposition to the military regime was relatively insignificant; and the Argentine regime faced what was probably the strongest armed left in Latin America at that time.[22] However, the scope and intensity of regime repression should not be confused with its form. The strength of the opposition does not account for the distinctive institutional matrix of each regime or the different organizational arrangements for dealing with subversion in each case.[23] Why did the Argentine military regime not prosecute more suspected guerrillas in military courts? Why were so few members of the Brazilian armed left disappeared? Why were Chile's military court trials so insulated from the civilian judiciary? These questions are important, because the institutional form of authoritarian repression can influence its breadth and intensity and, in particular, how open it is to resistance, challenge, and modification by victims and their supporters. Furthermore, the institutional form of repression may influence in important ways the attempts of a new government to engage in transitional justice.

This book advances a different argument to unlock the puzzle of legal variation in Brazil and the southern cone. It argues that to answer the questions above, one must study the timing and sequence of institutional changes in the realm of political repression. The key lies primarily in history, or more specifically, the cumulative influence of previous political decisions about institutions.

I argue that the variation can be explained primarily by the differing degrees of integration and consensus between judicial and military elites prior to those regimes, as well as the interaction between the legal system, defense lawyers, and civil society groups. Judicial and military elites constitute corporate status groups, each with its own powerful organization within the state apparatus, and these status groups strongly influence the development and application of law under authoritarian regimes.[24] Consensus is defined here as substantial elite agreement about the overall design, goals, and tactics of policy (Melanson 1991, 1–12). Key factors in the formation of consensus between the groups are the organizational contours of the military justice system, the extent to which the dominant military factions and their supporters perceive themselves to be threatened, the history of relations between military officers and the judiciary, and the degree of conflict between these groups over interpretations of national security law. My contention is that this kind of integration and consensus was highest in Brazil and lowest in Argentine, with Chile occupying a middle position.[25] My argument is historical, because I argue that political and social conditions in place before the formation of each political regime were important in shaping subsequent decisions by regime leaders. While policies that shaped the legal system under military rule were all put in place after military coups, conditions prior to the coups were important in shaping attitudes among and relations between judicial and civilian elites. The policy decisions that occurred after regime change were important because they formed systems that endured for a relatively long period of time. It is striking that once established, the basic legal orientation of the military regimes examined here did not fundamentally change during the course of their rule.

It might be objected that it is difficult to measure judicial-military integration and consensus independently of the variable they are supposed to explain —the legal strategy adopted by the military regime. It is difficult, but not impossible. In this book, I have used two indicators to gauge the degree of consensus and integration between military officers and judicial elites. First, the organization of the military justice system is a key variable. The degree of formal connection between military and judicial elites in the application of national security law matters. Where military courts are part of the civilian justice system, with the participation of civilian judges and prosecutors, as in Brazil, military and judicial elites are compelled, through their common participation in the same hybrid system, to construct and maintain a cross-organizational understanding of the concrete meaning and applicability of national security law. Where military courts at the first level are completely separate from civilian justice, as in Chile, the military can more easily act upon its own view of political justice, without regard for the ideas of civilian judges and lawyers. This variable can be discerned in the formal architecture of the military justice system, but its significance goes beyond the architecture itself and affects the attitudes, dispositions, and mutual understandings of military and judicial elites.

Consensus is harder to measure. Consensus refers to the extent of agreement across status groups about key national security ideas and how to apply them. To gauge consensus, I have examined the opinions of both civilian legal experts and military officers on national security legality, political trials, and the regime's treatment of opponents. These views can be found in newspapers, memoirs, academic studies, legal decisions, and specialized journals dealing with the military, the law, and military justice. This is a qualitative judgment, but consensus between military officers and civilian judicial elites can be inferred to be high, medium, or low, depending on the harmony between the military and civilian views expressed in these sources. I have coded Brazilian sources as reflecting a high degree of consensus, Chilean sources as indicating medium consensus, and Argentina as low consensus. The sources used for these judgments are referred to in the narrative that follows and are described in the appendix and references at the end of the book.

Consensus between and integration of military and civilian elites on national security issues does not imply "hegemony" or some other term connoting consensus beyond these elite groups. Many views of the political trials and national security legislation prevailed in all three of the countries analyzed here and can be found in the historical record. Defendants in the political trials certainly held their own views, and when they indicated that they accepted the legitimacy of the courts and the national security legality under which they were being prosecuted, this was usually done for tactical reasons and was unlikely to have been completely heartfelt. Evidence also suggests that defense lawyers who exalted the legitimacy of military courts during trials publicly questioned them and the national security legality they enforced in other venues.

Some scholars might prefer the more inclusive term "legal culture" to my terms consensus and integration. However, legal culture connotes many aspects of the judicial sphere that I do not cover in this book; therefore, I prefer to focus on institutions in the sense used by Douglass North, as the formal and informal rules regulating behavior, including both consciously created rules and those that evolve gradually over time (1990, 4). These rules include the internal rules of organizations such as the military and judiciary.

While I examine the Brazilian, Chilean, and Argentine cases along similar dimensions, I should mention three limitations of this study. First, when I examine the regimes' legal strategies, I concentrate primarily on the treatment of dissidents and opponents in courts, and not the many other aspects of legal policy under these regimes. This makes sense because political trials were important in shaping state-society relations and in revealing the concrete meaning of national security laws as they pertained to citizens. Second, I concentrate primarily on the Brazilian case, using the Argentine and Chilean cases to highlight the distinctiveness of the Brazilian trajectory of political justice. I also assert that only in the Brazilian case were defense lawyers able to significantly alter interpretations of national security laws. Third, for the Chilean case, I concentrate only on the period of "wartime" military courts from 1973 to 1978, due both to lack of data from the period after that and to clarify the comparisons of types of authoritarian legality made in the book.[26]

Studying judicial-military consensus and integration prior to and during military rule reveals new insights into the issue of regime legality. In Brazil, the 1930 revolution involved civilian-military cooperation that resulted in the organizational fusion of civilian and military justice in the 1934 constitution. Civil-military cooperation and integration remained a hallmark of the Brazilian approach to political crime. The repression initiated by the 1964 coup was highly judicialized and gradualist; the regime slowly modified some aspects of traditional legality but did not engage in widespread extrajudicial killing, even after the hardening of the regime in the late 1960s.

In Chile, in contrast, the military was much less closely associated with a civil-military political project in the interwar years. Instead, it disdained civilian politics, and gained a reputation for a "Prussian" degree of professionalization and autonomy. Military justice in the first instance was strictly separated from civilian courts. When the military occasionally intervened in local areas at times of conflict, it temporarily usurped judicial authority rather than working within civil-military institutions established by consensus, as in Brazil. This pattern can be seen again after the 1973 coup. The legality of the Pinochet regime was more radical and militarized than Brazil's, even after the adoption of "peacetime" military courts in 1978 and the ratification of the 1980 constitution.

Argentina represents yet another path that puts it in the lower right quadrant—radical and extrajudicial—of figure 1.1, a radical break with previous legality and a largely extrajudicial assault on regime opponents. If the Chilean military tended to usurp judicial authority, its Argentine counterpart tended to reject and override it altogether. Mediating conflict in a highly polarized polity, the Argentine military was prone to use force directly, and then induce a dependent judiciary to ratify its de facto power. Here we see the least amount of civil-military cooperation and integration in the judicial realm. While rulers in the period of military rule from 1966 to 1973 tried to build authoritarian legality along the lines of their Brazilian and Chilean counterparts, these efforts were reversed. This set military officers on a collision course with the judiciary as they concluded that a judicial solution to the problem of political crime would not work.

My argument therefore distinguishes between authoritarian regimes based on their approach to the law. I contend that under authoritarian rule, military-judicial consensus and integration moderates political repression by allowing for its judicialization. Under judicialized repression, defense lawyers and civil society opposition groups can defend democratic principles to some degree, even if this opportunity is highly constricted. Where the military views the judiciary with suspicion or outright hostility, on the other hand, it is likely to usurp judicial functions and engage in purely military court proceedings, as in Chile, or completely ignore the law altogether and treat defense lawyers and sometimes even judges as subversive enemies, as in Argentina. The scope for the defense of democratic principles is more limited in the former and almost nonexistent in the latter. The danger in military regimes is that the military will bypass or even destroy the judiciary and engage in all-out war with its perceived opponents; in such an outcome, defense lawyers and civil society groups must wait for the end of the authoritarian regime to demand justice with any hope of success.

In addition to demonstrating the applicability of the overall argument to the three cases, this book pursues another related goal: to analyze in depth political trials under those regimes—in Brazil and Chile—that used this tactic extensively. Because there has been so little scholarly analysis of these trials, it is important to describe them empirically and to confirm to what degree they were both similar and different.[27] Who was prosecuted in political trials in the military courts, how, and why? What happened to them in the courts? In much of the literature on authoritarian regimes, such legal maneuvers are regarded as relatively unimportant compared to the presumably more fundamental logics of dependent capitalist accumulation or national security ideology that are seen as having driven each regime's repression. Yet these trials were not mere charades that simply put a gloss of legality on the regime's repression. They were legal exercises conducted by individuals who seemed to believe in the legitimacy and coherence of the laws. These prosecutors and judges made careful efforts to examine vague national security laws and apply them to concrete instances of individual behavior, deciding what was or was not subversive. Although the regimes took power by force, their efforts to legalize and legitimize their repression were important to their consolidation.

This book therefore uses the historical record to explain how and why political trials were initiated, maintained, and abandoned under military regimes in Brazil, Chile, and Argentina. It is not an attempt to compare those regimes in toto. It is also not a study of the opposition to military rule. While some knowledge of the opposition groups that were targeted for repression is indispensable for understanding authoritarian legality, the goal of the book is to understand legal institutions, not opposition groups. The book is not a detailed study of national security ideology in each country nor an analysis of the entire legal structure that each regime created, although some understanding of the latter is necessary for the case studies. I do assume that the way in which the regimes dealt with opponents and critics is a vital element of their respective legal strategies and can be used as a way to characterize them comparatively.

The next chapter frames the issue and describes the political repression that was the context of the authoritarian regimes' legal strategies. I then trace the historical background to the distinctive approaches to authoritarian repression in Brazil, Chile, and Argentina, arguing that patterns of repression between the countries look similar at the beginning of the twentieth century, gradually emerging on slightly different pathways in subsequent decades. Chapter 4 examines the distinctive way in which political trials in Brazil worked, while chapters 5 and 6 deal with two distinctive institutional matrices, the Chilean and the Argentine, respectively. Chapter 7 returns to the analysis of Brazil, examining a variety of cases in which the boundaries between free speech and subversive propaganda, terrorism and ordinary crime, offenses against authority and legitimate criticism, and foreign and Brazilian ideas and behavior were drawn. Chapter 8 asks what difference the variation in the modes of repression made to the different patterns of transitional justice in each country. At the end of the book, I extend the analytical framework developed for Brazil and the southern cone to three European authoritarian regimes—Nazi Germany, Franco's Spain, and Salazarist Portugal—showing how the framework developed here, with some modification, can help understand the degree of judicialization of authoritarian regimes that are not ruled directly by the military. I also suggest that a further modification of the framework is necessary if it is applied to democracies by examining the case of the United States since September 11, 2001.

In the United States, unlike the southern cone military regimes, military-judicial consensus and integration are unlikely to be a moderating force on repression, because they reduce rather than expand the space in which defense lawyers and civil society groups can defend individual rights. The U.S. case suggests that under democratic regimes, military-judicial conflict, rather than cooperation, is a moderating force, opening up space for the defense of constitutional guarantees. In authoritarian regimes, in contrast, too much military-judicial conflict threatens to spur the military into extrajudicial repression; judicial-military integration and consensus provide a rule-bound system in which some physical guarantees for political prisoners can be preserved. The dynamics of political justice therefore may be very different depending on the nature of the political regime. Put another way, authoritarian legality must be studied within the broader political context of which it is a part.

2

National Security Legality in Brazil

and the Southern Cone in

Comparative Perspective

> The great question on the prison walls and one that has no
> easy answer is Why? Why did the terror take the forms that
> it took, and how was it possible to create the machinery to
> implement it, and why was no one able to stop it?
>
> Juan Linz, "Totalitarian and Authoritarian Regimes"

ON MARCH 31, 1964, the Brazilian military initiated a self-proclaimed revolution that deposed the elected president João Goulart. In the following days, the new government issued an "institutional act" that overrode the constitution, purged the state apparatus of supporters of the prior government, organized a witch hunt of alleged Communists in society, and initiated a dictatorship that was to become increasingly repressive over the next five years. The Brazilian military regime, which ended in 1985, was a prototype for a new kind of authoritarianism in Latin America.

Similar regimes soon appeared in nearby countries. In 1966 the Argentine military engaged in its own "revolution," ousting the civilian president Arturo Illia, closing Congress and ushering in a period of military rule that was to last until 1973. In Chile in 1973, the military intervened in a bloody coup, bombing the presidential palace of socialist president Salvador Allende, executing thousands of his suspected supporters, shutting down Congress, and inaugurating a repressive regime led by General Augusto Pinochet that endured until 1990. In Uruguay, a civilian president, Juan María Bordaberry, allied with the military to

MAP 1

SOUTH AMERICA
ARGENTINA
BRAZIL
CHILE

Map 1: South America: Argentina, Brazil, Chile. Map by Lynne E. Perry.

install an authoritarian regime in 1973 that survived (eventually without Bordaberry himself) until 1984. And in 1976 the Argentine military returned to power with a vengeance, inaugurating a ruthless "process of national reorganization" that included a dirty war against civilians, leaving tens of thousands disappeared and dead when the regime finally collapsed in 1983.

All of these regimes emerged in partially industrialized societies that, taken together, constituted the most economically developed region in Latin America. They had relatively large and capable state bureaucracies and used the state's technical capacity to intervene in society in new and more comprehensive ways. All of them pledged allegiance to the defense of "national security," a Cold War conception of political conflict that conflated the state with the nation and blurred the distinction between internal and external aggression, war and peace, Communist and non-Communist political activity, and armed attacks on the state, on one hand, and peaceful dissent and opposition on the other. All of these regimes, at one time or another, engaged in state terror, systematically monitoring, detaining, torturing, killing, and sometimes disappearing their own citizens. This took place with the tacit consent, and frequent complicity, of the U.S. government.

Patterns of Repression and Legality

The leaders of the military regimes in Brazil and the southern cone were concerned with the legality of their rule. Despite the fact that they had all come to power through force, these leaders strove mightily to frame their actions with a scaffolding of laws, a mixture of the old and the new. In all of their regimes there was a realm of extrajudicial state terror, on the one hand, and an area of routine, well-established legality on the other. For example, during the Argentine dirty war, citizens could take the federal government to court in civil cases and win, at the same time that fellow citizens were being plucked from the streets and executed by clandestine groups of state-sanctioned murderers.[1] But between these two poles there also lay a gray area in which the regime attempted to legalize its repression—by issuing decrees; rewriting constitutions; purging, reorganizing, and manipulating judiciaries; and promulgating new legislation.

Another tactic in the struggle to make repression lawful was "political justice," or the prosecution of the regimes' opponents in courts of law for offenses against national security. Political justice was part of the efforts of these regimes to make lawful some portion of the repression that they enacted. How big a portion that was, and exactly how it was made to be or to appear lawful, varied considerably. Political justice was also an attempt to reshape society to fit regime leaders' vision of what citizenship should be by prosecuting citizens for such crimes as the distribution of subversive propaganda, membership in banned organizations, offenses against authority, and sociopolitical nonconformism. For supporters of the regime, political justice was an attempt to realize national greatness and political correctness one defendant at a time. For its critics, it turned the country into a giant barracks, inappropriately applying military standards of behavioral discipline and attitudinal conformity to civilians.

Political trials under military rule in Brazil and the southern cone took place in legal systems in which rules and rational arguments mattered, but in which the ideal of the rule of law was far from fully realized. Within this gray area the law was not always what it appeared to be. Sometimes it never constrained power holders at all, but was instead only applied to selected enemies of the state, and even then arbitrarily and intermittently. Legal procedures under these military regimes were consistent with the rule of law in appearance, but not always in substance. They included courts in which judges lacked independence, impartiality, and irremovability; laws that were so vague as to allow almost any behavior to be punished; laws that were passed and then applied retroactively against offenders; defendants who were prosecuted more than once for the same crime; defendants who were convicted solely on the basis of confessions extracted under torture or their statements about their political beliefs; and judges who repeatedly ignored the security forces' systematic failure to comply with the law. Rules and procedures under these conditions were not mere façades, but the systems lacked one or more elements of a fair legal system, such as equality before the law, the prohibition of double jeopardy, the right of the accused to legal defense, the requirement that convictions be based on evidence, and the application of law to state officials and not just citizens. John Rawls calls such a system a deviation from "justice as regularity" (1971, 235). Jennifer Schirmer refers to it as a "military view of law" (1998, chap. 6). In the cases of Brazilian and Chilean political trials, the regimes' legality failed to protect detainees' basic human rights or to check the violent excesses of the security forces, and over-valorized the claims of the state at the expense of the citizen. However, just as virtual reality is not sheer fantasy but instead a carefully constructed reproduction designed to induce the experience of the real, this authoritarian legality did entail real record keeping and deference to fixed and clearly delineated procedures. This rule-boundedness often enabled defense lawyers to protect the lives of their clients, sparing them from arbitrary execution by the security forces.

Political justice under the military regimes of Brazil (1964–1985), Chile (1973–1990) and Argentina (1976–1983) was part of larger patterns of repression in each country. Repression varied from case to case in terms of its intensity, scope, timing, geographic reach, and change over time. Some basic features of repression in Brazil, Chile, and Argentina are compared in table 2.1. Authoritarian legality was part of these larger patterns of repression, and repression influenced the role that could be played by various actors in political justice: political prisoners, defense lawyers, police and military personnel, prosecutors, judges, the legal establishment, the military high command, and civil society organizations.

Brazil's repression came in two distinct waves. At the time of the military coup in 1964, the military and political police sought out suspected members of the Communist Party and known supporters of the prior government of João Goulart. The military created a federal intelligence agency, the SNI (Serviço Nacional de Inteligência or National Intelligence Service), to coordinate repression and relied heavily on the political police in the states (DEOPS, Departamento Estadual de Ordem Político e Social). There was relatively little lethal violence in this phase, and resistance to the coup was minimal. Repression was concentrated most heavily in the Rio de Janeiro–São Paulo–Belo Horizonte triangle, the most densely populated region of Brazil.

The first wave of repression in Brazil was therefore typical of most military coups, in that it was aimed at supporters of the deposed government. The second wave of repression occurred in the late 1960s, as an armed left emerged. This repression was more brutal, more widespread, and more centralized than the earlier wave, but was still fairly selective, since the armed left was small and lacked any kind of mass base. The military regime created feared special military-police units, the DOI-CODI (Departamento de Operações Internas, or Department of Internal Operations, and Comando Operacional de Defesa Interna, or Operational Command for Internal Defense), to root out "subversion" in each state and exchange information about the armed left with other agencies. There was considerable competition in this phase between the agencies involved in repression, including the political police and the intelligence agencies of each of the armed forces.

Unlike the first wave, which had targeted workers, military personnel, Communists, and supporters of Goulart, this wave was focused on shadowy groups within the armed left and their presumed support base, including stu-

2.1 Lethal violence by state forces and other indices of political repression in Argentina, Brazil, and Chile, 1964–1990

Category	Brazil 1964–1979	Chile 1973–1989	Argentina 1976–1983
Period of heaviest repression	1964, 1969–1973	1973–1977	1976–1980
Deaths and disappearances	284–364	3,000–5,000	20,000–30,000
per 100,000 people	0.21+	23.07–34.62	62.50–93.75
Political prisoners	25,000	60,000	30,000
per 100,000 people	17.36	461.54	93.75
Exiles	10,000	40,000	500,000
per 100,000 people	6.94	307.69	1,562.5
Number of people tried in military courts for political crimes (estimates)	7,367+[a]	6,000+[b]	350+
per 100,000 people	5.12+	46.15+	1.09+
Ratio of those tried in military courts to those killed extrajudicially[c]	23/1	1.5/1	1/71
Amnesty	8/28/79	4/19/78	9/23/83 (later annulled by Congress)
Main human rights report	*Nunca mais* (1985), secret project supported by the Archdiocese of São Paulo and the World Council of Churches	*Rettig Report* (1991), Rettig Commission appointed by President Aylwin	*Nunca más* (1984), Sabato Commission appointed by President Alfonsín
Population (1988)	144 million	13 million	32 million

Sources: Argentine National Commission on the Disappeared (1986); Projeto Brasil: Nunca Mais (1988); Chilean National Commission on Truth and Reconciliation (1993); Drake (1996, 29–30); Nino (1996, 64, 80); Miranda and Tibúrcio (1999, 12, 15–16, 633, 635).

[a]Counts only defendants in cases appealed to the STM.

[b]Counts only those tried in "wartime" military courts (1973–1978).

[c]To produce these ratios, I used the average of the high and low estimates of the killed and disappeared: 324 in Brazil, 4,000 in Chile, and 25,000 in Argentina.

dents, academics, journalists, and clerics. The Fifth Institutional Act of late 1968 (AI-5) eliminated habeas corpus in national security crimes, giving the security forces tremendous leeway in the treatment of detainees. Political killings and disappearances increased during this phase, which lasted until about 1975. Almost half of the disappeared were members of a rural guerrilla force that was wiped out by the army in northern Brazil in 1972–1974. Regime liberalization, which began in about 1974, gradually led to the dismantling of many of the most draconian national security laws. (AI-5 was abolished in 1978.) An amnesty in 1979 freed political prisoners and allowed the return of political exiles, while political repression was relatively mild from about 1978 to the formal end of military rule in 1985.

Despite Brazil's reputation for casual and informal attitudes to questions of law, the military regime was particularly concerned with the perceived legality of its actions.[2] Some aspects of its authoritarian legality are compared to those of Chile and Argentina in table 2.2. The military rulers did not suspend the constitution when they seized the reins of government in a coup d'etat and purged but did not close Congress. Congress functioned throughout the military regime except for a few months in 1968–1969. The constitution was selectively overridden with institutional acts and eventually replaced by a new constitution, with the consent of a controlled Congress, in 1967. This constitution, substantially revised in 1969, heavily concentrated power in the hands of the executive and was even followed by the promulgation of absurd, secret institutional acts that had the force of law even though almost nobody knew what they were. (The 1969 constitution was eventually replaced by a new constitution devised under the successor civilian regime in 1988.) The military regime has been described as a hybrid, in that it preserved more of the trappings of a democracy, including a functioning if restricted Congress and controlled two-party elections throughout the country, than other similar regimes in the region (Lamounier 1996, 168–69). Furthermore, the military regime's repression was relatively mild if one considers the incidence of lethal violence. While thousands of people were tortured, a relatively small number of around three hundred victims of state killings and disappearances have so far been recognized.

While lethal violence was low, a large number of people were subjected to political trials in Brazil. Most of these trials took place in military courts. (These courts are compared with other courts discussed in this book in table 2.3.) Military courts lacked independence and impartiality but were not purely military; they consisted of one civilian judge and four active-duty military officers who were not trained in the law and who were rotated in and out of the courts for three-month stints. The sentences in these trials could be appealed to a higher military court, and from there to the civilian Supreme Court. Investigations and trials were drawn-out affairs, often lasting two years or more from the date of the beginning of the lower court trial to the sentence by the military appeals court. Defendants could sometimes (but not always) remain at liberty during this period. This legal process guaranteed that of those who served time in prison, most were eventually given clearly delineated sentences. Most of these prisoners were released six years before the end of military rule itself, and all

2.2   Features of authoritarian legality in Brazil, Chile, and Argentina

Features	Brazil 1964–1985	Chile 1973–1990	Argentina 1976–1983
Declaration of state of siege at time of coup	no	yes	yes
Suspension of parts of old constitution	yes	yes	yes
Eventual promulgation of new constitution	yes	yes	no
Military courts used to prosecute many civilian opponents and dissidents	yes	yes	no
Military courts wholly insulated from civilian judiciary	no	yes	yes
Habeas corpus in political cases recognized in practice	1964–1968, 1979–1985	no	no
Purges of Supreme Court	some removals and court packing, 1969	no	yes
Purges of rest of judiciary	limited	limited	yes
Judges' irremovability revoked	yes	no[a]	yes

[a]The controls over the judiciary were largely internal in Chile, because the Supreme Court's power over the lower levels of the judiciary included the right to disqualify judges from service and to give them poor evaluations (Constable and Valenzuela 1991, 130–32).

were released by 1985. If one accepts that the ratio of those prosecuted in courts to those killed by the state tells us something about the legal strategy of a regime, than the Brazilian military regime's repression appears to have been more judicialized than its counterparts in Argentina, Chile, and even Uruguay. As table 2.1 shows, the ratio in Brazil was 23 to 1. In contrast, in Chile it was close to parity at 1.5:1, while in Argentina only one person was put on trial for every seventy-one killed extrajudicially.[3]

In Chile, the story of repression and authoritarian legality is quite different from that of Brazil. Chilean repression, triggered by the 1973 coup and led by the army, was much more massive and intense than Brazil's. The junta declared a state of siege throughout Chile and divided the country into zones directly controlled by the military commanders, with the army in control of most territory. The military targeted suspected supporters of the Allende government and in particular, members of the Socialist and Communist parties. This early repression was fairly uncoordinated and unselective, with military commanders in each region having a high degree of autonomy. Santiago was the primary focus, but

2.3   Comparison of courts analyzed in this book

Issue/Category	Brazil 1964–1979	Chile 1973–1978
Military courts	yes	yes
Wartime military courts?	no	yes
Civilian judges?	1 of 5	no[a]
Number of judges in first instance	5	7
Right of appeal?	yes	no
Judges trained in the law in first instance?	1 of 5	no
If appeal allowed, judges trained in law?	yes	no appeal
Prosecutor	civilian	military
Typical length of trial	6 months–1 year	days
Trial public?	yes	no
Death penalty existed	1969–1979	yes
Death penalty applied?	no	yes
Most common charges	membership in banned organization	violation of Arms Control Law and Law of State Security

[a]Civilian judges served in exceptional cases.

deaths and disappearances took place throughout the country in the first few months after the coup. Lethal violence was still quite high through 1974.

In 1975, as Pablo Policzer shows, regime repression became more selective and centralized (Policzer 2001). The creation of the DINA (Dirección Nacional de Inteligencia, or National Intelligence Directorate), a political police and intelligence agency controlled directly by President Pinochet, took day-to-day repression out of the hands of the military. The DINA was also involved in high-profile assassinations of critics of the military regime abroad, including the killing of former head of the army General Carlos Prats in Buenos Aires in 1974 and the 1976 bombing of former Chilean foreign minister Orlando Letelier in Washington DC. Evidence has since come to light that the Chilean military regime was also a leading force in the creation of Operation Condor, a network that linked the intelligence agencies of Chile, Paraguay, Uruguay, Argentina, Brazil, and the United States, and that exchanged information and coordinated abductions and assassinations throughout the region (Mariano 1998; McSherry 1999).

Despite its reputation as a rigorously legalistic country—there is a joke that during the Chilean coup, the tanks stopped at red lights—the Chilean military regime operated with far less concern for legal restraints than its Brazilian predecessor for the first five years of its rule. In the first few months after the coup, the number of people summarily executed by the army or police (*carabineros*) seems to have far outweighed those treated in some sort of judicial manner. Those that were prosecuted were tried in military courts composed only of military officers who acted as if the country were at war. Trials were rapid, and sentences sometimes harsh. There was no right of appeal for defendants, because the civilian Supreme Court refused to review the verdicts in military court trials. When Chilean military courts imposed the death penalty, the sentence was carried out, unlike the situation in Brazil.[4] In some instances judicial procedures were nullified by extrajudicial violence. For example, in late 1973 a "caravan of death" led by a general close to President Pinochet, Sergio Arellano Stark, moved around the northern provinces of the country, summarily executing prisoners who had been given lesser sentences in the military courts.[5] Such extralegal acts diminished over time, and the peacetime military courts that operated from 1978 to 1989 were closer to their counterparts in Brazil but were still more insulated from the civilian judiciary and more punitive. Also unlike Brazil, in Chile hundreds of political prisoners were still in jail at the time of the democratic transition. Overall, the Chilean military regime in the first five years of its rule was more radical in regard to traditional legality than the Brazilian one and resorted to unmediated force in more instances and on a wider scale.

As table 2.1 suggests, Argentine repression was the harshest of the three cases examined here and presents the most radical and extrajudicial approach to the law of all three military regimes. Argentine political violence grew out of a society polarized between supporters and opponents of former president Juan Domingo Perón, and increased gradually after the 1955 military coup that ousted Perón. An armed left emerged in the country in the early 1960s, and the 1966 coup brought another military regime to power. By the late 1960s, armed actions against military personnel by guerrilla forces such as the Montoneros and the ERP (Ejército Revolucionário del Pueblo, or Revolutionary People's Army) became a major concern of the government.

Repression increased markedly in 1973, when the military regime withdrew from power and permitted the restoration of a Peronist government. First without Perón, then with the aging leader himself, and after his death with his third wife María Estela Martínez de Perón (Isabel or Isabelita) as president, the spiral of political violence continued. Under Isabelita, the Triple A (Alianza Anticomunista Argentina) a paramilitary group reportedly coordinated by the president's advisor José López Rega, began a dirty war against the armed left. This escalated into a major military operation by the army in Tucumán province in 1975, and the 1976 coup came in part because of the military's desire to expand the dirty war nationally. Unlike both Brazil and Chile, therefore, Argentine repression began before rather than after the creation of the military regime.

As we have seen, Brazilian repression came in two waves, the second more intense than the first, while Chilean repression began with a ferocious spike at the beginning of the regime, and then subsided to a low level and selective lethality within two years. Argentine repression, in contrast, raged for four years after the military coup of 1976, subsiding somewhat in 1980, but continuing until the collapse of the regime. To a greater extent than either Brazil or Chile, this repression was clandestine and wrapped up in a cloak of "plausible deniability"—which only gradually became implausible—by the government.

Argentine repression was centered in the capital city of Buenos Aires, where half of the disappearances took place, but was also intensive in other cities such as Córdoba, La Plata, and Mendoza. Trade unionists, members of the Peronist and Radical parties, intellectuals, students, and journalists were all targeted by the repression. Unlike Brazil and Chile, in Argentina, judges and lawyers were also targeted by the regime—over one hundred lawyers for political prisoners disappeared between 1976 and 1983.[6] Because Argentine repression was so decentralized, with each branch of the armed forces having responsibility for different territories, the potential for random acts of brutality was higher than in Brazil and Chile. Some security units were selective, operating on the basis of intelligence, while others engaged in a high degree of arbitrary torture, killing, and looting based more on whim than information.[7]

In terms of its approach to the law, the Argentine regime stands out for its almost complete disregard for legal conventions. It convicted some 350 people in military courts,[8] but its main response to its political opponents was a fierce "war" in which the physical elimination of suspected subversives was conducted largely without judicial constraints. Courts were used primarily as a defensive mechanism to deny applications for writs of habeas corpus and to maintain the appearance of ordinary legality. This was done also in Brazil and Chile, but unlike in these two countries, in Argentina courts were largely unused as an offensive instrument of political repression of opponents. Instead, this task fell almost entirely to a front line of armed forces personnel, aided and abetted by military and civilian intelligence agencies and the police.

Despite their broad similarities, therefore, the military regimes of Brazil,

Chile, and Argentina exhibit remarkable variation in the pattern of their repression, their attention to legality, the relationship between courts and the security forces, and in their use of political trials. The cases represent a spectrum that moves from a high degree of judicialism and gradualism (with respect to previous legality) to a very radical break with previous legality and almost totally extrajudicial repression.[9]

Explaining Variation in Authoritarian Legality

How can we explain such variation? Like Lichbach and Zuckerman, we can identify structuralist, rationalist, and cultural approaches to the problem (1997). A large body of work explains patterns of political repression in terms of the economy, class structure, and international economic position of different countries. These essentially structuralist arguments posit an elective affinity between certain forms of political economy and the use of force by governments (see Ozlak 1981; O'Donnell 1980; Moore 1966; Rueschemeyer, Huber Stephens, and Stephens 1992). For example, Cardoso and Faletto (1979) and many other writers of their era (e.g., Hutchful 1986) saw a tight fit between strategies of dependent capitalist accumulation and authoritarian political regimes. In some versions of this perspective, internal class repression is a reflection of an international capitalist system in which violence by client states facilitates global exploitation by transnational firms and hegemonic states (see Wolpin 1986; Carleton 1989; Cardoso and Faletto 1979; Petras 1997).

This perspective suggests that increases in the scope and intensity of political repression should be attributed largely to objective characteristics of the political economy. For example, crises of capitalist accumulation that induce political leaders to embark upon radical restructuring inevitably lead to state violence directed at workers' movements that stand in the way of such restructuring. The most heavy-handed forms of repression are more likely in agrarian societies strongly dependent upon cheap and controlled labor; political repression is highly functional because it contains landowners' labor costs and ensures their profitability. Thus Central American repression can be expected to be worse than repression in more industrialized societies such as those in the southern cone of South America. Political repression is therefore mainly explained by the requirements of the owners of the means of production in the economy. Political repression is essentially class oppression.

Such a perspective has valid insights. However, it generally avoids explicit theorizing about the legal form that repression takes. What matters is the coalition of classes and states on each side of the division created by repression. In this type of analysis, the political and judicial institutions framing, regulating, and legitimating state repression are usually seen as epiphenomenal, less important than the material interests that serve as the driving force of the process.

However, all instances of political repression cannot plausibly be forced into the confines of a political economy approach. While some political repression is clearly driven by concerns about class conflict and the organization of production, other social cleavages such as religion, ethnicity, race, and nationalism can also come to the fore.[10] Political institutions and practices are not mere reflections of underlying material forces; they have a logic and an autonomy that must be appreciated in their own right.

In contrast, a rational choice perspective would locate the sources of the regimes' legal strategies in the self-interested strategic action of key actors inside and outside each regime. Trials or their absence are thus equilibria established to meet the short-term strategic interests of regime leaders in gaining acquiescence to their rule, the subjugation of rival factions within the regime, or some other goal.[11] Different approaches to the legal prosecution of opponents can be explained in terms of variation in challenges that regimes face, such as the degree of opposition or internal cohesion, and rational responses to those challenges.

Such a perspective has much to recommend it. As Barbara Geddes points out, in political conflicts in which the stakes are high and defeat could possibly result in loss of life for the losers, strategic action is more likely than where stakes are low. There is in fact much strategic action on the individual level in the cases reviewed here. However, Geddes also points out that while rational choice theory can often illuminate actors' ends-means rationality, it is much less able to elucidate why actors choose their goals in the first place.[12] More importantly, rational choice theory generally assumes that institutions are relatively efficient ways of solving particular problems—that a sort of "invisible hand" produces equilibria that solve dominant actors' main political problems, until those problems change and new institutions can be created to address them.[13]

However, past decisions can lock regimes into certain institutional arrangements even if they occurred by accident, and these arrangements can endure even after the features that made them attractive to key actors have disappeared (Pierson 2000, 264). Outcomes are thus not necessarily efficient, nor can institutions easily be remade, even when they constrain actors' pursuit of their interests. As the anthropologist Virginia Domínguez remarks (1986, 8–9), in explaining social outcomes, it is important to consider not just the choices that individuals make but the construction of the categories and institutions that structure their choices. Furthermore, individuals are usually not the isolated, atomistic actors of much rational choice theory but people embedded in networks and organizations that influence their choices (Tilly 1998, 16–25, 34). It is my contention that regime leaders in Argentina, Brazil, and Chile did attempt to use institutions for strategic purposes, but they could not remake those institutions just as they chose. The conditions that each set of leaders inherited— organizations, procedures, mentalities, and personnel—were different, and these shaped regime leaders' strategies in important ways, especially after military coups, when important policy decisions had to be made. Equilibrium analysis that assumes that choices are made on the basis of more or less similar prior conditions does not capture this vital feature—differing historical pathways— of the cases reviewed here. As Douglass North has said, "it is not an ergodic world," and we sometimes need non-ergodic tools to understand it.[14]

A different approach would be to deny any universalistic rationality to actors and posit instead the existence of distinctive legal and political cultures in each country. As with rational choice theory, this framework is grounded in plausible assumptions, in this instance about how distinctive patterns of meaning are formed in political systems and how these shape the nature of conflicts between groups. This approach looks at collectivities rather than individuals. Culture, a constitutive element in all social relationships, influences how signals between different actors are interpreted and acted upon and is thus crucial to understanding the intersubjective creation of political understandings and outcomes.[15]

However, in explaining the three cases discussed here, purely cultural approaches run up against conflicting and often ambiguous evidence about the differences between the political cultures of Argentina, Brazil, and Chile. Furthermore, recent historical work has questioned long-standing assumptions about national cultural differences, such as that Brazilians tend not to engage in violence for political reasons, underlining the need for caution in contrasting cultures.[16]

Furthermore, while culture can be studied as a dynamic factor and one that can be disaggregated below the level of the nation-state (as in explanations of "corporate cultures" or regional cultures), it sometimes becomes a static generalization about particular nationalities' tendencies toward political compromise, or violence, or some other type of behavior. It is reasonable to conclude, therefore, that a deep-seated, national cultural predisposition, as a variable, is too broad to explain the variation in outcomes dealt with here.

In contrast, the explanation offered in this book aims at theory that lies between the high generality of theories of the economic determinants of repression and distinctive national cultures, on one hand, and the methodologically individualist explanations of rational choice theory on the other.[17] It attempts to use the best insights of each approach while avoiding their limitations. Thus, not all features of authoritarian regimes' repression can be ascribed to the political economy; regime leaders' choices may often be rational, but they are constrained and shaped by prior institutional arrangements and understandings; and while culture is important, it cannot necessarily be captured by simple generalizations about national differences.

In reaching these conclusions, this study builds on two important bodies of literature. The first is on institutions and their development, the rediscovery in political science that "institutions matter."[18] The second is on "modes of transition," based on the insight that how regimes break down influences the quality of the successor regime (see, for example, Linz and Stepan 1996). It focuses on institutions or the "institutional matrix" of political repression under each regime. The institutional matrix constitutes the "rules of the game" or the "humanly devised constraints that shape[d] human interaction" between the regime and its opponents (North 1990, 3). It consists of formal rules (constitutional provisions, institutional acts and executive decrees, national security laws, procedural codes within the military justice system, penal regulations) and informal constraints (prevailing attitudes about national security and the treatment of political prisoners, the perceived threats posed by "subversives," and hegemonic ideas about the role of law in society and the proper limits of civilian dissent from and opposition to the military regime). The latter includes aspects of the wider political and legal culture in which repression took place.

According to economic historian Douglass North, "an essential part of the functioning of institutions is the costliness of ascertaining violations and the severity of punishment" (1990, 4). Therefore, a good place to analyze the nature of repressive institutions under military rule is the courts, where citizens accused of violating the political rules were prosecuted and often punished. This book therefore focuses mainly on the courts and especially military courts, where the bulk of political trials took place. It adopts a theoretical framework that borrows from the insights of historical institutionalism.[19] This approach is distinctive in that it sees the particular sequencing of events or processes as determinative of divergent outcomes.[20] More specifically, the book examines similarities and contrasts among countries over time and engages in "process tracing" with regard to specific institutional arrangements in one country over time (Collier and Collier 1991, 5).

Aside from this central insight, historical institutionalism as applied to the cases in this book relies on four other claims. First, outcomes are contingent— several of them may be possible at any given time, and no single outcome is likely to be inevitable or necessary. (In this respect, historical institutionalism shares with methodological individualism a concern for avoiding functionalist arguments.) With respect to the cases discussed here, this means that it was not necessarily inevitable that only the Argentine military regime, and not its counterparts in Brazil and Chile, embarked on a policy of mass disappearances. While Argentina's past powerfully influenced its descent into arbitrary mass terror, the rulers of Brazil and Chile might have opted for such policies as well had it not been for the successful adoption and maintenance of alternative arrangements. (And they did engage in some disappearances, although on a smaller scale than in Argentina.)

Second, large consequences may flow from relatively minor or contingent events; and third, particular institutional configurations, once adopted, can be very difficult to undo.[21] (Similarly, once institutions have been dismantled they —like Humpty Dumpty—can be very difficult to put together again.) Finally, state institutions are not moving on a single, synchronous path, but are instead part of different trajectories with distinctive starting and branching points (Orren and Skowronek 1995, esp. 310).

These theoretical insights have a direct bearing on the analysis of political justice in Argentina, Brazil, and Chile. Because sequence matters, the success or failure of early attempts to impose political justice on perceived opponents of the military shaped the military's subsequent approaches to the issue. In Brazil and Chile, early efforts largely succeeded, while in Argentina, they were dramatically overturned, leading the military to switch to a much riskier and more radical strategy. Thus, large consequences flowed from institutional changes that were not seen as momentous at the time.[22] Similarly, the overriding tendency in both Brazil and Chile was to stick with a particular institutional venue (military courts) and mechanism of political justice (prosecution for national security violations) regardless of the particular political groups that were targeted by the trials. As North has written, "established institutions generate powerful inducements that reinforce their own stability and further development."[23] Only in Argentina was a radical break with the past attempted, indicating that in political justice, as in many other political outcomes, the initial adoption of a particular path is difficult to undo. Finally, the history of institutions and methods of political justice are not strictly coterminous with the broader history of the military regime itself. In both Brazil and Chile, significant elements of the machinery of authoritarian political justice were constructed before the coups that created the regimes; in the Brazilian case, political trials were also largely abandoned several years before the end of the regime. The insights derived from historical institutionalism can be applied to the legality of many twentieth century authoritarian regimes, as well as those of Argentina, Brazil, and Chile. But not all aspects of the legality of these authoritarian regimes concern us here. Our focus is on a particular phenomenon—political trials.

Political Trials and Authoritarian Regimes

Political trials are trials in which criminal charges are brought against individuals for political reasons. They are staged by regimes to intimidate, delegitimize, and demobilize opponents.[24] In a well-known formulation, one scholar writes that in political trials, as opposed to common criminal trials, the "judicial machinery and its trial mechanics are set into motion to attain political objectives. . . . Court action is called upon to exert influence on the distribution of political power."[25]

Why would the leaders of an authoritarian regime choose to put opponents on trial? In approaching the law, leaders have two basic options. One is conservative. This is for leaders to proclaim themselves as protectors of the existing constitutional order, and to justify any deviations from traditional legality as temporary suspensions necessary to meet an extraordinary threat. The second is revolutionary. In it, dictators denounce the old constitution and herald the construction of a new and better order. In practice, most authoritarian regimes waver between these two forms of legitimation, and frequently change over time in one or another direction.[26] The second strategy is more radical, in that it puts authoritarian leaders into conflict with legal traditions and the legal establishment.

After choosing a basic legal framework, authoritarian leaders must decide whether or not to put opponents on trial. Some analysts assert that the nature and frequency of political trials vary by regime type. For example, Kittrie contrasts three models for dealing with political offenders: the totalitarian, the authoritarian, and the democratic. The first is the most severely punitive, in which political criminality is expanded to include even mild expressions of opinion contrary to the regime. In contrast, democracies are marked by liberal legislation that generally protects freedom of speech, excluding only such offenses as threats against public officials, and distinguishes between punishable acts against the government and permissible expression against it. Authoritarian regimes lie between these two poles, combining brutal suppression of dissent with occasional liberality in the treatment of dissidents and opponents (Kittrie 2000, 301–7).

However, this typology raises as many questions as it answers, and cannot explain the kinds of variation within regime type dealt with in this study. While regime type certainly helps us to see broad contrasts between patterns of political justice, by itself it is insufficient to explain the nature and timing of political trials.

Several plausible reasons for the use of political trials by authoritarian regimes can be identified. The first and obvious reason is to raise the cost of opposition—to intimidate it, label it criminal, tie it up in costly and time-consuming legal battles, and to prevent it from playing an effective political role. Trials are ingenious mechanisms by which to accomplish this because they individualize collective conflicts, accusing selected individuals of political crimes and therefore turning broad questions of political morality into apparently objective cases of guilt or innocence. The whole really can be greater than the sum of the parts with political trials, because such trials can serve as striking exhibitions of the costs of political opposition and dissent to others who might otherwise be inclined to actively oppose the regime. Trials can thus play an important role in the demobilization of oppositional social movements, even though any regime that deploys them also runs the risk of creating martyrs and inadvertently galvanizing its opposition.

A second reason for the use of political trials is the desire of regime leaders to use courts to justify their repression and to garner legitimacy or at least passive acquiescence to their rule. Courts carry heavy symbolic weight that can lend an air of gravity and judiciousness to even the most trumped-up charges and the most blatantly unfair proceedings. They can provide legitimacy both domestically and internationally. Domestically, they may reassure politically uncommitted citizens that the regime is not arbitrarily repressing its opponents, but instead allowing independent courts to follow traditional procedures in prosecuting criminals. Internationally, political trials may placate multilateral institutions, nongovernmental organizations (NGOs), foreign governments, investors, and citizens that the human rights of political opponents are being respected. Both at home and abroad, political trials can be "good for business," assuring capitalists that rights to property and contract will be enforced by a state committed to the rule of law. In short, political trials are useful in the game of public relations engaged in by all political regimes.

Political trials are especially attractive to authoritarian leaders because some of the perceived legitimacy of courts can rub off on the regime even if the outcomes of political trials are manipulated through the creation of special courts, control over the selection of judges, or other means. Furthermore, political trials are usually one among a gamut of repressive practices that can be applied to opponents, including summary execution, disappearance, torture, exile, and cooptation. Because of this, they should be analyzed as one element in a larger pattern of interaction between regimes and their opponents.

A third reason regimes use political trials, closely related to the second, is to create a psychological effect among the public, or in Kirchheimer's words, to create effective political images that cast certain political actors as villains and others as heroes. Courtrooms are ideal places to create such images because trials make good theater, as the ubiquitous courtroom scenes in novels, films, and plays suggest. Many political trials are aimed as much at the general public as they are at partisans on either side of the regime-opposition divide. As Kirchheimer writes, trials "elevate the image [of the political enemy] from the realm of private happenings and partisan constructions into an official, authoritative, and quasi-neutral sphere" (Kirchheimer 1961, 422). Trials also create an official story of guilt and innocence that can acquire an air of unquestioned veracity when disseminated and repeated among the public. They can become part of a historical memory that reinforces unthinking acceptance of a regime's rule.[27]

Fourth, political trials can be responses to intraregime conflict and rivalry. They may be designed to monitor and restrain the state's repressive forces, or they may be concessions to certain factions within the regime that want to strike more aggressively against regime opponents. Perhaps the most famous examples of the use of trials in intraregime conflict were the Stalinist show trials of 1936–1938, in which the entirety of Lenin's Politburo still in Russia was arrested, accused of treason and sabotage, and executed (Lane 1985; see also Shklar 1964, 201). The assumption that political trials are always a proportionate and rational response of a unitary actor—the regime—to its foes is therefore not always correct. As Stanley points out in his study of political violence (1996, 12), state repression is often grossly disproportionate to the extent of opposition, and states often provoke rather than suppress opposition through indiscriminate acts of coercion. Furthermore, states are not always unitary actors—they contain bureaucratic components that follow different goals and often compete with and contradict one another. In Stanley's view, "states can operate 'protection rackets', manipulating the appearance of mass opposition, or in fact generating it through inflexibility and brutality in order to secure ongoing political and economic concessions from social elites."[28] Such a dynamic can be at work in political trials, which may have as much to do with factional struggles within a regime as they do with struggles between a regime and its enemies.

Finally, political trials can stabilize regime repression by providing a relatively predictable set of rules governing the punishment of oppositional and dissident behavior. What John Carey (2000) calls "parchment"—the formal, written, rules of national security legislation, military court procedures, and the like—can generate mutual expectations among political actors that then stabilize and reinforce the institutions involved in political repression. Trials can also serve as monitoring mechanisms conveying information about the activities of the opposition and the security forces to regime leaders (McCubbins and Weingast 1984). In this sense, political trials can work, from the point of view of the leaders of authoritarian regimes, by facilitating the normalization of new or reorganized repressive institutions and stabilizing the regime's rule.

Political trials are tempting to authoritarian rulers, in summary, because they may demobilize popular oppositional movements; garner legitimacy for the regime by convincing key audiences that it "plays fair" in dealing with opponents; create positive political images for the regime and negative ones for the opposition; help one faction gain advantage over others within the regime; and stabilize the repression by providing information and a predictable set of rules around which opponents and regime officials' expectations can coalesce.

Political trials can also vary according to whether they are aimed at supporters of a prior regime or active, current opponents; target members of the state apparatus or members of the opposition in society; are conducted in military courts (with or without civilian participation), special civilian courts, or ordinary civilian courts; the degree to which they convict defendants and pass death sentences; whether they take place in a context of widespread extrajudicial killings by state agents, or few such killings; the degree to which the regime respects its own laws, both inside and outside the courtroom; and perhaps most importantly, the political values espoused by those who stage the political trials.

Despite these important differences, most political trials share certain characteristics. The first is that prior political conflicts and especially prior judicial-military cooperation influence the nature and targets of political trials. The second is that even the most radical regimes usually fail to create entirely new forms of legality and legal institutions, and most authoritarian regimes tend instead to rely on modified forms of the old legality and judiciary, which constrains them in significant ways, despite their efforts to bend law to their own ends through the purging of judicial personnel, the passage of special legislation, and the like. Third, most practitioners of political justice enjoy almost complete impunity. Even in the most heinous instances of the use of courts for political revenge, as in the People's Courts in Nazi Germany, for example, judges are rarely made accountable for their actions, but simply remain in office, blending into the background of the new, post-authoritarian regime (see Müller 1991). For this reason, some effects of political trials are likely to endure. Beyond the deaths of those sentenced to execution in the courts, long-running instances of political justice are likely to create precedents and legal mind-sets that justify the status quo and perpetuate authoritarian attitudes after the regime that nourished them has disappeared. Finally, political trials are not often studied, because their records are usually hidden or destroyed by rulers anxious to keep them from the public. However, the records of the Brazilian and Chilean political trials are quite ample. The characteristics of these sources, and my selection of cases from them, are described in appendix 1.

3

The Evolution of National Security Legality

in Brazil and the Southern Cone

> An immense and bewildering subject opens up before one
> who contemplates the diversity of arrangements and insti-
> tutions through which justice is variously administered in
> modern states.
>
> Mirjan R. Damaška, *The Faces of
> Justice and State Authority*

MILITARY REGIME LEADERS in the 1960s and 1970s in Brazil and the southern cone made choices about how to deal with opposition and dissent. Yet their
dilemmas were not entirely new. Military leaders had faced similar challenges in
the past, and their responses to those challenges were often decisive in shaping
the trajectory of political change in Latin America. After World War I, the broad
features of national security legality developed along similar lines in Brazil, Chile,
and Argentina, influenced by the common pressures of interwar ideological
conflicts and economic collapse, the rise of U.S. hegemony after World War II,
and the creation of a hemispheric Cold War security system that reinforced the
tendency of Latin American militaries to focus on domestic rather than external threats.

While the basic patterns of development across the three cases were broadly
similar, each country was on a slightly different path with regard to national security legality even before its military coup. Brazil was marked by relatively high
levels of judicial-military cooperation and a preoccupation with legality, at least
in the treatment of members of the political elite. In Chile, despite four decades

of constitutional civilian rule from 1932 to 1973, a highly insulated military usurped (or was sometimes assigned) judicial functions during periods of protest in local areas. And in Argentina, political polarization between a powerful elite and highly mobilized labor movement facilitated the military's periodic seizure of dictatorial powers. To present the basic patterns most starkly, we see a contrast in the cases between military cooperation with, usurpation of, and rejection of judicial authority. While it cannot be said that all of the variation among the regimes' legal strategies could have been predicted on the basis of conditions existing prior to the military coups—Chile's violent and only partially judicialized repression in 1973 would have been particularly difficult to anticipate—many of the main features of authoritarian legality under each regime were created well before military rule.

Brazilian distinctiveness in the area of national security law can best be explained with reference to the impact of the political turmoil of the 1920s and 1930s on the military, the special relationship between the U.S. and Brazilian armies after World War II, and the historical time period in which the Brazilian military regime was created. Other factors, such as the French military mission in the interwar years, seem to be less salient in explaining the Brazilian outcome.

Background to Political Repression

A variety of scholars have pointed out the special attributes of Latin American legal development. Argentina, Brazil, and Chile all shared some of these attributes. For example, Brian Loveman focuses on Latin American constitutions of the nineteenth and twentieth centuries that granted presidents broad latitude to declare a state of emergency and to suspend fundamental rights under circumstances that they deemed appropriate.[1] Whereas European constitutions often required parliamentary approval when such measures were advocated by prime ministers, Latin American constitutions usually gave presidents unilateral power to suspend fundamental rights.[2]

Below the constitutional level, Latin American legal systems have tended to be strongly hierarchical and oriented to the implementation of state policy, rather than the pluralistic coordination of competing interests.[3] More specifically, they have tended toward inquisitorial procedures in the area of criminal law (Kant de Lima 1995, 2). Latin American elites have usually taken institutions from Europe or the United States as the reference point for their own reforms, either as models that could be imitated, or impossible ideals that would never work, due to their own societies' "backwardness." As Máximo Langer points out, when Latin Americans enacted their first criminal codes in the late nineteenth and early twentieth centuries, their model was outdated Spanish legislation developed under the absolutist monarchies, not the newer codes constructed under the influence of European liberal reforms (Langer 2001, 2). Both of these features—broad presidential latitude in declaring a state of emergency, and an inquisitorial criminal code and procedure—made the law a particularly effective instrument for political persecution in Latin America.

Ideologically, Latin America has long been a hybrid combination of an Iberian tradition of a "hierarchical, diversified, and functionally compartmented social order" (Morse 1964, 124) with Western liberalism's emphasis on individual liberties, formal equality before the law, the separation of powers, and the disciplining of even executive power by the observance of formal rules. Changes in liberal practice after the beginning of the last century led to corresponding changes in Latin America. According to Ingraham, a relatively liberal, nineteenth-century view of political dissent gave way, around World War I, to a much more repressive conception of the requirements of national security in Western Europe and elsewhere. This authoritarian trend dissolved the distinction between external and internal threats to national security, so that certain forms of domestic opposition to the government came to be seen as treasonous, especially after the Bolshevik revolution of 1917 (Ingraham 1979, 219–20).

The rulers of many Latin American states embraced this view, especially when heavy European immigration in prior decades produced concern over the internalization of "foreign" threats. In developed countries, too, the state security apparatus was hardened in the 1920s and 1930s (Loewenstein 1942, 134). The post–World War II ascendancy of the United States in the Western Hemisphere and the political polarization of the Cold War reinforced and supported the institutionalization of this attitude toward dissent, which could be found in virtually all the industrialized countries as well as Latin America. For example, several European states changed their laws in the 1950s to facilitate the prosecution of Communists, fascists, and other dissidents thought to be engaged in subversion.[4]

However, in the context of weak civil societies and states with relatively dependent judiciaries and strong militaries, the turn toward a repressive conception of national security went farther in Latin America than it did in most other regions. In twentieth-century Latin America, large masses of disenfranchised people were effectively deprived of access to the courts, and the citizenship rights of the lower classes were generally unrecognized, especially in rural areas. Furthermore, in the civil law tradition, judges were seen, not as the creators of law through interpretation, as in the Anglo-American common law, but as enforcers of law that was created only by the executive or legislature. This is not so much a philosophical bias inherent in civil law systems as a sociological fact.[5] The role of judges in Latin America was thus often seen as "that of a civil servant who performs important but essentially uncreative functions"; this reflected the relative weakness of the judiciary vis-à-vis the executive there (Gardner 1980, 55).

Strong executives, weak judiciaries, inquisitorial criminal justice systems, disenfranchised masses, and elite fear of subversion thus form the general background to the cases discussed here. More specifically, in Argentina, Brazil, and Chile, military involvement in politics in the interwar period solidified certain attitudes within the officer corps about national security and popular organizations. In Brazil, the military never ruled directly in the twentieth century until the 1964 coup, but was a pillar of the dictatorial regime of Getúlio Vargas (1930–1945). In Argentina, the military ruled directly in the last century between 1930–1932, 1943–1946, 1955–1958, and 1966–1973 before the coup d'etat of 1976 (Waisman 1999, 75). And in Chile, the military was intensely involved in politics between 1920 and 1931, with a military president, Carlos Ibáñez del Campo, ruling from 1927 to 1931 and de facto military control from 1924 to 1927 (Collier and Collier 1991, 169–78). Thereafter, formal civilian control over the military was maintained until the 1973 coup, although the military had a large number of prerogatives and was highly insulated from civilians.

Just as each country experienced political interventions, and in two cases direct rule by the military, each country also experienced a populist experiment.[6] Occurring in the middle decades of the twentieth century, these experiments polarized political actors between their supporters and conservative opponents. The opponents eventually included the majority of the officer corps of the armed forces in all three countries, as nationalist-populist sympathizers were purged from the ranks in the post–World War II years. And in all three countries, classical liberal notions of the rule of law were used by opponents of populism to denounce the latter's demagoguery and subversion.

In Argentina, the populist experiment was the government of Juan Domingo Perón from 1946 to 1955. In Brazil, it was the return of the former dictator Getúlio Vargas—this time as an elected president—from 1950 to 1954. Chile did not have a comparable period in the post–World War II era until the election of Salvador Allende, but it had a short-lived populist interlude during the socialist republic of presidents Marmaduke Grove Vallejo and Carlos Gregorio

Dávila Espinoza in 1932, and had strong Socialist and Communist parties. The historical backgrounds to all three military regimes discussed here therefore exhibit common patterns.

Modes of Political Repression

In considering our three cases, the rhetoric that the regimes themselves used is misleading. The Brazilian military regime that began in 1964, which glorified itself as the harbinger of a revolution, was the most conservative of the three.[7] On the other hand, the reactionary rhetoric of the Argentine juntas of 1976–1983, including their references to a "process of national reorganization," masked a revolutionary disdain for the traditional legal order and an all-out extrajudicial war on their perceived enemies. Chile lies somewhere between these two poles. The section that follows outlines basic patterns of military-judicial relations and modes of political repression prior to the most recent military regimes in each country.

Brazil

In Brazil, both the practice of using the law to repress political opponents and the doctrine of national security were far older than the military coup of 1964. The practice of judicial repression of political opposition is thus to some extent a feature, not just of the 1964–1985 regime, but of the Brazilian state.

To a greater extent than in Chile or even Argentina, the centralization of state power in Brazil's confederal political system was accompanied by a delicate balancing act of accommodating local, private power. In this sense the central state was somewhat less autonomous and powerful and more societally embedded than in the other two cases, "unable to rule effectively without striking bargains with, and gaining the cooperation of, private groups . . . keenly conscious of the fragile limits of its authority" (Uricoechea 1980, 54). National power rested on a dualism between the central state and its expanding bureaucracy and a landed oligarchy divided by competing networks of kinship and patron-client ties.

Brazilian society, with its history of slaveholding on a grand scale and the preservation of an empire until 1889, was more hierarchical and conservative than its counterparts in the southern cone, which had gone through larger mass mobilizations during the independence wars and had been more influenced by republican ideas. According to Leonardo Avritzer, "the Brazilian elites watched the main events of the Hispanic American independence and agreed to sacrifice republicanism in order to maintain the country as a national unit. This has led it [*sic*] to sacrifice not only the republican element of national liberation, but also the idea of civic equality."[8]

Despite the generally conservative trajectory of Brazilian political development, the military and in particular the army was not as conservative a force in Brazil as it sometimes was in Chile and especially Argentina. The army's refusal to chase runaway slaves contributed to abolition in 1888, while it was the military that ended the empire and declared a republic in 1889. The positivism of the late nineteenth century was replaced in the 1920s by *tenentismo*, a movement of junior officers that shared certain characteristics of positivism, such as the belief in the military's ability to unify and modernize the nation.

Beattie writes that the adoption of conscription in 1916 changed the status of the enlisted men (*praças*) from untouchables to respected members of the community and reinforced the army's claim to be the primary vehicle of national integration and the introduction of hygiene and physical and moral fitness to the lower classes. He argues that the spread of belief in eugenics preceded and justified the introduction of the draft in Brazil in 1916, whereas in Chile and Argentina, where conscription had been introduced in 1901, the draft preceded the emergence of eugenic thought.[9]

After World War I, political repression in Brazil was marked by periodic use of exceptional state powers and the linkage of political dissidents with common criminals in official pronouncements. Under the Old Republic (1889–1930), an insurrection in 1924 touched off a wave of trials of political opponents and the "cleansing" of cities such as São Paulo and Rio de Janeiro (Pinheiro 1991, 87–116, 320–22). Under the presidency of Getúlio Vargas (1930–1945), a Communist uprising (*intentona*) in 1935 elicited a strongly repressive response. The uprising was seen by the military high command not only as an attack on the state and therefore the nation but, in this view, as a "betrayal from within," because the plot had some support from within the armed forces.[10]

The government's response to the *intentona* was the enactment of a series of repressive measures, including state of siege powers, a new law of national security, and the power to fire military officers, civil servants, and even private employees suspected of being Communists. Then minister of justice Vicente Ráo complained to the lower house of Congress (Câmara dos Deputados) of "the dolorous anachronism of liberal democracy which disarms the state in its struggle against its enemies" and said that it was necessary to change outmoded "judicial traditionalism."[11] To this end, the regime created the National Security Court (Tribunal de Segurança Nacional, TSN) for the prosecution of those accused of political crimes.

The TSN was established on September 11, 1936, by Law Number 244, before the creation of the dictatorial New State, or Estado Novo. It remained in existence until 1945, and tried thousands of suspected Communists, fascist *integralistas* (after their failed insurrection of 1938), and merchants accused of violating the regulations of the Estado Novo's "popular economy." Many of the convicted were sentenced to long prison terms, although none were executed. Initially part of military justice, it was made a separate, predominantly civilian tribunal in 1937. The special powers of its civilian and military judges, such as the right to decide by "free conviction" rather than the weight of the evidence, made the court a place in which the distinction between political dissent and subversion, fundamental to constitutional government, could be repeatedly ignored.[12]

An observer of the justice system under Vargas who did considerable research on the TSN was moved to write, "Brazil has always enjoyed the reputation of possessing the ranking class of lawyers and jurists in South America. The Brazilians are by nature a law-abiding people who hold the legal profession no less than the administration of justice in high esteem. The foreign observer who digs only a little under the surface is surprised to encounter everywhere that essential feature of the Brazilian character, *judicialismo*, that is, the tendency to subject the social dynamics to rules of law, the effort to head off eventual conflicts by finding neat and incontrovertible legal solutions in advance. The Brazilians are an extraordinarily legalistic people . . ." (Loewenstein 1942, 106).

While the National Security Court died with the Estado Novo, its existence was important in that it had been experienced by the generals who came to power in 1964. It had been abolished fewer than twenty years before the 1964 coup and was part of the repertoire of repression known and available to the military. In Chile the model of previous judicial repression known to military officers was quite different, whereas after the 1976 coup in Argentina there was a lack of a viable model that had been successfully institutionalized in the past.

The post–World War II era saw the rise of the United States to global dominance, the Cold War, and a new era of concern for national security. Brazil's close ties to the U.S. military, furthered by the Brazilian Army's participation in the Italian campaign under U.S. command,[13] were strengthened in the late 1940s and 1950s through U.S. military aid and the formation of transnational communities in international organizations involving both Brazilian and U.S. policymakers. These communities reinforced shared ideological orientations and contributed to the development of a Brazilian version of national security that creatively adapted the U.S. model. The paternalistic authoritarianism of this time is reflected by the popularity of the work of Francisco José de Oliveira Vianna, an influential law professor and author.[14]

After a brief liberalization that followed the removal by the military of the dictator Getúlio Vargas, a Cold War crackdown took place in Brazil in the late 1940s. The Communist Party, briefly legal, was outlawed again in 1947. A series of purges in the 1950s weakened the power of nationalist-populists in the armed forces, enabling a conservative vision of national security to prevail within the military and its civilian support base (Smallman 2002, 121–75). Getúlio Vargas returned to the presidency in 1950, this time as an elected nationalist-populist with a working-class base. Despite this development, the military pushed for and obtained a new national security law in 1953 that redefined crimes against the state and the political and social order (Law 1,802 of January 5, 1953). This law was more externally focused than later national security laws passed by the military regime, referring in article two, for example, to attempts to submit the nation to the sovereignty of a foreign state. However, it was quite illiberal and made it illegal to reorganize or try to reorganize a banned political organization (article 9—this was clearly aimed at the Communist Party), to make public propaganda that preached hatred between races, religions, or classes (article 11), and to organize a public meeting or rally that had not been authorized by political authorities (article 19). It is significant that for the first few years of the military regime that came to power in 1964, the 1953 national security law was seen as a more than sufficient legal basis on which to prosecute suspected Communists, trade unionists, and supporters of the deposed Goulart government.

The Brazilian military was seriously divided at several important political moments in the 1950s, especially in the crisis around the election of President Juscelino Kubitschek in 1954. A civilian-military alliance opposed Kubitschek's ascension to the presidency, and only a serious countermovement of military and civilian leaders (which emerged again during the crisis surrounding João Goulart's ascension to the presidency in 1961) ensured the presidency for Kubitschek (see de Abreu et al. 2001, 3300–302). The eventual defeat of the anti-Kubitschek forces within the military led an editorial writer for the newspaper *O Estado de São Paulo* to write, "Imbued with the false respect for the law and demonstrating a legalistic fetishism incompatible with the gravity of the situation, they [the Brazilian military] did not dare cut deeply enough to remove the gangrene, which had invaded the nation."[15] The gangrene in question was of course the *bête noir* of the Brazilian right and the internationalist military, Communism.

It could almost be said that the coup that brought the Brazilian military to power took place not once but twice—first in 1961, when the military high command unsuccessfully opposed the succession of Vice President João Goulart to the presidency, and again in 1964. The events of 1961 are important for two reasons. First, they illustrate the strong opposition to conservative military intervention on the part of Goulart's support coalition. Second, they suggest how this opposition, which persisted after the 1964 coup, reinforced the military high command's legalism and influenced its subsequent legal strategy.

The 1961 crisis was set off by the abrupt resignation of President Jânio Quadros on August 25, 1961. This act made the vice president, João Goulart, the constitutionally designated successor to Quadros. At the time of Quadros's resignation, Goulart was traveling to China on an official visit. However, the Quadros government's military ministers declared that Goulart's political past made him unfit to assume the presidency.[16] Goulart had been minister of labor under President Getúlio Vargas in the early 1950s and was seen by the military high command as too closely linked to Vargas's legacy, the trade unions, and the Communist Party. The military ministers' position created an impasse that lasted for several days and involved an intense dispute between "legalists" in favor of Goulart's ascension to the presidency, on one side, and supporters of the military ministers on the other.

On the evening of August 25, the president of the lower house of Congress, Pascoal Ranieri Mazzilli was sworn in as interim president in the absence of João Goulart. Goulart himself flew to Montevideo to await the outcome of the conflict. On August 30, the military ministers published a manifesto to the nation in which they spoke in the name of the armed forces and reiterated their opposition to João Goulart's presidency. According to the document, if Goulart became president there "would be unleashed in the country a turbulent period of agitation on top of agitation" (Barbosa 2002, 177–78).

The manifesto split the armed forces. While the navy and air force were largely with the high command, the army was divided, and the National Security Council, composed of both civilians and military officers, refused to support the manifesto (Johnson 1964, 210). Governor Leonel Brizola of Rio Grande do

Sul (and Vice President Goulart's brother-in-law) led a strong civilian-military campaign in favor of the constitutional succession of Goulart. Working with generals who supported him, Brizola pushed hard for Goulart's presidency. Despite the unity of the military ministers, many officers and enlisted men favored Goulart and the constitutional succession.

The situation was tense and the possibility of civil war loomed. The military ministers prohibited the return of Vice President Goulart and mobilized the First and Second Armies in anticipation of a clash with the Third Army in Rio Grande do Sul. General Orlando Geisel, working for Minister Denis, ordered General José Lopes Machado to move against Governor Brizola, who was "outside of legality," and even suggested that Lopes Machado use the air force to bomb the governor's palace.[17]

The impasse was resolved in a compromise when the Congress formed a mixed commission of senators and deputies to study the issue. The commission proposed an amendment to the constitution making a parliamentary regime, so that the new president would have to share powers with a prime minister along the lines of the French Fifth Republic. On September 2, 1961, the Congress approved this in constitutional amendment number 4, a remarkable feat of constitutional engineering that put in place the only instance of parliamentarism in Latin America. With this maneuver the military ministers were mollified and Goulart was persuaded to take the presidency with reduced powers. Goulart was sworn in on September 7, 1961.

Goulart immediately removed the military ministers from power while changing the entire cabinet. Remarkably, he did not punish the military ministers beyond this, and all three of them became leading conspirators of the coup that definitively removed Goulart from the Brazilian political scene in 1964.[18] Goulart staged and won a plebiscite that ended the parliamentary regime and restored the presidency's powers in January 1963, but his rule was to be short lived.

The 1961 crisis sets Brazil apart from Chile and Argentina. In it, we see the intense collaboration between civilian jurists and military officers to create national security legality that became the hallmark of the Brazilian military regime. Despite the fact that the supporters of Goulart called themselves "legalists," the civil-military conspirators against him also saw themselves as upholders of a different, more conservative legalist tradition. They did not succeed in 1961, but they prevailed less than three years later.

Even before the coup, the proponents of an authoritarian legalism began to transform Brazil's legal system. For example, military courts successfully claimed jurisdiction over cases of political crime by civilians. In 1963, two civilian trade unionists from São Paulo were convicted in a military court in Brasília. Their ostensible crime was to distribute campaign literature on behalf of an army sergeant running for city council on the ticket of the Partido Trabalhista Brasileiro (PTB, or Brazilian Labor Party, the party founded by Getúlio Vargas after World War II; Simas 1986, 16–20). Such cases became commonplace after the passage of the Second Institutional Act by the military regime in 1965, but the precedent for them antedated the coup itself.

The Brazilian subsystem for dealing with alleged political criminals was thus far more integrated with the regular civilian judiciary than were its counterparts in Argentina and Chile. In the 1934 constitution, military justice had been placed within the civilian court system, and it was never removed.[19] Military officers serving in the military courts remained in the chain of command and served in the court for only three months. Because only the civilian judge had legal training, he often heavily influenced decision making by the court. Lawyers in the court were mostly civilian: the prosecutors were from the Ministério Público Militar (the Military Public Ministry, the prosecutorial arm of military justice) and most defense lawyers came from a small, select group of civilian attorneys who defended political prisoners. Furthermore, as we have seen, cases could be appealed all the way up to the civilian Supreme Court throughout the military regime. (This contrasts sharply with the Chilean military justice system from 1973 to 1978.)

Under the Brazilian military regime, though, some people from the judiciary were purged,[20] judges lost their irremovability, and the Superior Military Court and Supreme Court were manipulated (with the removal of independent judges and court packing) to ensure that they were not too oppositional.[21] Torture was also widely used as a basis for confessions in political trials. Furthermore, after 1965, the lower levels of the regular civilian judiciary had no jurisdiction over political crime. For example, the state Supreme Court of São Paulo, which had a long constitutionalist tradition, maintained a critical posture toward the military regime's use of military courts against civilians.[22] Military-civilian cooperation in the judicial sphere in Brazil, therefore, was limited, and excluded important civilian jurists. But it was still far more extensive than in the other two cases.

Chile

Chile presents many parallels with Brazil. As in Brazil, an oligarchic, somewhat representative regime (the Parliamentary Regime, 1891–1924) started to unravel in the 1920s (Sater and Herwig 1999, 3). Like the Brazilian military, the Chilean military then became increasingly involved in politics, as the labor question and later the depression disturbed political arrangements. Like Vargas in Brazil, Carlos Ibáñez del Campo emerged as a caudillo in the interwar years to declare a new order (the "New Chile"), only to be forced out by the military in 1931. Like Vargas, Ibáñez came back as an elected president in the 1950s. Vargas's and Ibáñez's political careers are therefore similar, even though Ibáñez was an active-duty military officer when he first came to power (Vargas was a former officer) and Ibáñez was more conservative in his second term as president (1952–1958) than was Vargas (1950–1954).

Like the Brazilian military, the Chilean armed forces included many officers who were hostile to both liberal democracy and socialism and were instead supportive of moderate, top-down reforms. Like the *tenentes* in Brazil, military writers heralded the military's ability to school the nation in nationalist and civic virtues (Loveman 1988, 211). And as in Brazil, some Chilean military officers took part in "revolutions"—in this case, the removal of interim president General Luís Altamirano in 1925[23] and the coup led by Colonel Marmaduke Grove Vallejo in December 1931.[24]

In addition, the Chilean military, like its Brazilian counterpart, could also lay claim to a tradition of legalism. In the words of two acute observers of Chilean politics, "The [Chilean] republic had long stood as a bastion of civilized, 'legalistic' behavior in a region of tyrants and revolutionaries; its officials prided themselves on scrupulous attention to constitutional norms and legal procedures. Law was the most prestigious profession, and judges, although not highly paid, enjoyed considerable status in a legally conscious society" (Constable and Valenzuela 1991, 116).

However, several factors distinguish the Chilean military from its Brazilian counterpart. The first is its "Prussianization." There were five German military missions to the Chilean army between 1885 and 1931, and these made it more vertical, cohesive, and rigid than the Brazilian army, and more separate and autonomous from civilian politicians.[25] The description of a "state within a state" has been used to describe the Chilean military's political role during this period, a term that is less appropriate to the Brazilian armed forces. Second, this

"Prussian" cohesiveness and rigidity can be seen in the army's dealings with internal "disorder," which tended to be highly repressive and free from civilian control. For example, in the nineteenth century, the war against the Araucanians (Mapuches) in the southern part of the country was a war of extermination (Sater and Herwig 1999, 20). And in La Coruña in 1925, soldiers machine-gunned protesting workers and destroyed their homes with field artillery, killing some six hundred to eight hundred people, including captured prisoners and the wounded.[26]

The third difference with Brazil concerns policing. Ibáñez transferred the centralized police force, the *carabineros*, from the Interior Ministry to the War Ministry in 1925, giving the Chilean army control over national policing. This control was unparalleled in Brazil, where state-level police forces were commanded by governors. Ibáñez used the *carabineros* and army to repress labor organizations, the Communist Party, anarchists, and other political opponents. He deployed his policing power freely, as when he defied civilian president Arturo Alessandri's order and used the *carabineros* to violently break up labor demonstrations in the port of Iquique in May and June of 1925 (Nunn 1989, 121–22).

In addition, when labor protests broke out in Antofagasta and Tarapacá in the same period, the commander of the First Army Division, General Florentino de la Guarda, declared a state of siege and martial law and tried protestors as "communist revolutionaries" in military courts (Nunn 1989, 122). He did this on the orders of civilian president Alessandri, but the point here is that political justice was dispensed directly by the military itself and not in a civilian court as in the Brazilian TSN. The military also engaged in the detention and exile of political opponents in the 1920s (Nunn 1976, 161–64). What we see in the Chilean interwar years is a lower level of civilian-military and especially judicial-military cooperation than in Brazil, with the military retaining more characteristics of an impenetrable, hierarchical, and separate institution.

These characteristics persisted in the post–World War II years, even as the Chilean military retreated to a constitutionalist position. As in Brazil, the beginning of the Cold War brought a hardening of the state's legal apparatus vis-à-vis potential and actual opposition and dissent. In 1948 the Chilean Congress passed the Law for the Permanent Defense of Democracy (Law 8987) in response to the fear of Communism prevalent in that era. Called the *ley maldita* (damned or accursed law) by its critics, this measure, among other provisions, outlawed the Communist Party, prohibited its members from participation in labor unions, and set up zones for the banishment or "relegation" of presumed subversives (Loveman 1988, 254). The Communists were repressed heavily for the next ten years, and the new law was used to prevent rural labor organization and to crack down on the urban labor movement.

When the *ley maldita* was passed, Augusto Pinochet Ugarte, the future dictator, was the captain of an infantry regiment in Iquique. In his memoirs, he recounts that in the aftermath of the law's passage he moved his troops around Iquique arresting Communist "agitators," using a list of names provided to him by military intelligence. He took the detainees to a military base in Pisagua, where more than five hundred of them were locked up, and where Pinochet became military commander in January of 1948. According to Pinochet, a group of congressmen led by Socialist senator Salvador Allende appeared in Pisagua and asked to visit the prisoners. Pinochet told them that they did not have permission to make such a visit, and that if they attempted to do so, he would shoot them. The congressmen then went away. Asked by an interviewer whether he would have carried out his threat, Pinochet replied, "I believe I would have done what I said as the orders were not to accept any visitors, much less these gentlemen, who only came to agitate the prisoners."[27]

This anecdote alerts us to the power and autonomy of the Chilean military in the judicial realm. A mere army captain detained political "criminals" and prevented everyone, even members of Congress, from visiting "his" prisoners. There is no mention of the civilian judiciary in the story. A previous generation of scholars emphasized the singularity of the Chilean military's constitutionalism in the 1932–1973 period (see Loveman 1988, 229; and Drake 1991, 269). This record is unique, but what is also striking is how Chile's constitutional settlement left a large role for autonomous military intervention in political and legal matters at the local level. Loveman ascribes this to the legacy of the 1924 coup and the Ibáñez administration (1924–1927; Loveman 1988, 193–94, 224). Regardless of the cause, it is misleading to describe the Chilean military's professionalism as consisting of political "noninvolvement."[28]

The Law for the Permanent Defense of Democracy was abolished in 1958 by President Ibáñez prior to his departure from office. The Communist Party was thus made legal again, ending ten years in which it was underground. In the same year, President Allesandri and Congress also approved Law 12,927, the Law of State Security. This law contained a very broad and illiberal definition of crimes against the state. Article 4 declared that anyone who "in any form or by any means rises up against the constituted government or provokes a civil war" is committing a crime against state security. This article also prohibited inciting members of the Armed Forces, including the *carabineros*, to indiscipline or disobedience (article 4, letter b) and divulging information either within or without the country to "perturb the constitutional order, the security of the country . . . [and] the stability of values" (article 4, letter g). Public desecration of the flag was also expressly prohibited by the law.

During the 1960s, different administrations started to widen their right to declare states of exception that allowed them to suppress constitutional guarantees without a previous authorization from Congress. This declaration was used by the executive, especially to suppress strikes in the copper mines. Once again, the pattern of direct military suppression of labor protests continued. In 1966, during the Frei government, the departments of El Loa, Tocopilla, Rancagua, and Chañaral were declared emergency zones due to a copper strike. The decree authorized the army to enter the town of El Salvador, which it did, in order to put an end to the workers' demands. The army and *carabineros* subsequently killed seven people and wounded thirty-five, according to official figures. After the massacre, debates in Congress included criticisms of the government of President Eduardo Frei Montalva, and in particular the defense minister Juan de Dios Carmona, responsible for the troops' actions. However, the Legislation, Constitution, and Justice Committee of the Senate concluded that the miliary acts in El Salvador were the sole responsibility of President Frei (Manns 1999, 175–80). The Senate therefore in this instance deferred to the executive's prerogative to impose martial law in zones of social conflict where workers' demands were deemed to threaten order.[29]

Here again we see that despite its strict adherence to constitutional constraints prior to 1973, the Chilean military shared its Brazilian and Argentine counterparts' concern for the maintenance of a particular vision of domestic security. Hernán Vidal professes to find in the Chilean military a vocation to exercise "a redemptive social function of the application of violence" (Vidal 1989, 125). And a textbook on the armed forces written by a Chilean military officer and published in 1972 shares very similar language with Brazilian and Argentine documents of the same era. It reveals the military elite's self-conception as a guardian against subversive propaganda and "psychosocial warfare" (Roldan 1972, 61–66, 173–80).

When the military took power in a coup in 1973, it declared a state of war and imposed wartime military courts on civilian supporters of the Allende Popular Unity government. Military courts had been used to try civilians during the War of the Pacific (1879–1883) and in the labor disputes of subsequent eras. Whereas for both Brazilian military officers after 1964 and for Chilean officers after 1973, subjecting civilian political opponents to prosecution in courts was something that had occurred within living memory, the model of political justice in Chile was very different from the Brazilian one. While Brazilian political trials had taken place through the cooperation of military and judicial elites in a hybrid system that fused the military and civilian judiciaries, in Chile, the trials had been purely military affairs in a system that insulated military courts from the civilian judiciary at the first level, and gave military commanders sole discretion over prosecutions in their areas. Furthermore, unlike the Brazilian military regime, the Chilean regime felt under threat from subversion throughout its rule, and preserved its subsystem for dealing with political crime right up until the transition to democracy.

As in Brazil, Chilean military attitudes to subversion were shaped largely before the coup. Like their Brazilian and Argentine counterparts, many Chilean military officers saw the development of working-class political movements and the arrival of European immigrants in the early twentieth century as threatening to a conservative vision of national identity (Smallman 2002, 26). Under Allende's Popular Unity government, the Chilean army had asked for and received the passage of an arms control law that allowed them to arrest and to try suspected members of the armed left. It was this law that became the most common charge against political prisoners after the coup. Like the 1963 prosecution of trade unionists in Brazil, the arms control law in Chile signals an active military role in combating the left before the military takeover. Again as in Brazil, political prosecutions in Chile in the first few years after the coup were largely based on laws that had been passed before the military took power. A further discussion of the prelude to the military coup in Chile can be found in chapter 5.

Argentina

The Argentine approach to the problem of opposition was the most radical of the three cases examined here. The military regime of 1976–1983 largely dispensed with any kind of legal strategy, and engaged in total and merciless war on the alleged agents of subversion. To some extent, this propensity toward extrajudicial and radical approaches to political repression can be seen in earlier Argentine history.

Many basic patterns, however, are familiar to students of the Brazilian and Chilean cases. As with the Brazilian and Chilean militaries, the Argentine military was riven by divisions connected to the larger political conflicts around it. Many of its officers were both hostile to liberal democracy and anxious to forestall the left, and supportive of a nationalist and reformist orientation to labor and economic problems. Like the Brazilian and Chilean officers, Argentine officers also took part in a "revolution" that took place only one month before the Liberal Alliance's armed revolt in Brazil in 1930. Again like their counterparts in Brazil and Chile, Argentine officers were influenced by foreign military missions, in this case from Germany.[30]

However, Argentina does exhibit important differences from Brazil and Chile. Perhaps most fundamentally, the Argentine military found itself in the midst of a political system in which "no constitutional authority is strong enough to prevent a determined president from imposing his will, even if this involves violation of the law and the constitution itself" (Potash 1989, 105). This volatile hyper-presidential system was polarized between very strong popular and labor movements (represented politically by the Radical and later Peronist parties), on one hand, and intransigent and powerful agrarian and financial elites on the other.

The military's role in the violent repression of labor can be seen in the interwar years. In January 1919, during the *semana trágica* (tragic week), the police and members of the Patriotic League (with many army officers involved) and Labor Association engaged in a violent sweep of working-class areas of Buenos Aires, ostensibly looking for subversives and "Bolsheviks." The Russian-Jewish community was particularly affected, and an estimated seven hundred to eight hundred people were killed, with thousands injured and arrested (Collier and Collier 1991, 147; see also Nino 1996, 42). The military was even more directly involved in *La Patagonia trágica*—the rural equivalent of the *semana trágica*— which took place in 1921–1922. In this action, the army violently repressed striking workers on sheep ranches, killing an estimated one thousand to two thousand workers (Collier and Collier 1991, 148).

Argentine officers' political opinions may not have been inherently more conservative than those of their fellow officers in Brazil and Chile. However, their political role was. This was due in part to structural factors, especially Argentina's deep polarization between a large and highly mobilized movement of the industrial working class, and a wealthy, powerful, and intransigent ruling class dominated by agrarian and financial interests. Such a polity saw "direct confrontations among the associations of different class and sectoral groups, in which the state and political parties played only a weak role in mediating and aggregating societal interests" (Collier and Collier 1991, 148). In it, there was less room for judicialized repression, whether by hybrid civil-military courts as in Brazil, or purely military courts as in Chile. Instead, the direct application of force by the military often prevailed.

If political polarization shaped the military's role, it also affected the judiciary. Nino remarks that a striking feature of Argentine politics is ideological dualism in the judicial realm: liberals were not democrats and vice versa (1996, 44). While this dualism existed throughout Latin America, it crystallized most clearly in Argentina. Oteiza (1994, 47–48) points out that the judiciary was rarely able to stake out an independent position vis-à-vis the other branches of state power within this political system. The Supreme Court, in particular, became a protagonist in the successive political conflicts. From its acceptance of the 1930 coup, through frequent purges when governments changed, to the refusal to grant writs of habeas corpus during the 1976–1983 military regime, the court became a handmaiden of executive power (see also Nino 1996, 47–48).

In 1930 the military ended Radical rule and ushered in a decade of electoral manipulation and repression. Unlike the Brazilian military's association with a project of working- and middle-class inclusion under Vargas, or the Chilean military's role in the relatively inclusive 1925 constitution, the Argentine military before 1946 was associated not with progressive reforms but with the oligarchic closure of the political arena. After the 1930 coup, the first president was General José Félix Uriburu, who had been an opponent of the Radicals' pro-labor policies and a member of the Patriotic League (Collier and Collier 1991, 154).

As the historian Tulio Halperín Donghi notes (1993, 194, 203), in interwar Chile (and, we could add, Brazil), the military's role was "as arbiter between the country's political elite and the forces of democratization," whereas in Argentina, the military sided more clearly with the oligarchic elite. This role did not necessarily make the military consistently more violent than its Brazilian and Chilean counterparts. For example, Potash reports (1969, 58–59) that under the Uriburu government's martial law from September 1930 to June 1931, five persons, including two anarchists, were executed by firing squads, while many foreign-born trade unionists were deported and torture was widespread. This violence does not seem to be worse than that of Chile and Brazil in the same period. However, it may have committed the military to a political posture that in the future would lead it to the use of more and more violence.

The Argentine military also seems to have been more insular and more reluctant to work with civilians than its Brazilian and Chilean counterparts.

McSherry (1997, 37) interviewed a retired military officer in 1992 who said, "the generation of the 1880s was the last sociological group where you had both civilians and the military who knew each other, who fought together for their country [in the war against Paraguay] . . . nobody paid much attention at first, but by the 1930s, [officers and civilians] went into their own ghettos, and the civilians were too busy making money. When these things begin to happen, I think you have a sort of wall, a very difficult wall to climb, a very high one." The contrast between Argentina and Brazil, where civil-military cooperation in the judicial realm was much higher, should be noted here.

Furthermore, the Argentine military hierarchy was not broken in the interwar period. Again the contrast is especially stark when compared to Brazil, where junior officers had embedded themselves within a civilian-military movement to "republicanize the Republic" and had risen up against some of their own generals in the 1930 revolution. The 1924 coup d'etat in Chile also defied military hierarchy. But no successful revolt against military hierarchy occurred in Argentina in the interwar years. In addition, factionalism within the Argentine armed forces was more intense than in Brazil and Chile, while military-judicial relations were more strained, with more judicial opposition to military notions of national security than in either Brazil or Chile.

After Argentina's 1930 revolution, the military grew in size and importance within the state apparatus. The officer corps doubled in size between 1930 and 1945, the personnel under the officers' control tripled, and Argentina's arms industry expanded, reflecting its status as the leading Latin American industrial power of that era (McSherry 1997, 39–40).

With the growth of the armed forces, domestic security issues became increasingly militarized. For example, in 1941, civilian president Ramón S. Castillo declared a state of siege, lifting constitutional guarantees. States of siege were invoked several times again until 1963. In 1942, a special police unit inside the Ministry of the Interior was created to apply "vigilance over and suppression of anti-Argentine activities." In 1943, the military stepped in again to directly take charge of the executive branch. The 1943 coup coalition consisted of military officers, small and medium-sized industrialists, and some leaders of organized labor. The navy, traditionally linked to Great Britain and the United States and with liberal rightist sympathies, generally opposed the coup, but the army largely supported it (McSherry 1997, 40–41).

Populist nationalist elements temporarily gained the upper hand in the Argentine military with the rise of Juan Domingo Perón to the presidency in

1946. Unlike Chile, where a populist experiment lasted for less than a year in 1932, Perón's rule survived for nine years, until 1955. Perón offered something to both pillars of the Argentine social order: substantial material concessions to organized labor, and anti-Communism to the military. However, the management of this uneasy coalition proved to contain too many contradictions.

The 1955 coup against Perón, which united most of the armed forces' high command, the Catholic Church, and the agrarian and financial elites, was bloody. It triggered Argentina's descent into a spiral of violence. Post-1955 governments vainly tried to crack down on "Communism," now expanded to include radical Peronism. Decree-Law 18,787 of 1956 outlawed Communist activity, defining Communists as those affiliated to the Communist Party or any other party forming part of "the communist movement." Decree-Law 4,214 of 1963 gave a more technical, detailed definition of Communism, and included in it any activities carried out "because of, or motivated by, or for the reason of communist ideology."[31] With Peronism driven underground, the actual Communist Party was no longer the most important threat to the managers of the national security apparatus. As an incipient armed left appeared, the military used military courts to try suspected guerrillas in the early 1960s. And in 1966, the armed forces took power once again.

Unlike the coups of 1930, 1943, and 1955, in which the military described its intervention as a temporary "cleansing" of the body politic, the 1966 coup signaled the military's intention to remain in power indefinitely. In this sense it resembled the 1964 coup in Brazil, although in the Argentine case the "revolution" was more radical. For example, the new regime replaced the entire Supreme Court, repeating a pattern established previously in Argentina. More importantly, it abandoned any attempt to pose as a provisional government or prepare the ground for a return to democracy. Instead, it modified the constitution, called its decrees "laws," and used the term "governor" rather than *interventor* for its appointed replacements in the provinces. In the words of legal expert Enrique Groisman, "For the first time, a 'de facto' government avoided a commitment to return to the constitutional order and behaved as if it had founded a distinct legitimacy" (1983, 8). Furthermore, it established a personal autocracy around General Juan Carlos Onganía.

The Argentine military regime of 1966–1973, while short lived, was repressive in much the same way that its Brazilian and Chilean counterparts were. For example, the universities were purged, and Decree-Law 17,245 of April 1967 prohibited all activity on university campuses related to "forms of militancy, agitation, propaganda, proselytism, or indoctrination of a political character" (McSherry 1997, 64). Less well known is the regime's Decree-Law 17,401 for the repression of Communism, promulgated on August 29, 1967. Its definition of Communism is much more flexible than in previous laws such as 18,787 of 1956 and Decree-Law 4,214 of 1963. The 1967 measure gave the secretary of State Information the right to determine whether individuals were Communist. This determination was made in secret.

The consequences of being categorized as a Communist by the state were severe. They included the loss of the following benefits and rights: an ID card; state employment; a professorship in a public or private university; a radio or TV transmission license; permission to own a printing press; ownership of property in areas deemed to be of national security interest to the state; and positions in professional associations (either as employers or employees). Naturalized Argentine citizens could also lose their citizenship and be deported if found guilty of Communism under this law. Also, anyone convicted of proselytizing activities—that is, spreading subversive propaganda or propaganda inimical to the public order, motivated by Communist ideology—was liable to a sentence of one to eight years in prison under Decree-Law 17,401 (Gobierno de Argentina 1967, 27B:1633, 1634, 1636).

Despite the drastic loss of rights of those deemed to be Communist by the state, the procedures for an appeal of the initial determination were stacked against citizens. As in some of the Brazilian and Chilean military court trials, the burden of proof effectively lay with those accused—they had to prove that they were not Communist.

Decree-Law 17,401 shows that the Argentine military regime of 1966–1973, like its counterpart in Brazil, was committed to some sort of judicialization of its repression. In the note from the executive power justifying the law, the then justice minister Jaime Perriaux declared, "It would be very easy and comfortable to say that the ordinary judicial system of Argentina and her Western brothers completely lacks efficacy and for now has to be abandoned, at least in a certain sense. It is my firm belief that this solution would be premature, and that the Argentine state must respond to the challenge of these [terrorist] acts, showing the necessary capacity to modernize and modify its institutions in order to respond with greater efficiency" (Gobierno de Argentina 1971, 31B:1265). Here we see dedication to a project of authoritarian legality that did not exist in 1976–1983.

However, regime leaders were frustrated in their attempts to realize such a project, in part because of enduring judicial independence. While President

Onganía appointed new members to the Supreme Court and a new attorney general, all lower court judges continued to enjoy irremovability. Lower court autonomy was even slightly increased, because while Congress had the power to remove judges, the 1966 coup leaders had closed Congress. Thereafter, they transferred responsibility for removing judges to the judiciary itself. As Arceneaux shows (2001, 36), provincial governors were allowed a one-time purge of the courts at the time of their appointment by the military regime, but afterwards, "any guarantees of immovability established in the provincial constitution would hold." The result was that the "higher levels of the judiciary were subservient to the executive, but not the lower ones." For example, a lower court found in 1968 that the government did not have the authority to close certain news magazines, although the decision was eventually overturned by the Supreme Court (Arceneaux 2001, 36–37).

Understanding the 1966–1973 military regime in Argentina is crucial to understanding the subsequent 1976–1983 regime. For our purposes here, two of the earlier regime's features deserve attention. First, it clearly ratcheted up the level of internal repression and constructed a foundation of national security legality that was still largely in place in 1976.[32] However, compared to the military regimes of Brazil and Chile, the 1966–1973 military regime in Argentina was also more massively and seriously opposed by various political forces, and consequently constrained. Because of this, the regime was forced to preserve more elements of a pre-authoritarian, civilian judicial system in which defendants' rights and the possibility of contestation of regime policies continued to exist.

After the "Cordobazo" of late May 1969—a weeklong uprising of students and workers in Córdoba that spread to Corrientes, Rosario, and Tucumán and was put down by the army—the regime was on the retreat (Arceneaux 2001, 59). In June 1969 President Onganía was ousted in a "coup within the coup," and the subsequent governments of Generals Levingston and Lanusse sought an exit strategy for the military regime.

Under Levingston and Lanusse, the strength and autonomy of the lower levels of the judiciary forced the military regime into ad hoc judicial solutions to the problem of political opposition, in particular the creation of a National Penal Court in 1971. This civilian court prosecuted hundreds of political prisoners in the brief period of its existence. The eventual withdrawal of the military from power led to the election of a Peronist government in 1973. The strong opposition to military rule triumphed in the Peronist restoration, the National Penal Court was dissolved, and all political prisoners were freed and then amnestied. This contributed to the accumulation of frustration within the military and the later adoption of dirty war tactics in 1975 at the regional level, and in 1976 at the national level.

The Argentine military regime of 1966–1973 was therefore trying to construct the kind of authoritarian legality that existed under Brazilian military rule, and it is analyzed in more detail later in this book. However, resistance to military rule was stronger in Argentina than in Brazil, and political polarization was more severe. This led to the abandonment of the military's original project and an abrupt change of regime in 1973. As will be argued in chapter 6, this switch of regime induced the military to adopt a radical change of course and to largely repudiate its prior strategy of legalism.

Historical Trends and Variations

At first glance, it might seem that the authoritarian legalities of the military regimes in Brazil, Chile, and Argentina in the 1960s and 1970s were ad hoc, short-term adaptations to extraordinary and entirely new circumstances, and that as such, they had little relation to previous historical developments. Indeed, some might argue that the legal outcomes completely belied previous patterns. Nevertheless, the tendencies found in each regime had some precedents in earlier periods. These tendencies can be seen in the interwar years, and were reinforced by subsequent developments in the post–World War period. The outcomes of pre-coup attempts by the military in each country to cooperate with civilians in the revision of institutions to meet the perceived threat of subversion substantially match subsequent strategies under military rule. They also influenced the options of military regime leaders before they took power. In each country prior conditions affected the post-coup decisions that created new authoritarian legal systems, each of which remained largely in place throughout military rule.

The Brazilian institutional matrix, in the 1930s and again in the 1960s, was the most gradualist and involved the most judicial-military cooperation. The National Security Court under Vargas was a civilian-military hybrid, as were the military courts of the 1960s. The military was closely connected to civilian political elites and did not administer justice on its own. The Chilean institutional matrix was that of a military state within a state, as in labor conflicts before the coup in which the armed forces declared martial law and tried labor leaders in their own, insulated courts. The Argentine military found itself in an oscillating political system marked by strong polarization between popular political forces and economic oligarchies, in which political competition repeatedly spilled over the boundaries of constitutional limits. In such a system, the military's power as a political moderator was most likely to be used in extrajudicial ways via pure force, since a lack of consensus about the rules of the game made judicial repression complicated to organize.

The Brazilian armed forces were at the other end of the spectrum among our three cases, developing a reputation as a military reluctant to apply force decisively, unilaterally, and extrajudicially. This orientation can best be explained by reference to the legacy of *tenentismo* in the 1920s and the 1930 revolution, the close ties between the U.S. and Brazilian armies, and the historical period in which the Brazilian coup took place.

The first factor created a pattern of close consultation between military officers and civilian political leaders and, in the legal sphere, the integration of the civilian and military judiciaries. The U.S. influence played a role in the tendency of the military to couch its positions in legalistic language. The fact that the 1964 coup took place during the waning days of the Alliance for Progress and not later was probably also significant, in that the reformist orientation of that era had not yet been replaced by the starker anti-Communist realpolitik that could be seen in the 1973 coup in Chile.

The fact that unlike the Chileans and Argentines, the Brazilian army had been visited by a training mission from France rather than Germany is probably less significant than the factors listed above. The French mission in 1920 may well have turned the officer corps' attention more fully to national problems, but it seems unlikely that political differences between republican France and imperial Germany would have been decisive in shaping attitudes toward the law. The French army, after all, waged a brutal and largely extrajudicial campaign against anticolonial forces in Algeria in the late 1950s and early 1960s, and it is French counterinsurgency doctrine that is most often cited as the primary intellectual influence on Argentine military officers who engineered the dirty war.[33] Therefore, although more research undoubtedly needs to be done on this topic, to cite the French training mission as an explanation for Brazilian distinctiveness seems rather implausible on its face.

Conclusion

The legal systems of the Brazilian, Argentine, and Chilean military regimes were, at least in general terms, quite similar. Compared to other legal systems around the world, they were strongly hierarchical, relying heavily on documentation and the exclusive authority of state institutions. Similarly, they were oriented toward policy implementation rather than the resolution of conflicts in a more pluralistic sense (Damaška 1986, 181).

Common internal and global pressures influenced the similar development of national security legality in Brazil and the southern cone. The success of the Bolshevik revolution in 1917 and the subsequent rise of Communist parties, the economic depression of the 1930s, and the rise of working-class movements with significant participation by foreign-born workers and Communist, anarchist, and socialist influences alarmed judicial and military elites and led them to devise new legal safeguards for the preservation of order. The rise of the United States after World War II created a new hemispheric alliance system that eased Latin American leaders' fears of external aggression and gave militaries freer rein to focus on internal security threats. National security law was increasingly oriented toward domestic political actors in the decades after World War II.

Despite these commonalities, these regimes did not exercise their powers of repression in identical ways. If we look within the legal systems at the specific relations between military officers and judges, we find quite distinctive patterns in the construction of authoritarian political justice in each case. This variation was not the result of long-term legacies stemming from the colonial or nineteenth-century experience. Instead, history mattered in particular and conjunctural ways. Of particular importance were the relations between military and judicial elites within each country.

The Brazilian approach to legality was marked by greater judicial-military cooperation and greater concern about formal legality in the treatment of political opponents, at least those who were members of the political elite, than in the other two cases. In Chile, the military tended to usurp or be assigned judicial authority, rather than work to integrate itself within the civilian judiciary, as in Brazil. And in Argentina, outright end runs around the judiciary by the military were common, with subsequent judicial ratification of the de facto results of military power.

I ascribe Brazilian distinctiveness in the use of law to three factors: the legacy of *tenentismo* in the 1920s and the 1930 revolution, the close ties between the U.S. and Brazilian armies, and the historical period in which the Brazilian coup took place. The first factor caused a break in military hierarchy and saw junior officers engage in a program of national reform in alliance with civilians. The second factor influenced Brazilian military officers in the direction of maintaining certain liberal appearances in the creation of their regime, while the third factor was important because the early 1960s was an era of reformism that had not yet given way to the more hard-line Cold War confrontations of the 1970s.

This is not to argue that in 1960 there were overwhelmingly obvious, tell-tale signs that militaries would behave in the legal sphere exactly as they did. The transition of the Chilean military from a force with a reputation for a rigid adherence to constitutionalist principles to one engaged in a coup d'etat and massive internal repression is perhaps the most surprising of our cases. Nevertheless, I argue that even in Chile, pre-coup attempts by the military to meet the perceived threat of subversion foreshadow the later legal strategies of military regime leaders. In Chile, civilian politicians periodically granted considerable autonomy to the army to impose martial law on political protestors, enabling the military to behave as a relatively closed, autonomous, hierarchical body imposing its view of order on the nation.

Therefore, in each country prior conditions affected the post-coup decisions that created new authoritarian legal systems, each of which remained largely in place throughout military rule. The 1961 succession crisis in Brazil shows the highly legalistic orientation of the country's military and its tendency to cooperate with judicial (and congressional) elites. The substantial resistance to the high command from "legalists" within and without the armed forces tempered hard-line tendencies within the military and impressed upon military leaders the imperative that their future actions appeared to conform, at least outwardly, to legal and constitutional traditions. This imperative did not constrain them from staging a coup d'etat less than three years later, but it is significant that this was the only coup of the three discussed in this book that was partially justified in constitutional terms. I turn now to this historical moment and its aftermath.

4

Political Trials in Brazil

THE CONTINUATION OF A CONSERVATIVE TRADITION

No oppression is so heavy or lasting as that which is inflicted
by the perversion and exorbitance of legal authority.

Joseph Addison

AUTHORITARIAN LEGALITY WAS closer to the legal system of the prior
regime in Brazil than it was in Chile and Argentina. There was more gradualism
and continuity in the Brazilian case, and this can be seen in the records of political trials. Analysis of the history of judicial and military institutions bests accounts for this distinctive outcome.

The 1964 Constitutional Coup

The 1961 compromise that allowed João Goulart to become president papered
over but did not end the conflicts in Brazilian politics. On one side were the
landowning and industrial elites of São Paulo, Minas Gerais, and Rio de Janeiro,
the internationalists within the military (most of the higher officers), and many
members of the middle class. On the other were union leaders, the peasant
leagues, university students, public sector employees including some enlisted
men in the armed forces, and some elected politicians. The United States was
an important actor in these conflicts, clashing with the administration of João
Goulart on a number of economic and security issues, eventually throwing its

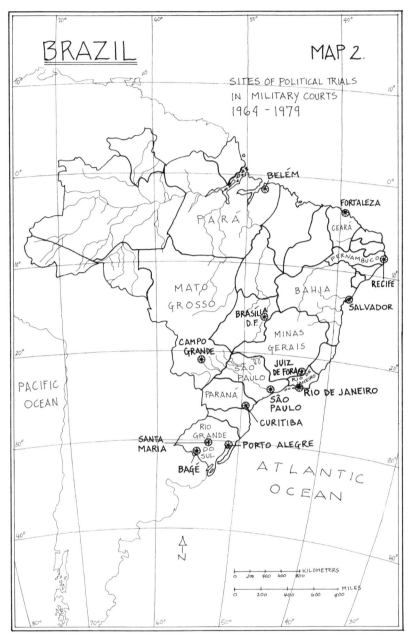

Map 2: Location of political trials in military courts, Brazil 1964–1979. Map by Lynne E. Perry.

weight behind the coup, and facilitating the coup's justification in constitutional terms.

The coup was triggered by General Olympio Mourão Filho on April 1, 1964, and succeeded quickly. The first step in justifying the action was to characterize it as a defensive measure. In the words of then U.S. ambassador to Brazil Lincoln Gordon, Goulart's purpose "was to put an end to constitutional government in Brazil in the interest of establishing some sort of personal dictatorship" (quoted in Skidmore 1967, 410–11, note 26). This justification remained suspect, however, because Goulart never made the preemptive dictatorial moves that his opponents claimed he was contemplating. Goulart's executive decrees of March 13, 1964, nationalizing oil refineries and expropriating land adjacent to federal highways, railways, and reservoirs, were fully within the president's powers, even if they were controversial.

After the coup, the Brazilian military was eager to portray the coup as having come "just in time." Military officers claimed to have seized documents in the state of Minas Gerais that revealed a large-scale national plan on the part of the Communist Party to seize power.[1] Ironically, the Communist Party had criticized Goulart for reforming too quickly and for being an adventurer, and reacted to the coup passively (Horowitz 1970, 210).

Talk of Communist conspiracies and the president's dictatorial intentions were not the only elements in the attempt to legitimize the coup. The coup was also presented by some of its defenders as constitutional. This presented various problems, because the coup had involved several obvious breaches of the prior constitution. First, the president of the lower house in Congress, Pascoal Ranieri Mazzilli, assumed the presidency, even though the 1946 Constitution authorized him to do this only if the incumbent president "abandoned" the presidency (article 79). João Goulart was still in the country when Mazzilli was elected president in Congress on April 2, 1964; Goulart had only fled to Rio Grande do Sul to avoid capture by the military. Furthermore, only 150 members of the Senate and lower house voted to elect Mazzilli, less than the required quorum.

Furthermore, on April 11, 1964, Congress elected General Humberto de Alencar Castelo Branco to the presidency, transferring power from Mazzilli to the new president on April 15. This was a violation of article 139 of the 1946 Constitution, which prohibited chiefs of the Army General Staff from running for election to the presidency until three months after vacating their posts. While unconvincing, the constitutionalist claims were aimed at holders of centrist and

moderate opinions within and outside of the military. The constitutional justification for the coup in Brazil far outweighed such claims—which were practically nonexistent—in the cases of the 1973 Chilean and 1976 Argentine coups.

The U.S. government was closely involved with the Brazilian coup plotters.[2] President Johnson recognized the new government in Brazil with great
haste—his telegram to interim President Mazzilli arrived on April 2, one day
after the coup began. (Because of the negative publicity surrounding this recognition, the United States waited for almost two weeks to recognize the military
government in Chile after the 1973 coup.)[3] The telegram stated that the United
States "admired the resolute will of the Brazilian community to resolve . . . difficulties within a framework of constitutional democracy and without civil strife"
(reprinted in U.S. Department of State 1964, 610).

Some members of the Brazilian Congress evidently felt that the 1964 coup
could be resolved along the lines of the 1961 crisis. They elaborated a proposed
emergency act of Congress to temporarily give the Supreme Military Command
full powers to act. If this proposal had been accepted by the military, the military's powers would have been formally delegated by Congress, which would
have retained the right to revoke them. This might have limited the dictatorship
in important ways. Nevertheless, the military ministers in the Supreme Military
Command rejected this proposal and authorized Francisco Campos and Carlos
Medeiros to draft what later became known as AI-1, in which the military granted
itself powers on the basis of a revolutionary mandate, without submitting itself
to congressional constraints.[4]

What is especially important about the Brazilian coup when compared with
the Chilean and Argentine cases is the participation of civilian jurists who not
only legitimized the military's actions in legal terms, but also provided links between the military and the civilian judiciary. Francisco Campos, Antônio Neder,
and Carlos Medeiros are three leading figures from the judiciary whose trajectories before and after the coup show this connection. Medeiros, a lawyer and
jurist who had held important posts in the Estado Novo and Kubitschek governments, was appointed by President Castelo Branco, the first president of the
military regime, to the Supreme Court in 1965. Neder, an opponent of Vargas,
was a key coup conspirator appointed by Castelo Branco to the Federal Resources
Court (Tribunal Federal de Recursos or TFR) and by President Médici to the
Supreme Court in 1971. Campos, the best known of these figures, was a major influence on the legality of the Estado Novo. After the 1964 coup, he was appointed
by the new government to a seat on the Inter-American Legal Commission.[5]

Other military coups and military regimes have had juridical collaborators: lawyers and judges willing to give the imprimatur of legality to the use of force. Under the Brazilian military regime, organizational relations between the military and the judiciary were very close, such that many members of the two organizations shared the same vision of national security law and communicated with each other frequently. This feature cannot be found to the same degree in the other two cases.

The Coup's Aftermath

After the coup, the new regime inaugurated "Operation Clean-Up" (Operação Limpeza) to root out potential threats to what it defined as the nation's security. Tens of thousands of people were detained, many for just a short time, in the first few months after the coup (Alves 1987, 59–60). As authorized by the First Institutional Act (AI-1), and in cooperation with the police, it set up inquiries (Inqueritos Policial-Militares, or IPMs) to investigate and root out Communists and their collaborators in the civil service, universities, state-owned firms, and trade unions. AI-1 also vested the executive with extraordinary powers, including the power to suppress the political rights of anyone for ten years. Under this provision, between the coup in 1964 and 1973, the regime deprived a total of 517 people of their political rights (to vote and run for office), stripped 541 elected officials of their mandates, forcibly retired 1,968 government workers, and fired another 1,815 government workers.[6] Among the officials affected by this purge were 68 members of Congress, former presidents Kubitschek, Quadros, and Goulart, and numerous labor leaders.

The IPMs potentially affected anyone associated with the Goulart government or its popular base. The IPMs were most active in the three most populous states of the country—Rio de Janeiro, Minas Gerais, and São Paulo—with Pernambuco in the northeast and Rio Grande do Sul in the south other important poles of repression. Of those purged from government agencies, 69 percent were removed in 1964 and 16 percent in 1969. Therefore, 85 percent of those purged were removed during the twin peaks of repression during the military regime—the original coup of 1964, and the "coup within the coup" at the end of 1968 (dos Santos, Monteiro, and Lustosa Caillaux 1990, 256).

The military itself was a major target of the purges. Of all of those purged from the state in 1964, 44 percent (1,147) were members of the armed forces, spread fairly evenly across the army, navy, and air force (dos Santos, Monteiro, and Lustosa Caillaux 1990, 246, 251). Trade unions also suffered from government intervention. Ministry of Labor officials removed 432 trade union leaders in 1964 and 1965 and replaced them with politically reliable substitutes. The top states where this occurred were, in order, São Paulo, Minas Gerais, Rio de Janeiro, Bahia, and Pernambuco.

The purges were part of an overall repressive strategy that involved a substantial degree of information gathering, coordination, and selectivity. This repression was clearly not as violent in lethal terms as the repression of the later military regimes in Chile and Argentina. However, the Brazilian repression was broad. A commonly cited estimate is that fifty thousand were imprisoned for political reasons at some point during the length of the regime's rule, while as many as twenty thousand people may have been tortured. An estimated ten thousand people went into exile, most of them returning after the passage of an amnesty in 1979. In addition, hundreds of faculty and students were removed from universities (Chiavenato 2000, 131).

Conservative vs. Revolutionary Legality

In chapter 2, I argued that there are two basic types of dictatorship, conservative and revolutionary. In the conservative type, an already existing legal entity authorizes the dictatorship, the old constitution remains a point of reference, and the dictatorship does not exercise legislative powers. A revolutionary dictatorship, in contrast, rejects the need for legal continuity, conjoins executive and legislative power, and attempts to legitimate itself by invoking the "will of the people" or the revolution rather than the prior constitution (Arato 2000a).

The Brazilian military regime of 1964–1985 was a hybrid, a curious mixture of these two types. The regime never fully resolved the basic contradiction between conservative and revolutionary approaches to legality, and experienced continuous tension between the two. In the words of an editorialist for the newspaper *Jornal do Brasil*, "The coexistence of the constitution and the [institutional] act . . . is a typically Brazilian solution, trying to reconcile the legal process with the revolutionary process."[7] However, when we compare the Brazilian military regime's approach to the law with the approach of the Chilean and Argentine regimes of the 1970s, we can see that the Brazilian system of legal repression entailed far more conservatism than the other two.

The faction that was initially dominant within the regime, led by General Castelo Branco, saw its role as that of a caretaker that would clean up the political system of corruption and subversion before restoring civilian rule (Gordon 2001, 53; Fragoso 1975, 108). The so-called soft-line or Sorbonne group around Castelo Branco went to the trouble of arranging an election of the new president in Congress in order to legitimate his mandate within the terms of the existing constitution—something that was not done later in Chile or Argentina, where Congress was instead shut down. In his inaugural address, Castelo Branco declared, "my government will be one of laws" (Couto 1999, 190).[8] The military wanted the Congress to pass antisubversive legislation to facilitate a purge of government offices; only when it became apparent that Congress was reluctant to act did the executive issue AI-1. AI-1 designated a six-month period from April to October of 1964 to punish alleged subversives. It suspended the job guarantees (*vitalicidade* and *estabilidade*) of all state employees to allow investigations and purges (Couto 1999, 194), and declared itself exempt from any kind of judicial review.

The prologue to AI-1 reveals tension between the revolutionary and conservative impulses of the coup makers in the armed forces and the act's ultimately conservative inspiration. The act declares grandiosely in its second paragraph that "the victorious revolution, as a constituent power, legitimates itself." It also proclaims the radical idea that the revolution "issues juridical norms without by doing so being limited by the normality prior to its victory."

However, as if to assure conservatives, AI-1 goes on: "To demonstrate that we do not plan to radicalize the revolutionary process, we have decided to maintain the 1946 Constitution, limiting ourselves to modifying only those parts of it that relate to the powers of the president, so that he can accomplish the mission of restoring economic and financial order in Brazil and take urgent measures to drain the Communist boil, whose purulence has infiltrated not just the top of the government, but its administrative dependencies." The act also limited its provisions to the period up to January 31, 1966, or the end of President Goulart's mandate. This makes it far more temporally limited and unambitious than similar declarations that accompanied the 1973 and 1976 coups in Chile and Argentina, respectively.[9]

In a speech in 1964, Castelo Branco described the purge enacted by the coup makers in the following terms: "it inexorably follows timetables and conditions required so that everything proceeds in a serious atmosphere. The purge cannot give itself up to wild action and must give to the nation the impression that justice is done according to the law in all cases" (Couto 1999, 184–85). The immediate targets of the purge were Communist militants and their sympathizers who, in the eyes of the new regime, had tried to ally with the Goulart government to create a "syndicalist republic."

U.S. Ambassador Lincoln Gordon, in a speech delivered at the Superior War College (Escola Superior de Guerra, or ESG) on May 5, 1964, just a month after the coup, articulated one influential position on the witch hunt then going on in Brazil. Gordon said (1964, 16), "Evidently, any policy of limitation of political liberty must be exercised with maximum caution, with full procedural safeguards to assure that it is directed solely against genuinely subversive conspiracies and not against simple non-conformities or differences of political opinion with the authorities temporarily in power. The risk of abuse is very serious. The late Senator McCarthy became a symbol of such abuse and we absolutely do not want to see the repetition of that experience. But we could have an even worse danger if free societies feel paralyzed before organizations that have no respect for the rules of the democratic game or for the basic consensus that makes the permanence of civilized society possible. And, in our opinion, international cooperation through the intermediation of organizations such as the OAS [Organization of American States] can be a very valuable supplement for the action of each country to protect itself against these types of subversive organizations."

However, many leaders within the regime were not content with the position staked out by Castelo Branco and encouraged by Ambassador Gordon. Hard-liners and especially younger military officers did not like the "legalistic prejudice" of AI-1 and felt that what they saw as the mildness and restraint of the repression, due in part to the regime's preoccupation with returning the country rapidly to institutional and constitutional normality, would allow the "Communist threat" to remain active. For these officers, the new regime was self-limiting to such an extent that it tolerated subversion. They saw civil liberties as a Trojan horse for the Communists. Hard-liners had wanted the new regime to close Congress and the Supreme Court and to rule on the basis of the "force of the facts" as a fully revolutionary regime, not on the basis of the old constitutional order (Couto 1999, 184–85).

AI-2

Hard-liners scored a significant victory with the enactment of the second institutional act, AI-2, in October of 1965. From a legal standpoint, AI-2 represents the crucial turning point and foundational document of the regime, rather than the later and more infamous AI-5. Unlike Chile and Argentina, where the basic frameworks of repression were established coterminously with the coups, AI-2 in Brazil came eighteen months after the beginning of military rule. The preemptive nature of the Brazilian coup gave the military more room to maneuver, and the ambiguity surrounding the military's role lasted longer than in either Chile or Argentina. But AI-2 established the basic framework for repression that was maintained until the liberalization of the late 1970s.

AI-2 allowed the president to declare a state of siege to repress subversion, and unlike AI-1, did not limit the time period for political punishments. Castelo Branco had originally been against the measure. He said that "to combat the Communist threat, one cannot put the nation in a Nazi straightjacket, mistreating Brazilians by a regime in which some civilians want to grab the top of the sword of the military in order to dictatorially put the blade in their fellow-countrymen who oppose their ambitions." Castelo Branco instead wanted Congress to grant him exceptional powers. Only when Congress did not go along with his wishes did he reluctantly decree AI-2.[10]

AI-2 was the triumph of a more radical vision of the "revolution." AI-1, passed only nine days after the coup, sounded revolutionary, but in essence it was conservative, because it defined itself in relation to the presidential mandates existing within the prior legal order, and saw the regime as a temporary project to rebalance the existing political system. AI-2, in the words of Nehemias Gueiros, represented the regime leaders' decision "that it was not possible to reconcile, in such a short time, the revolution with formal [traditional] legality" (Couto 1999, 197). AI-2 confirmed that authoritarian legality would be different from the old legal system.

The Evolution of Authoritarian Legality

If AI-2 represented an attempt to put the legality of the regime on a new footing, subsequent acts were part of an effort to definitively "institutionalize" the revolution in legal terms. Castelo Branco and his moderate Sorbonne group were not able to control the presidential succession, so the ascension of General Artur da Costa e Silva to the presidency in 1967, like the passage of AI-2, is typically interpreted as a victory of hard-liners. The Costa e Silva government then tried to engage in the legal consolidation of the revolution, passing seven institutional acts, more than any other military government, and creating a new constitution, promulgated in 1967.

However, the armed left grew during this time. An unsuccessful bomb attack on then general Costa e Silva at Guararapes airport in Recife in late July 1966 was the most significant sign that a reaction of at least part of the left to increasing repression was to engage in an underground guerrilla war against the regime.[11] The regime countered this threat on December 13, 1968, with its most infamous institutional act, AI-5.

AI-5 was the most radical legal step taken by the military regime. The act declared that "notably subversive acts coming from the most distinct political and cultural sectors prove that the juridical instrument that the victorious revolution gave to the nation for its defense, development, and the well-being of its people are serving as the means to combat and destroy it [the revolution]" (text, Heller 1988, 649). This statement was the closest that the Brazilian military ever came to repudiating the judiciary and the legal rules of the game that had been created to guide the struggle against alleged subversion and terrorism. AI-5 changed those rules yet again, most notably by eliminating habeas corpus in cases of national security crime, and thereby institutionalizing the use of confessions extracted under torture as a basis for the repression and prosecution of opponents and dissidents. However, unlike its Chilean counterparts in 1973, the Brazilian military did not take political prisoners entirely out of the jurisdiction of the civilian judiciary nor did it, like the Argentine military in 1976, decide on a completely extrajudicial strategy of repression. That the Brazilian path of legal repression was the most conservative and gradual of our three paths can therefore be seen most clearly in the moment of greatest potential rupture, the declaration of AI-5.

General Hugo de Andrade Abreu, a major figure in the military regime, justified AI-5 in terms of the threat of terrorism. "The struggle against terrorism explains the arbitrariness," he explained in his book *O outro lado de poder* (The Other Side of Power). "National security came to have temporary precedence over individual rights: it was as if we were at war, when all the force of the country had to be directed toward victory" (quoted in Couto 1999, 253).

In a similar vein, an editorialist for the *Jornal do Brasil*, a leading Rio de Janeiro newspaper, declared that "repression is a corollary of terrorist violence. It is the price we have to pay so that the path of peaceful evolution that we all want is not disturbed." Note the bizarre illogic of this statement: state torture and killing must be carried out so that Brazil can develop "peacefully." This is a frank admission that "peaceful evolution" entails violence against a minority. But the editorial writer went on to note that "repression can assume—and unfortunately has assumed—dangerous and negative aspects. Arbitrariness is transferred to lower levels and frequently ends up in unable hands, with the risk of generating intranquility among citizens in the name of national security. . . . Terror must be fought, but it is not acceptable that the whole of society is punished for crimes that are the responsibility of only a few who are marginal to the law."[12]

Note the conservatism of the editorial writer. It is acceptable for the state to use violence against the armed left, but only in small doses and in ways that do not affect the rest of society. Officials at "lower levels" are incapable of handling arbitrary power with responsibility and good judgment—hence the "dangerous and negative" aspects of the repression are due to the power that these "lower levels" have acquired within the police and the military. Consequently, state violence must be rigidly controlled from the top—it must be selectively applied only to those people who are really subversive, and it must be of limited duration. The point of view here is of course the opposite of revolutionary—it is a call for the defense of society as it is, for the avoidance of major change, and for the maintenance of traditional social relations, hierarchies, and values.

Mário Pessoa, one of the chief ideologists of national security law, shared this conservative outlook. Pessoa paradoxically called AI-5—an act now generally seen as representing the height of authoritarian rule in Brazil—an "instrument for the preservation of democracy."[13] Another apologist for military rule, General Augusto Fragoso, said that AI-5 represented the military's commitment to "democracy that reconciled the security of the state—or, better said, national security—with the security of human rights; aware, not irresponsible democracy; militant, not remiss democracy; participatory, not immobile democracy; ordered, not chaotic democracy; vigorous, not suicidal democracy; democracy, in other words, that impedes the arbitrary and distinguishes between the legitimate political opposition and subversive and ideological contestation" (1975, 116). This rhetoric does not reach the level of rhetorical violence of the Chilean and Argentine juntas' pronouncements, which referred to the need for wholesale reorganization of society. Instead, it continually seeks legitimacy in democracy rather than Christian civilization or some other potentially less liberal abstraction.[14] Although there were revolutionary elements in the Brazilian military regime that sought unfettered repression and an abandonment of traditional legal frameworks altogether, they never triumphed to the extent that they did in Chile and Argentina.

The Ideological Justification of the Political Trials

Mário Pessoa was the author of the 1971 book *O direito da segurança nacional* (*National security law*), used by the military to claim a legal justification for its actions. Pessoa refers (p. 270) to national security law as something unpleasant but necessary for the preservation of Brazilian democracy. He describes the law of national security as a Byzantine system of (1) institutional acts, (2) the federal constitution, (3) complementary acts based on the institutional acts, (4) decree-laws, (5) and complementary and ordinary laws.[15] By 1971 the system had swollen to a bewildering array of 160 separate legislative acts.

Despite Pessoa's rationalizations, Brazil's national security legality was not constitutionalism in the ordinary sense. It constitutes, in Arato's terms, a dictatorship established by extralegal means (Arato 2002, 463). According to Pessoa, however, the executive was to use this power only for essentially conservative goals. For Pessoa, national security law was defined as "that complex of juridical norms, codified or not, that objectively seek to confer on the state the maintenance of the socio-political-juridical order, indispensable for the safeguarding of national values or characteristics" (1971, 243). A handful of subversives threatened that order, and therefore had to be dealt with expeditiously by a form of exceptional or transitory justice. Pessoa goes to great pains to stress that the application of martial law is not special law or the application of a special court, because the latter is permanent. National security trials were seen as temporary expedients that would not be continued indefinitely.

In Chile and Argentina, on the other hand, national security legality took on a more radical or revolutionary tinge. The military governments sought to extirpate deeply rooted popular causes and parties (Peronism in Argentina, the support base for President Allende's Popular Unity government in Chile). The perception of threat was far greater in these governments, and their measures for confronting the threat were correspondingly more severe and thoroughgoing. More than in Brazil, these regimes attempted to create radically new orders rather than just preserve the old, as we shall see in later chapters.

Pessoa's conception of national security exalted executive discretion and thereby put the state above the law, unlike rule of law notions that emphasized the submission of the state to constitutional strictures. Thus "Liberty signifies that the state is not subordinate to any law, save that which it accepts voluntarily" (1971, 261). Or "the substance of state liberty is found in its domination over men within the territory. And . . . this liberty means the unlimited exercise of that power" (1971, 262).

Pessoa's treatise on the appropriateness and legality of Brazil's repression and its political trials was part of a larger effort by the Brazilian government to legitimate itself before both domestic and international audiences. Pessoa's writings were aimed primarily at the former, while Brazilian diplomacy strove to influence the latter. Brazilian diplomatic responses to denunciations of torture in the country frequently cited the characteristics of its military justice system, and in particular the revision of sentences by courts of appeal, as evidence of the system's fairness and impartiality.[16] Conservatism was used as a legitimating device both at home and abroad. While the attempt at legitimation was not universally accepted by either domestic or international public opinion, it did give the regime cover to engage in arbitrary repressive action.

The Courts and the Treatment of Defendants in the Political Trials

The military justice system that processed political prisoners consisted of various actors. Security personnel, generally members of the military and police, apprehended suspects. Defense lawyers were contacted by family members of prisoners to locate their loved ones within the security apparatus, and defend them in court if necessary. Civilian prosecutors worked in the Military Public Ministry and prepared cases for trial; they were lawyers chosen by examination who could be promoted to judge. Civilian judges were also career civil servants who often dominated legal judgments because their colleagues on the bench were military officers shuffled in and out on three-month terms. Military officers did not value their service in the military justice system because it was not helpful to their careers. The STM was the court of military appeal where cases from the regional military courts were often sent. Above the STM was the civilian Supreme Court. Finally, a network of civil society groups monitored court decisions and pressured for change. The most important of these were the Brazilian Bar Association (OAB, or Ordem dos Advogados do Brasil), the justice and peace commissions (Comissão de Justiça e Paz, or CJP), and the amnesty committees (Comitês Brasileiros pela Anistia, or CBAs).

Judges in the court system all covered up the systematic torture of prisoners and probably would have been expelled if they had not. While judges in rare instances acquitted defendants because of allegations of torture in the late 1970s, this did not occur in the hard-line 1968–1974 period nor did any judges investigate allegations of torture.[17] Outside the courts, extrajudicial killings did occur.[18]

Military justice had twelve military court districts (Circunscrições Judiciárias Militares or CJMs), with jurisdictions corresponding to the territorial base of the military in the area (naval district, the army's military region, and the air force's regional aerial command). Each CJM had at least one military court (*auditoria militar*), which was the first instance of military justice in that area (see map 3). Each court was composed of four military officers and a civilian judge, and a prosecutor and court-appointed defense lawyer (Vannucchi Leme de Matos 2002, 38).

In a study of cases involving 202 defendants from the urban guerrilla group ALN (Ação Libertadora Nacional, or National Liberationist Action), Vannucchi Leme found that the courts followed the position of the prosecutors 60.89% of the time (2002, 61–63). However, hierarchy mattered in military justice. At the level of the STM, where cases were prosecuted by a federal military justice prosecutor (*procuradoria da justiça militar*), the STM accepted the charges for 88.48 percent of the defendants. But the federal prosecutor rarely changed the verdicts and sentences of the lower level courts; it maintained the sentences from these lower courts in the cases of 87 percent of the defendants.

When cases went to the civilian Supreme Court (STF), they were handled by the civilian federal prosecutor's office (Procuradoria Geral da República, equivalent to the U.S. Attorney General). In Vannucchi Leme's ALN sample, the Supreme Court accepted the arguments of the civilian federal prosecutor in 66.66 percent of the cases (2002, 63). This is lower than the rate at which the STM accepted the charges of its military prosecutors, reinforcing the reputation of the STF for having a slightly higher degree of independence than the STM. (Military personnel, unlike civilians, did not have the right to appeal their cases to the STF.)

Brazil's political trials involved thousands of defendants; 7,367 defendants had their cases appealed to the Superior Military Court during the fifteen years that such trials took place under the military regime. Those defendants were charged with 11,750 crimes, within which the largest category was belonging to a banned organization (42 percent). If we add this to the 11.7 percent of the charges that were for participation in a group or mass movement, we can see that over half of all charges were for the crime of membership or participation in groups or movements opposed to the military regime. Only 12.5 percent of all the charges were for violent or armed action. And 12.7 percent of all charges—more than the charges for violent actions—were for the mere expression of ideas, while a further 5.9 percent were for the possession of subversive material (Projeto "Brasil: Nunca Mais" 1988, 12).

These data challenge Pessoa's justification of the trials as necessary primarily to protect Brazilian democracy from the armed attacks of a small number of terrorists. In fact, the profile of the defendants described above suggests instead that Brazil's political trials were a broad-based effort to intimidate and silence a large number of people who were actual or potential critics of military rule, and to win over the "silent majority" of Brazilians to passive acquiescence or even active support of the regime.

How did the courts deal with this wave of accusations against presumed opponents of military rule? Acquittal rates do not by any means represent the whole story of the trials. They do not capture the time spent in prison by defendants awaiting trial nor do they reflect the capacity of public trials to intimidate and demoralize the opposition. However, acquittal rates do tell us something about the application of the law in the courts, and especially the severity with which national security laws were applied. Low acquittal rates indicate the courts' willingness to sanction the repression of the security forces and to further punish political prisoners. High acquittal rates represent the courts' formal recognition of the rights of individuals over and above the claims of the state for security.

A remarkable feature of the Brazilian political trials is their relatively high acquittal rate. One source indicates that the acquittal rate at the level of the regional military courts was 48 percent (Heinz 1992, 90). My sample of 257 cases involving 2,109 defendants reveals an acquittal rate that is even higher: 54 percent in the regional military courts.[19] The Superior Military Court (STM) acquittal rate is higher still—60 percent—but this is based on a sample of only 40 cases. However, if we supplement the data with newspaper sources, we find a similar figure. An article on the front page of the Rio newspaper *Jornal do Brasil* on January 25, 1971, declared that the STM acquitted seven hundred defendants in 1970 while convicting only five hundred—an acquittal rate of 58 percent. We can also see from the article that the military regime actively disseminated the notion that the STM was relatively mild in its judgments, and the closed nature of military justice leads to the conclusion that the source of the story was the STM itself.[20]

The military justice system also punished violent crime more severely than nonviolent crime. In my sample of 257 cases from the regional military courts, the acquittal rate for nonviolent crimes was 57 percent, but it was only 43 percent for violent crimes. The corresponding figure is a 46 percent acquittal rate for violent crimes in the Superior Military Court and 73 percent for nonviolent crimes (for 40 cases involving 204 defendants). These data, while not comprehensive, suggest that Brazilian national security legality did not overturn the traditional and conventional distinction in criminal law between violent and nonviolent crime. While some ideologues of the regime declared that crimes involving the dissemination of ideas were more dangerous than crimes involving guns, the military courts seem not to have accepted this principle in their rulings, and instead relied on the more familiar precept that armed political criminals were more dangerous than their unarmed counterparts.

If we turn from the acquittal rate to the sentencing of political prisoners, we see from a sample of 246 of the cases involving 1,830 defendants that the average sentence for those convicted of political crimes in the regional military courts was 47 months, or slightly less than four years. Surprisingly, defendants convicted of violent crimes received sentences of five months less, on average, than defendants convicted of nonviolent crimes. However, at the Superior Military Court level this disparity was sharply reversed. Although based on a sample of only 40 cases, these data show that those convicted of violent crimes received average sentences of over seven years, as opposed to those convicted of nonviolent crimes, whose average sentence was sixteen months. In these cases the Superior Military Court appears to have reimposed the conventional criminal law distinction between violent and nonviolent crime on the military justice system. Once again, the evidence suggests that Brazil's authoritarian legality had strong elements of continuity with the "normal" or pre-authoritarian justice system.

Interestingly, a sample of court cases from the archive shows that acquittal rates varied considerably by state. The number of cases in some states is not large, and various plausible explanations for the variation could be entertained. However, the pattern appears to reflect Brazil's federal and decentralized character. While most literature on the military regime stresses its centralization of political power compared to the 1945–1964 period, it should also be noted that this centralization in a country as large and diverse as Brazil could only go so far, and at least when it comes to the military courts, central authorities left a large amount of discretion in the hands of local power holders.

Table 4.1 shows the variation in the acquittal rates by the location of the regional military court. However, the types of cases handled by each court cannot

4.1 Acquittal rates in national security trials in regional military courts by location of court, Brazil, 1964–1979

Court location	No. of cases	No. of defendants	No. of acquitted defendants	Acquittal rate (%)
Southeast				
São Paulo	54	301	171	56.81
Rio de Janeiro	56	936	492	52.56
Belo Horizonte	7	58	45	77.59
Juiz de Fora	18	89	65	73.03
Regional total	*135*	*1,384*	*773*	*55.85*
South				
Paraná	19	78	31	39.74
Rio Grande do Sul	21	116	102	87.93
Regional total	*40*	*194*	*133*	*68.56*
Center-West				
Mato Grosso	1	2	1	50.00
Brasília	9	34	20	58.82
Regional total	*10*	*36*	*21*	*58.33*
Northeast				
Bahia	12	95	35	36.84
Pernambuco	31	224	84	37.50
Ceará	13	61	51	83.61
Regional Total	*56*	*380*	*170*	*44.74*
North				
Pará	5	33	30	90.91
Total	*246*	*2,027*	*1,127*	*55.60 (average)*

Note: These data and the other figures presented in this chapter are from a sample of cases. For an explanation of the source of these data, see appendix 1.

be ascertained from the table. The acquittal rates alone do not allow one to conclude that one court was more severe or more lenient than another.[21] We do know that the focus of the armed left's activities was the Rio de Janeiro–Belo Horizonte–São Paulo axis, and table 4.1 shows that courts in these cities did not have the lowest acquittal rates. Rio de Janeiro and São Paulo, which dealt with the bulk of the cases in both our sample and the entire universe of cases, had acquittal rates that were very close to the average for all the regional military courts. Surprisingly, courts in more peripheral areas such as Paraná, Bahia, and Pernambuco had the lowest acquittal rates, while courts in other peripheral states such as Pará, Ceará, and Rio Grande do Sul had the highest acquittal rates.

Without detailed knowledge of particular cases, the precise reasons for this variation remain elusive. However, the data suggest that the treatment of political crime varied considerably from state to state under Brazil's military regime,

4.2   Average sentences in national security trials in regional military courts
by location of court, Brazil, 1964–1979

Court location	No. of cases	No. of defendants	Average sentence (in months)
Southeast			
São Paulo	52	263	26.88
Rio de Janeiro	52	799	55.79
Belo Horizonte	7	58	97.15
Juiz de Fora	18	89	33.70
South			
Paraná	18	75	31.04
Rio Grande do Sul	21	116	27.35
Center-West			
Mato Grosso	1	2	120.00
Brasília	9	34	11.71
Northeast			
Bahia	11	83	19.37
Pernambuco	29	148	77.52
Ceará	13	61	14.90
North			
Pará	5	33	6.00
Total	*236*	*1,761*	*45.77 (average)*

even though the military justice system in which such crimes were prosecuted
was a uniform federal system with ostensibly the same rules and procedures
and body of law. Military regimes in Argentina and Chile, as we shall see later,
dealt with the problem of political subversion in a far more centralized way.
Brazil's political trials therefore exhibit characteristics of its state: strongly confederal in nature, consisting of a loose coalition that allowed substantial autonomy to power holders in its constituent parts.

The same pattern of regional variation can be seen in the sentences handed
down by the military courts, as shown in table 4.2. The average sentences in the
courts range from ten and eight years, respectively, in Mato Grosso and Belo
Horizonte to six months in Pará and just under a year in Brasília. Furthermore,
courts with high acquittal rates such as Rio Grande do Sul and Ceará also gave
very low average sentences for those convicted (twenty-seven and fifteen months,
respectively), while the court in Pernambuco was at the other end of the spectrum on both counts, with low acquittal rates and a high average sentence (about
six and a half years).

4.3 Acquittal rates in national security trials in regional military courts by year of alleged crime, Brazil, 1964–1979

Year of alleged crime	No. of cases	No. of defendants	Acquittal rate (%)
1961	2	38	92.10
1962	4	36	22.22
1963	11	167	53.28
1964	80	1,117	51.65
1965	2	16	68.75
1966	6	26	46.15
1967	10	64	64.06
1968	48	266	60.52
1969	40	147	70.74
1970	16	40	80.00
1971	12	53	30.18
1972	6	9	77.77
1973	1	2	100.00
1974	4	6	100.00
1975	2	2	100.00
1976	1	1	100.00
Total	245	1,990	55.48 (average)

Brazilian courts treated defendants differently in yet another way. As can be seen in table 4.3, the acquittal rate in our sample of cases varied substantially by the year of the alleged crime. The most significant trend is that after 1972 the acquittal rate rises (in our sample, to 100 percent). This shows that after the defeat of the armed left in 1973, courts became more lenient. (Cases took about two years to come to judgment, so a crime allegedly committed in 1973 was normally judged in 1975.) Furthermore, acquittal rates rarely dipped below 50 percent, except in judging crimes committed in 1962, 1966, and 1971, suggesting that the goal of those managing the courts was not necessarily to convict and incarcerate the maximum number of opponents and dissidents, but to raise the costs for and frighten those who might otherwise have opposed the regime.

There appears to have been no great pressure from the security forces to make military justice more punitive than it was. General Adyr Fiúza de Castro, a former head of army intelligence during the military regime, said in 1993 that the great majority of political prisoners "returned to the life of a petite bourgeois. . . . And we thought that 45 days [the maximum time to detain someone before legal proceedings had to begin, as laid down by AI-5] were sufficient punishment when there was not a crime involving death, when it was only bank robbery, graffiti-writing, this, that . . . I, at least, thought that it was sufficient for, in the majority of cases, the comrade to abandon his subversive activities" (quoted in D'Araújo, Dillon Soares, and Castro 1994, 66).

Table 4.3 allows for another important observation. The verdicts of the cases in this sample do not conform neatly or simply to the conventional tripartite division of Brazil's military regime into an early, consolidating phase (1964–1968), a second highly repressive phase (1969–1974), and a third liberalizing phase (1975–1985; see, for example, Alves 1987; Costa Couto 1999; Skidmore 1988). No such pattern emerges from the data. The severity of judicial repression does not match the severity of the physical repression. Instead, the courts appear to be "countercyclical," moderating political trends by making rulings that mitigate the ferocity of earlier phases of repression.

For example, at the time of the 1964 coup, the military purged its own ranks of participants in the legalist movement that had prevented a military coup in 1961, but table 4.3 shows that in our sample of cases, over 90 percent of the thirty-eight defendants accused of participating in the 1961 movement were acquitted. Conversely, the lowest acquittal rate comes not in the highly repressive period but in the early phase of the regime, for crimes committed in 1962. Similarly, the acquittal rate in forty cases of alleged crimes committed in 1969, a year of high repression after the passage of the Fifth Institutional Act, was much higher than that of six cases from 1966, a year seen in the conventional narratives as much less repressive than 1969.

The acquittal rates by the year the verdict was reached—as opposed to the year of the alleged crime—present a similar picture. In my sample, there were 394 acquitted defendants out of 929 (42.41 percent) in cases decided in the five-year period 1964–1968, and 691 acquitted defendants out of 1,103 total defendants (62.65 percent) in cases judged in the comparable period of 1969–1973. In other words, acquittal rates in the more permissive early phase of the regime were lower than in the more physically repressive phase. The judicial sphere, even in courts as manipulated and clearly biased in favor of the regime as the Brazilian military courts, seem to have had some "relative autonomy" from the political sphere and made judgments that were not necessarily in lockstep with the political trends of the time.[22]

To add to the complexity of the picture, acquittal rates vary considerably depending on the professional background of the defendant. Discounting cases

4.4   Acquittal rates in national security trials in regional military courts
by professional background of defendant, Brazil, 1964–1979

Professional background of defendant	No. of cases	No. of defendants	Acquittal rate (%)
Journalist	3	5	40.00
Military	42	759	46.11
Student	63	306	49.01
Politician	30	167	58.08
Trade Union	39	421	66.74
Religious	14	100	93.00
Merchant	2	2	100.00
Total	193	1,760	55.40 (average)

involving merchants (which are too few to be conclusive but do reveal how few businessmen were prosecuted), the most striking finding pertains to defendants from the religious orders. As table 4.4 shows, members of the clergy, who were mostly from the Catholic Church, were especially likely to be acquitted. This suggests that even though under the military regime traditional church-military deference and mutual cooperation broke down to some extent (see Serbin 2000), the military courts were still reluctant to convict members of the church, whose alleged subversion was often defended as the teaching of an updated and socially conscious version of traditional Catholic doctrine. In our sample of cases, members of the clergy were acquitted at a rate of 93 percent, while journalists and members of the military were acquitted only 40 and 46 percent of the time, respectively.[23] The figures for journalists are too sparse to draw broad conclusions, but the fact that 409 of 759 military defendants were convicted (53.89 percent) suggests that judges in the military courts—who were overwhelmingly active-duty military officers themselves—may have taken the traditional military view that accusations of violations of discipline and hierarchy within the armed forces were very serious and worthy of punishment when there was any evidence of guilt. Such violations were also the normal caseload of military courts. The Brazilian military regime particularly feared opposition from renegade military personnel such as Captain Carlos Lamarca, and punished military personnel accordingly.[24]

In contrast, and surprisingly, given the regime's general orientation toward "demobilizing" labor, in our sample of cases the courts acquitted trade union defendants at an above average rate.[25] National security law in Brazil selectively

4.5   Acquittal rates in national security trials in regional military courts by charge, Brazil, 1964–1979

Charge	No. of cases	No. of defendants	Acquittal rate (%)
Robbery	2	4	25.00
Murder	2	69	28.98
Membership in a banned organization[a]	5	58	32.75
Military insubordination	30	561	39.92
Destruction of property	2	2	50.00
Subversive propaganda[a]	114	577	57.53
Assault	2	13	69.23
Trade union activity[a]	37	386	78.75
Offense against authority[a]	26	34	79.41
Total	220	1,704	54.99

[a]Crimes that were introduced or redefined in national security legislation under the military regime

criminalized some trade union activities while preserving the legality of more innocuous ones. Judges in Brazil's military courts did not uniformly rule against members of the unions in their judgments. In fact, they were more likely to convict students, whom they more strongly associated with new forms of subversion, than they were to convict trade unionists. The latter were recognized members of the corporatist capital-labor structure that had been created in the 1930s and 1940s and was not dismantled by the military regime. While the military regime certainly controlled labor by preventing strikes and the autonomous organization of workers in the workplace, it did recognize the rights of trade unions to continue functioning and did not, as its counterparts in Chile and Argentina did, attempt to suppress almost all forms of trade union activity.

If we turn to an analysis of the trials according to the charges brought against defendants, we can see once again the conservatism of Brazilian legal repression. The most striking aspect of table 4.5 is that three of the four charges for which the courts produced the highest acquittal rates—subversive propaganda, trade union activity, and offense against authority—were also nontraditional charges that had been introduced or redefined by the military regime's national security legislation. On the other hand, charges that were part of long-standing legal traditions (robbery, murder, military insubordination, destruction of property) had much lower acquittal rates. The only exception to this general pattern is the charge of membership in a banned organization, which

4.6 Sentences of those convicted in national security trials in regional military courts, Brazil, 1964–1979

Sentence	No. of defendants	Percentage
up to 12 months	447	15.81
13–24 months	540	19.09
25–36 months	514	18.18
37–48 months	276	9.76
Subtotal: 4 years or less	*1,777*	*62.84*
49–60 months	171	6.05
61–82 months	425	15.03
83–120 months	102	3.61
Subtotal: between 4 and 10 years	*698*	*24.68*
121–180 months	220	7.78
181–240 months	64	2.26
241–360 months	33	1.17
more than 360 months	36	1.27
Subtotal: more than 10 years	*353*	*12.48*
Total	2,828	100.00

was the most common charge in the total universe of cases. This charge had been modified by the military regime to include many more groups beyond the traditional listing of the Brazilian Communist Party. In this particular sample, the acquittal rate for this charge is below the average, indicating the importance of this legal instrument in the incarceration of political prisoners.

Turning now to the sentences of those convicted in the courts, we can see from table 4.6 that roughly 63 percent of all those sentenced in the regional military courts received sentences of four years or less. On the other hand, only 12.48 percent of all convicted defendants were sentenced to ten years or more in prison. This confirms the picture presented here so far, that the national security trials in Brazil were part of a more modest and conservative form of legal repression than what we will see in Chile (chapter 5) and Argentina (chapter 6).

Finally, an examination of the time actually served in prison by a sample of 1,608 defendants in Brazilian political trials reveals that fully a quarter of defendants served thirty days or less in prison, while only 18.5 percent served more than one year. This confirms journalist Elio Gaspari's observation that many of the most severe punishments under Brazil's authoritarian legal system were meted out not in the courts themselves but in the detention centers where suspects were initially interrogated and tortured.[26]

Civil Society and the Trials

If national security trials are a form of political theater, then it is important to examine how they were covered and framed by the regime and the media and how ordinary people and the leaders of civil society associations came to think about them.[27] In general, it seems accurate to say that the military regime was able to successfully frame the trials, at least during its rule, as the prosecution of dangerous terrorists, subversives, Communists, and their accomplices, a necessary mechanism to ensure the security and well-being of ordinary and law-abiding Brazilians. Jeffrey Lesser asserts that "the total of perhaps ten thousand participants [in the armed left] were considered by the majority of the population to be terrorists."[28] Or in the words of the *Jornal do Brasil* editorial writers, "Peace must be maintained, so that the nation can amplify its prosperity, its well-being and security, without adherence to outdated privileges. Terrorism is limited to a minority of fanatics condemned to failure until their total eradication."[29]

However, in Brazil, some semblance of a public sphere that allowed for contestation endured throughout military rule. An important example of this can be seen in the case of Teodomiro Romeiro dos Santos, a nineteen-year-old member of the PCBR (Partido Comunista Brasileiro Revolucionário, Brazilian Revolutionary Communist Party) sentenced to death in 1971 for the killing of an air force sergeant working for the security forces.[30] The death penalty had been created by the military regime on September 27, 1969, partly in reaction to the kidnapping of the U.S. ambassador.

Teodomiro's death sentence provoked a flurry of criticism and commentary in the Brazilian press. National deputy Clóvis Stenzel, vice-leader of the government in the lower house of Congress, declared that the defendant was capable of recovery because he was only nineteen years old. The archbishop of Salvador, Dom Eugenio Sales, said that he was surprised and saddened by the sentence handed down in his archdiocese and declared himself to be against the death penalty. Lawyer Heleno Fragoso, the author of the then new penal code in Brazil and a defense lawyer for political prisoners, condemned the death penalty as incompatible with human dignity. Fragoso was joined in this opinion by another defense lawyer for political prisoners, Heráclito Sobral Pinto. The general secretary of the Conference of Brazilian Bishops (Conferência Nacional dos Bispos do Brasil), Dom Ivo Lorscheider, also spoke publicly against the death sentence. Even the conservative newspaper *Jornal do Brasil* in Rio de Janeiro published an editorial against the death penalty.[31]

Teodomiro's defense lawyer appealed the death penalty verdict to the STM. The public outcry did seem to have an effect. On June 14, 1971, the STM revised Teodomiro's sentence to life imprisonment.[32] Then on March 7, 1975, the civilian Supreme Court reduced Teodomiro's sentence yet again to thirty years in prison.[33]

The outcome could have been different. There were voices at the time for a more hard-line response to the armed left. For example, the military prosecutor's brief in the case when it was appealed to the STM (dated April 16, 1971) said, "The regime that does not defend itself does not deserve to survive."[34] At the funeral of the victim the then governor of Bahia Antonio Carlos Magalhães warned against those "few skeptics who out of complacency or omission help the aims of the criminals" (*Jornal da Bahia*, Oct. 29, 1970). And a policeman at the funeral reportedly asked Governor Magalhães to create a death squad in Bahia, saying that there should be groups like that all over the country "to liquidate the Communists."[35]

This was a potential branching point in the history of Brazilian political repression in which the Brazilian military regime might have descended to the level of the Argentine dirty war. Death squads were active in São Paulo at the time and sprang up in other places in the country. The military justice system might also have become more punitive. Prosecutors in other military courts asked for the death sentence to be awarded against defendants after the Teodomiro case. However, the STM decision to reduce Teodomiro's sentence eased rather than raised tensions, and the option for more draconian legal repression and a sharp increase in extrajudicial lethal violence was not taken.

The evidence suggests that the death sentence had strong support within the military itself, and that judicial moderation of the military's attitude was important to the outcome. After Teodomiro was convicted, the General Staff of the Fourth Army held a press conference in which military officers defended the death penalty for the "barbarous crime committed by the two terrorists."[36] The prosecutor in the case at the first level, when he urged the application of the death penalty, told the judges "not to listen to siren songs and to be deluded by juridical details."[37] Other prosecutors also imitated their colleague in Salvador. A prosecutor in the military court in Juiz de Fora, Minas Gerais, asked for the death penalty in a case that began just before Teodomiro was sentenced.[38] A few days later a prosecutor in Ceará asked that the death penalty be applied to nine defendants in a military court case.[39] And in Recife a prosecutor asked for the death penalty for three terrorists accused of killing an air force officer.[40] A death sentence for Teodomiro could have led to an escalation in the severity of punishments in the military courts. Instead, the STM decision may have influenced the movement of military justice away from this particular path.

Under Brazil's authoritarian regime some public contestation still existed, the actions of the military courts could be criticized, and judges in the courts could respond to public opinion on some level, thus reining in the animosity of the armed forces at the killing of one of their own. Similar evidence of the existence of a limited public sphere under Brazilian military rule can be seen in the case of Alexandre Vannucchi Leme, a student and member of the ALN tortured to death by the security forces in 1973. Kenneth Serbin (2000, 206–12) shows how church and student leaders protested the killing and held a mass for Vannucchi Leme at the Sé Cathedral in São Paulo in late March 1973.

Perhaps an even more extraordinary example of the continued existence of some degree of contestation in Brazil under its military regime is the case brought by São Paulo prosecutor Hélio Bicudo against a death squad led by political police operative Sérgio Fleury. Fleury apparently led a death squad that worked for drug traffickers, killing their rivals for a fee.[41] Bicudo brought charges against Fleury and some of his colleagues for a series of killings of alleged drug traffickers. These charges, filed in civilian court, reached the Supreme Court in March 1971[42] and constituted one of four independent cases brought against Fleury's death squad by various prosecutors in the Ministry of Justice.[43] By that time, Fleury had been active in the antisubversion campaign and had the protection of high governmental authorities, so Bicudo was unable to get a favorable ruling from the Supreme Court. However, it is notable that at the height of the regime's repression, prosecutors could bring legal actions against members of the security forces that were accepted by the judiciary, discussed, ruled on, and reported in the media. This contrasts sharply with the later Argentine military regime. At a March 1981 press conference in Washington, D.C., for example, General Roberto Viola, then president of Argentina, was asked by reporters about human rights in his country. He responded by saying, "You are suggesting that we investigate our own security forces—absolutely out of the question" (Lewis 2002, 241).

Military-Judicial Cooperation

The mode of legal repression under each of the last military regimes in Argentina, Brazil, and Chile was the result neither of ineradicable historical or cultural predispositions or legacies, nor of the creation of instantaneous institutional equilibria. Instead, the past mattered in specific, contingent, and limited ways. In particular, prior efforts by the military in each country to collaborate with civilians in the adaptation of institutions to meet the perceived threat of subversion influenced the options of authoritarian leaders even before they took power. In Brazil (and as we shall see next, in Chile) the military court was an important component in the arsenal of organizational solutions to the problem of opposition and dissent, one that had the support of significant segments of the judiciary and civilian political elites. The use of military courts to try opponents gave a veneer of legality to the regime's repression and processed political prisoners in an orderly and well-documented manner.

The rhetoric of the regime was "revolutionary," but its actions in the legal sphere were gradual, incremental, and conservative. Even when it had evolved into a more hard-line dictatorship and issued the draconian AI-5, the regime never broke with the civilian judiciary. An overarching consensus between military and judicial elites as to the proper organization of repression endured throughout the regime. The institutional expression of this consensus was the military court as a venue for the prosecution of civilians accused of violations of national security law. The Brazilian military court was a hybrid institution involving high levels of civilian-military cooperation.

The preservation of the military courts as an instrument for prosecuting dissenters and opponents kept the Brazilian military regime on a legalistic if not constitutional path. Originally employed to purge Communists and supporters of Goulart from the state apparatus, the use of the military courts expanded to include members of the new armed left who were committed to overthrowing the regime. This ensured a modicum of procedural standardization in the treatment of political prisoners, even though the regime in some cases chose to ignore its own legality and to kill and disappear armed leftists who were considered to be particularly dangerous. But this extrajudicial dirty war never grew to Chilean or Argentine proportions.

Data from the political trials confirm the view of Brazilian legal repression as basically conservative. Acquittal rates were high, sentences relatively light, and the courts were more willing to convict people accused of traditional crimes than crimes that had been newly defined in the burgeoning national security legislation. Considerable contestation of the treatment of prisoners in military justice also occurred in the public sphere. Chilean legal repression, in contrast, was more radical and more draconian. It is to the Chilean case that I now turn.

5

"Wartime" Legality and
Radical Adaptation in Chile

> We may note that Decree Law No. 3655 granted further
> authority to wartime military tribunals to punish "with the
> utmost rigor terrorist actions planned from outside the
> country that damage the noble values of the country and
> seek to destroy the very foundations of our national being."
>
> Report of the Chilean National Commission
> on Truth and Reconciliation

THE BRAZILIAN MILITARY regime used peacetime military courts to prosecute political dissidents and opponents. It selectively overrode the previous constitution with institutional acts, then produced another constitution more to its liking. Torture was widespread, but disappearances were rare and political trials in military courts left some room for the defense of the accused, involved civilian participation on the bench and at the bar, and included the right to appeal. The death sentence, handed down by regional courts four times and asked for by prosecutors on several other occasions, was never formally carried out. The courts moved slowly—trials typically dragged on for two years from the time of the initial charges to a verdict, and an appeal could prolong the process another one or two years.

The Chilean military regime, created nine years after its Brazilian counterpart, was both more draconian and more radical in legal and institutional terms. The Chilean military declared a state of siege and executed hundreds of people without trial at the time of the 1973 coup. Torture was common, and most pros-

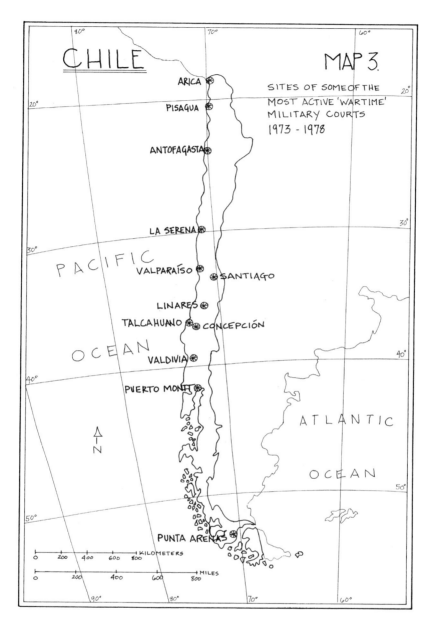

Map 3: Location of some of the most active military courts, Chile 1973–1978. Map by Lynne E. Perry.

ecutions that did take place occurred in "wartime" military courts, insulated from the civilian judiciary, for the first five years of the regime.[1] In these courts the defendants had few procedural rights, no effective right of appeal, and faced rapid verdicts and sentences, including the death penalty.

Chilean national security legality is therefore intermediate between the Brazilian case and the Argentine one. The Chilean military regime, like its Brazilian predecessor, was conservative in some respects. A preexisting organization —military courts—and some elements of prior legality were used to prosecute civilians. But Chile represents a path not taken by Brazil in other respects. Its repressive strategy was more radical and less judicialized than Brazil's.

The Chilean military regime's legal weapons of choice were old laws—the Law of State Security, passed in 1958, and the Arms Control Law, passed under Allende in 1972. The regime saw itself at least in part as defending a social and legal order that had been threatened by the Allende government. In doing this, it used much higher levels of violence against its opponents than the Brazilian regime did, and its coup was a rollback coup and not a preemptive one. When one looks at the treatment of defendants in the national security trials, there are some surprising points of similarity with Brazil, despite the obviously greater severity of punishments. However, the Chilean military regime was also committed to substantial change in the economic, political, and legal spheres, and this radicalism is missing in the Brazilian case.

Parallels and Connections between the Brazilian and Chilean Coups and Military Regimes

The Brazilian ambassador to Chile at the time of the 1973 coup, Antônio da Camara Couto, had such tight relations with the new military regime that he was referred to by some as the "fifth member of the junta." The ambassador coordinated the persecution of Brazilian exiles in Chile, and under his direction, the Brazilian embassy became a base of operations for the conspiracy against the Allende government. He received news of the coup exultantly (Rabêlo and Rabêlo 2001, 158–59).

Brazil was one of the first countries to recognize the military junta in Chile (Rabêlo and Rabêlo 2001, 158). Along with Uruguay, Brazil announced its recognition on September 13, 1973, sending its ambassador to meet with the new regime's leaders. The U.S. government, anxious to avoid the appearance of unseemly haste in welcoming news of a coup (as in Brazil in 1964), waited another eleven days to announce its recognition (Davis 1985, 374). The Brazilian ambassador to Chile ordered embassy functionaries to deny visas to the family members of Brazilians wishing to return to Brazil (Rabêlo and Rabêlo 2001, 158). He also facilitated the visit to Chile of Brazilian policemen to interrogate people in the National Stadium. It is customary to highlight the role of the U.S. government in the coup in Chile; less attention has been paid to the role of the Brazilian government.

There are other connections and parallels between the Brazilian and Chilean military regimes. Leading figures in the Institute of Research and Social Studies (IPES or Instituto de Pesquisa e Estudos Sociais), a private anticommunist think tank in Rio, claimed that prior to the coup they advised Chilean opponents of Allende and that São Paulo businessmen gave money to the Chilean opposition. Couriers delivered the money to groups including the right-wing paramilitary organization Patria y Libertad (Fatherland and Liberty). One observer wrote that the Brazilian coup of 1964 "appears to have been used as a model for the Chilean military coup. The private sector played a crucial role in the preparation of both interventions, and the Brazilian businessmen who plotted the overthrow of the left-leaning administration of João Goulart in 1964 were the same people who advised the Chilean right on how to deal with Marxist President Allende."[2] Both Nathaniel Davis, then U.S. ambassador to Chile, and his predecessor reported on the strong support from the military government of Brazil to the coup plotters in Chile (see Davis 1985, 332, 362).

A Brazilian historian said after the Chilean coup that the Chilean military's "allegations that the 'Communists' had been preparing a massacre . . . were so scandalously identical to ours, one almost presumes that they had the same author." "Plan Z" was an alleged plan by the Popular Unity (Unidad Popular, or UP) government leaders to murder Chile's senior military officers and carry out a takeover. This was a justification for the coup, but the junta never produced evidence for Plan Z (Davis 1985, 370–71).

The parallels between Brazil and Chile can be summarized as follows. In each, a left-wing government promoted reforms and was opposed by business, the military, much of the middle class, and the United States. Each coup was backed by the United States. After each coup, the military claimed that there had been an imminent left-wing plot to subvert the nation. In both coups, many civilian politicians initially thought that military intervention would be short term, but each turned into a long-term regime, lasting twenty-one years in Brazil and seventeen years in Chile.

There were other connections between the two countries. Many Brazilian exiles were present in Chile at the time of the 1973 coup—around three thousand, according to one source. Some were rounded up in the police-military dragnets of the time, and five were killed (Mariano 1998, 96–98). Immediately after the coup, the Chilean Ministry of Defense sent to the Brazilian government a list of Brazilians held in the National Stadium in Santiago, as well as a list of Brazilians who had obtained refuge in the Argentine Embassy in Santiago.[3] This cooperation later developed into a full-blown regional operation to share intelligence information and cooperate in the apprehension and exchange of alleged subversives.[4]

Notwithstanding the parallels and links, there are important differences between the two regimes. The extent of mobilization and reform under Allende's government was far greater than under Goulart in Brazil. The Chilean military leaders led a much more violent coup and relied far more on violence during their rule. Military power within the new regime was high in Chile, but in Brazil military power was exercised with much closer cooperation with civilians. In Chile, the leaders of the new military regime acted with indifference to the views of civilian political forces, even conservative politicians. In the words of U.S. ambassador Davis, "the attitude of General Washington Carrasco seemed representative of the new government's view: 'The politicians have already worked a lot in this country. Now it is only fair that they take a long rest'" (Davis 1985, 372). As we shall see, the Chilean military also provided quite a rest to Chile's judges.

The Erosion of Consensus on the Rule of Law, 1970–1973

Chile is correctly seen as a particularly rule-bound and orderly society in comparison to much of the rest of Latin America. Chilean social scientist Genaro Arriagada writes, "One of the most characteristic political realities of Chile is the importance of legality as a superior standard to which all behaviors and the resolution of conflicts between people and institutions are referred. . . . Legality is the foundation of the government's legitimacy." (Hilbink 1999, 12–13)

However, there is a difference between legality per se and legality produced by a process of democratic debate, participation, and consensus.[5] In the years prior to military rule, and despite the reputation that Chile then enjoyed for having a successfully consolidated democracy, a basic consensus among political leaders about the legal framework of the political game gradually unraveled. At the same time, the executive acquired enhanced powers and the political role of the military was amplified. These tendencies were so strong that the main legal weapons of the military government that took power in 1973 were already in place before the coup itself.

Under the government of President Allende, elected by a slim plurality of votes in 1970, the executive took a position far more favorable to workers, putting it on a collision course with the judiciary, and creating tension within the military. President Allende and his advisors talked of substituting "class justice" with "popular justice." They also suggested that the People's Assembly, a unicameral Congress that they wanted to replace the existing bicameral legislature, should appoint Supreme Court justices (Hilbink 1999, 184–85).

These proposals were part of a widening rift that led to a collision between the Allende government and the judiciary. For example, on January 5, 1971, a supporter of the Allende government in Congress derided "the classist position" of the Supreme Court, which he called "openly antipopular." The congressman further protested against this "justice for the rich, justice put at the service of a class."[6] These statements elicited strong responses from politicians of the right and center-right.

The Minister of Justice Lisandro Cruz Ponce, also in January 1971, widened the rift by praising the popular courts created by activists of the MIR (Movimiento de Izquierda Revolucionario, Movement of the Revolutionary Left) in land invasions and affirmed that the government planned to establish similar courts in the major cities of the country.[7] The popular courts were a little like alternative dispute resolution mechanisms proposed as part of judicial reform packages in the contemporary era. However, in the polarized and politicized period of the Allende government, they were seen by the government's opponents as attempts to subvert the justice system.

The Christian Democratic Party opposed the legislation to create the popular courts. The Christian Democrats declared that "the creation of the popular courts is an attack on the rule of law, in which the existence of a hierarchical, structured, and independent judiciary is essential."[8] They also said that the creation of the courts involves "grave risks . . . to citizenship."[9] Lacking congressional support, the Allende government eventually abandoned its proposal to create the popular courts (Hilbink 1999, 186). But the debate about the proposal suggests how polarized conceptions of legality were prior to the Chilean military coup.

Under Allende, workers became emboldened and began to organize land invasions and factory takeovers. For example, in 1970 and afterwards the MIR organized a series of urban land invasions in Santiago and rural land invasions from Talca to Temulco in the south of Chile. The MIR both supported Allende's Popular Unity government and criticized it from the left (Olavarria 2002, 87, 90). Critics of the government charged that the Allende government did not enforce court orders to evict land invaders and return properties to their original owners.

In response to this, in October 1972 the Supreme Court sent a letter to President Allende that mentioned "the absolute necessity of instructing his cabinet to instruct in turn their subordinates to adhere strictly to the decisions that, in the exercise of their constitutional attributions, emanate from the ordinary courts of justice" (quoted in Panish 1987, 701). However, Panish claims that the Interior Ministry did not change its policies after this letter, and instead circulated an internal memo instructing all mayors and governors not to enforce any legal judgment in favor of property owners unless the Minister himself ordered them to do so.

In March of 1973 the President of the Chilean Supreme Court, Enrique Urrutia Manzano, gave an interview with the press in which he declared that "in a rule of law, judicial decisions are respected normally" and complained about the Allende government's failure to obey judicial decisions. He also attacked critics who claimed that judges were classist and biased and defended the idea that judges could judge impartially.[10] Chile's main newspaper, *El Mercurio,* defended the Supreme Court president's position in an editorial.[11]

In May 1973 the Supreme Court denounced the "breakdown of the legal order of the country." It went on to deplore the "illegal acts of the administrative authorities who are illicitly interfering with the proper exercise of the judicial power" (quoted in Panish 1987, 701–2). Right-wing political parties sided with the Supreme Court in alleging that the Allende government disrespected labor law in resolving labor-management disputes. During this time nationalizations of banks, coal mines, and a host of other industries was occurring. While some observers such as Robert Barros insist that "the Allende government did not violate the law when implementing its economic policy," the point is that a large segment of the right and center-right argued that it did, thus eroding any preexisting consensus about the rule of law (Barros 1996, 168).

Elizabeth Hilbink sums up this impasse: "All of the Allende government's efforts to secure greater cooperation from the judiciary or control over legal outcomes were to no avail. The opposition majority in Congress, the Comptroller

General, and the Supreme Court simply did not share the government's goal of fundamentally transforming the legal system or its outcomes. As an increasingly frustrated Allende administration turned to ever more controversial means of proceeding with its 'revolution through law,' the Supreme Court joined, and at key moments led, the chorus of protest against the government's alleged illegalities" (Hilbink 1999, 190).

Therefore, unlike in Brazil before the 1964 military coup, in Chile there was a serious rift in executive-judicial relations before the military coup. This rift widened before Allende's downfall. Allende answered the Supreme Court's criticism by saying that he was obligated as president to guarantee peace and public order, and that this obligation gave him the right to enforce judicial decisions selectively. In Allende's vision, his higher duty as president to guarantee social peace required him in some instances to ignore court decisions and to respond to demands from below for the redistribution of property. This offended Supreme Court justices' conservative vision of the law, and they responded by writing him another letter that declared, "The President has undertaken the task, especially difficult for him since he knows the law only through hearsay, of determining for this Supreme Court the rules for the interpretation of the law, a duty which in the matters entrusted to it, belongs exclusively to the judiciary and not to the executive" (quoted in Panish 1987, 702).

Political polarization under Allende's Popular Unity government led to the creation of armed groups on both the right and the left. Violence began to break out in various places.[12] Allende promised to "oppose reactionary violence with revolutionary violence" if it was true that landowners in the south were planning to create centers of armed resistance to his government.[13] He said in a speech to a national meeting of the parties in the Unidad Popular that his government "would not be the first to initiate hostilities, but it will react with all the rigor of military force and the power of the people if antirevolutionaries decide to turn the table."[14]

In 1972 the Chilean Congress debated a bill to modify the 1958 Law of State Security in order to transfer arms control—the confiscation of unauthorized arms and the prosecution of the owners of these weapons—from civilian to military authorities. The law (number 17,798), approved on October 21, 1972, did just that, giving the army the role of arms control and military courts the jurisdiction to try arms control violators. The new law prohibited people from carrying arms without the previous permission of the military authorities (article 5). It also prohibited not only the possession of unauthorized arms but the formation of private militias or armed groups (article 8). The act began to be enforced in June 1973.

Both the left and the right alleged that the new Arms Control Law was being unfairly enforced, but the point is that this was a major increase in military power prior to the coup. Unlike Brazil, where military courts made small efforts to prosecute civilians prior to the 1964 coup, in Chile the military gained jurisdiction over a crucial issue—the legality of bearing arms—well in advance of its seizure of state power.

In summary, the 1973 coup in Chile was preceded by a gradual dissolution of a prior inter-elite consensus on the constitutional and legal rules of the game. There had been no equivalent of this process in Brazil. In Hilbink's words, the Allende government shifted "from an initial commitment to work through the formal legal system to its acceptance of mass mobilization and direct action to achieve social justice" (Hilbink 1999, 190–91). This was part of a descent into what Samuel Huntington calls "praetorian" politics, with armed groups of the right and the left directly confronting one another (Huntington 1968, 192–98). Some place the blame for this outcome squarely on the shoulders of the Allende government itself. Others highlight the illiberalism and inflexibility of the Chilean judiciary, as well as the authoritarianism of the right, as major factors in the outcome.[15]

The 1973 Coup, Wartime Legality, and the Radical Adaptation of Legal Institutions

The Popular Unity government oversaw a three-year period of extensive mass mobilization and ambitious nationalizations of private companies on a scale that far surpassed the timid gestures of President Goulart in Brazil. In January of 1972, for example, the Popular Unity government unveiled a list of ninety-one firms to be nationalized. These firms were part of the country's key business conglomerates and included major banks and large producers of consumer durables, food, pulp, paper, and construction materials. Silva writes that the owners of these firms saw the Christian Democratic Party as incapable of defending their interests in Congress and within the existing, constitutional rules of the game (Silva 1996, 49). During the political polarization that took place under Allende in Chile, as we have seen, a major rift between the judiciary and the executive branch occurred, and this rift affected the military.

Unlike the Brazilian coup of 1964, the Chilean coup of 1973 was a rollback coup rather than a preemptive coup (Drake 1996, 32–33). The original *bando* (edict) justifying the military's intervention made much of the alleged violations of the rule of law by the Popular Unity government. In the new regime's first declaration of its right to "total power," drawn up by the heads of the four branches of the armed forces on September 12, 1973, the junta declared its commitment to "restore Chileanness, justice, and the broken institutionality" of the country. The third article of the same declaration declared that the new government would guarantee the independence of the judiciary (quoted in Cavallo, Salazar, and Sepúlveda 1997, 14).

Similarly, the Supreme Court was far more involved in the formation of the new military government than its counterpart in Brazil was. The president of the Supreme Court, Enrique Urrutia Manzano, issued a declaration on September 12, fewer than twenty-four hours after the beginning of the coup, congratulating the armed forces. The newly formed junta also consulted with Urrutia Manzano about the choice of minister of justice.[16]

The minister of justice was one of only two positions (ministers of education and justice) in the new cabinet held by civilians in the first post-coup government. Both of the civilians appointed to these positions worked for the military. The rest of the positions were divided up between members of the armed forces. This highly militarized cabinet received the blessing of judicial elites on September 18, seven days after the coup, when the Supreme Court justices were present at a religious ceremony to bless the government. And the junta members received a warm welcome from President Urrutia Manzano in the Supreme Court palace on September 25, just three days after the regime had dramatically expanded wartime military court jurisdiction vis-à-vis the civilian judiciary. Later, the junta appointed Urrutia Manzano to represent Chile at the inauguration of Juan Perón as president of Argentina on October 12, 1973 (Cavallo, Salazar, and Sepúlveda 1997, 15–19).

The *bandos* issued by the new military government in the days following the coup reflect the coup makers' claim that the Allende government had repeatedly violated the constitution and the law. Bando Number 5, issued on September 11, 1973, declared that "the government has placed itself at the margin of the constitution on multiple occasions, resorting to dubious, arbitrary actions and twisted and ill-intentioned, or even flagrantly erroneous interpretations of it which, for various reasons, have occurred without sanction."[17]

However, as in Brazil, there was tension within the armed forces between revolutionary and conservative approaches to the law. The first sign that the Chileans would be less conservative than the Brazilians came with the discussion about how long the military would stay in power. As we have seen, the original Brazilian solution was to declare an intention to occupy power only until the end of the mandate of the deposed president. This solution was also discussed in Chile, but no such self-limitation was ever declared (Cavallo, Salazar, and Sepúlveda 1997, 17).

Once the military regime was secure in its power, the Supreme Court went in the other direction in its relations with the executive. Instead of feuding with the executive about the law, the Supreme Court now turned a blind eye to abuses of power. While the 1925 constitution gave the Supreme Court the legal authority to review decisions made by the military courts, it refused to do so.

During the first eight months of rule by the junta after the coup in Chile, the institutional configuration and project of the new regime were relatively open. Barros writes that "unlike their Argentine or Brazilian counterparts, the Chilean armed forces did not have at hand extensive past experience of coup-making or military rule to draw upon—these things had to be worked out along the way."[18] The first few days of the coup were a "situation of total legal exception and absolute de facto rule"; military command had replaced ordinary civil and penal law and the constitution was suspended. The new regime's *bandos* were attempts to justify and explain its actions (Barros 2002, 40).

The *bandos* in the first few days of the regime declared a state of siege, imposed a curfew, summoned individuals to the Ministry of Defense, prohibited public assembly, authorized summary executions of people caught engaged in armed resistance, and closed the national Congress. The junta temporarily suspended the legal capacity of the Controlaría General de la República (auditor general) for preventive legal review of administrative decrees and resolutions. This decision widened the discretionary power of the executive by eliminating a form of prior judicial review (Barros 2002, 41–44). In the same way, the Brazilian military eliminated judicial review of its institutional act in AI-1. Unlike in Brazil, however, within days of the coup a group of prominent constitutionalists set to work to draft a new constitution. The legal scholars Jaime Guzmán, Sérgio Diez, Jorge Ovalle, and Enrique Orúzar were entrusted with constructing a new constitution to replace the 1925 document (Cavallo, Salazar, and Sepúlveda 1997, 17).

Decree-Law no. 5 of September 22, 1973, was the first decree-law to modify pre-coup legislation. This decree-law modified the military justice code to allow military personnel to use deadly force against anyone attacking the armed forces. It also modified the Arms Control Law (Law 17,798) and the Law of State Security, increasing penalties for a variety of offenses and introducing the death penalty for certain violations in time of war (Barros 2002, 45, n. 21). Most crucially for our purposes, it transferred cases involving violations of these two laws from peacetime military courts to wartime military courts.

Barros explains, "From the outset, the junta took great pains to link its exceptional powers to authority and powers conferred by the prior constitutional and legal system, particularly to declare states of exception and assure juridical continuity in the state administration. However, this articulation with earlier law did not involve limiting the junta to exercising only prior, valid legal powers" (Barros 2002, 72). The junta manipulated emergency powers, for example, far beyond that allowed by the 1925 constitution. Article 72 number 17 of the 1925 constitution allowed the president under a state of siege to transfer people from one department to another and to place them under house arrest. It did not sanction extrajudicial summary executions, which is what the regime engaged in after the coup. The junta also extended its state of siege powers to include the authority to exile people from Chile on the grounds of state security. As in Brazil, there were also secret laws; the Chilean military regime created ninety-eight secret or partly secret laws between 1973 and 1985.[19]

Therefore, the junta had it both ways. It used prior legality to supply a framework of order and state organization that could be used as a source of rules and authority when it suited the junta's interests. But it did not limit itself to the prior legal framework in exercising its power (see Barros 2002, 79). It combined revolutionary and conservative approaches to the law—a distinguishing feature of all three military regimes analyzed in this book—but it did so in a way that was more radical than its Brazilian predecessor, and less radical than its Argentine counterpart.

The Caravan of Death

The "caravan of death," a military mission that took place shortly after the 1973 coup, reveals the radicalism of the Pinochet regime in the legal realm. The caravan deliberately violated the regime's own legality. It exercised brute force against victims who posed no threat to those in authority and was directed by top leaders of the regime. It stands in contrast to the more constrained repression in Brazil after the 1964 coup.

In the aftermath of Chile's coup, local military commanders established military courts to quickly try local individuals associated with the previous Allende regime. These prisoners were usually found guilty and sentenced to various prison terms (a few were executed). Subsequently, between October 4 and 19, an "officer delegate" of the commander in chief of the army and president of the military junta, Augusto Pinochet, arrived by helicopter in several mostly northern towns and demanded to "review and expedite cases" and "harmonize the criteria" applied in them. While this special emissary, General Sergio Arellano Stark, dined and chatted with the local commander, officers in his entourage clandestinely rounded up selected political prisoners and executed them. By the end of the caravan's journey, seventy-five Chileans had been murdered in this way (Verdugo 2001).

The caravan's route went from Santiago to Cauquenes in the south and then La Serena, Copiapó, Antofagasta, and Calama in the north. The caravan presented a dilemma to regional army commanders. These officers had often enjoyed cordial relations with local government officials and lived among the townspeople; they also took pride in the Chilean army's reputation for bureaucratic correctness and adherence to legality. The caravan's stark and brutal executions presented the generals with the delicate question of what to tell people in the community about what had happened, and whether or not to let family members recover the bodies, some of which had been mutilated. As in any political crisis, some people responded more bravely and honestly than others—one commanding officer protested personally to Pinochet, let family members recover the bodies, and eventually resigned from the military; others remained silent, rationalized that it was not their responsibility, and ordered the dead to be placed in unmarked mass graves.

There are two contending explanations of the caravan. The first, offered by General Arellano in his own defense, is that the military intelligence agency the DINA (Dirección de Inteligencia Nacional, or National Intelligence Directorate) already existed at the time of the coup. Without Arellano's knowledge, DINA agents were placed in his entourage, creating a parallel command structure of the kind that existed in Nazi Germany and Stalin's Soviet Union. While Arellano innocently reviewed judicial sentences, his erstwhile subordinates carried out the executions behind his back, at the DINA's instruction. However, this explanation is implausible.

Instead, as Patricia Verdugo argues, it is more likely that Arellano had authorization from Pinochet, recruited his subordinates himself, personally selected the victims, and knowingly supervised their executions. Pinochet ordered the deletion of a reference to the caravan in General Lagos Osorio's report of the executions in his area, indicating that Pinochet wanted "plausible deniability" of the operation. The caravan, Verdugo concludes, was a message from the "hard-liners" within the military's coup coalition, to wavering military personnel and civilians alike, that the new military regime was there to stay and should not be resisted. The caravan thus arose from the "urgency of acquiring all power" for the junta and forestalling demands to return to civilian rule (Verdugo 2001, 226). This urgency was so great that it led the coup leaders to ignore their own carefully contrived legality, as represented by the wartime military tribunals. This is therefore an internal explanation for the executions, as the regime was not remotely threatened by the prisoners that it killed; the latter were already in detention, some had been charged with relatively minor offenses, and many had given themselves up voluntarily. This reinforces the important point that authoritarian legal and repressive strategies cannot be explained in terms of perceived threats to regime security alone; instead, intraregime dynamics often play an important role.

If the caravan was sent out to consolidate power, whose power was it consolidating? Robert Barros argues that Pinochet was not as powerful as many scholars think he was, and the regime was more of a collegial pact between the branches of the armed forces than a personalistic dictatorship (1996, 2001, 2002). Pablo Policzer argues that Pinochet interpreted the caravan to mean that using the regular military chain of command to carry out antisubversive terror would be difficult, given the resistance of the officer corps. This induced him to establish the DINA at the end of 1973. The caravan therefore may have played a role in the distinctive nature of coercion in the Chilean military regime (2001). For our purposes, what the caravan reveals is the audaciousness of the Chilean legal strategy in comparison to the Brazilian—first because the military courts used for prosecution were wartime military courts wholly insulated from the civilian judiciary, and second because even these courts' verdicts were selectively ignored by hard-liners intent on terrorizing potential opponents.[20]

In Brazil, the prolongation of military rule was accomplished by the gradual

ascension of hard-liners within the regime and administrative decrees cancel-
ing the 1965 elections and reforming the party system. Though unconstitutional,
these decrees were accomplished in a legalistic fashion. In Chile, in contrast, the
inner circle around Pinochet unleashed a campaign of terror that violated even
the draconian legality of the military courts—a reign of terror designed to convince military and civilian skeptics not to oppose long-term military rule. As
Barros writes, "To a large degree the ferocity of the coup was driven by symbolic
and disciplinary objects, not martial strategy: a massive display of force would
set an example and demonstrate the futility of resisting the new authorities—a
message equally directed at military officers and conscripts as to Chilean society
at large" (Barros 2002, 121–22).

Framing and Defending the Political Trials

Despite the violence of the coup, many people were subsequently put on trial.
Some justifications for the political trials in Chile, as in Brazil, were essentially
conservative. Bando Number 5, for example, claimed that the military was as-
suming power in order to "re-establish the economic and social normality of
the country [as well as] the peace, tranquility and security that were lost."[21]
However, the perception of threat was greater within the Chilean military than
the Brazilian, and the regime sometimes took a much more militant, if not mes-
sianic posture toward its presumed enemies. The "Declaration of Principles of
the Government of Chile," for example, issued in March 1974, six months after
the coup, declared that the "armed forces and the police do not set timetables
for their management of the government, because the task of rebuilding the
country morally, institutionally, and economically requires prolonged and profound action," which in turn implied "the absolute imperative to change the
mentality of the Chileans." In the same document, the military junta declared
that it "considers it as part of its mission to inspire a new and great civilian-
military movement . . . whose aims will deeply and lastingly reflect the aims of
the present government."[22] This is more revolutionary than conservative in its
implications. Like the Soviet and Cuban revolutions that took on the mission of
creating a "new man," the Chilean regime declared its intention to create Chileans
with a new mentality—and to accomplish this change through a political movement. At least on the rhetorical level, the Chilean military regime does not
adhere to Linz's ideal-type of authoritarian regime, which is described as es-

chewing the kind of mass mobilization common to so-called totalitarian regimes (see Linz 1975).

The Chilean military regime went even further in later pronouncements. On the third anniversary of the coup that brought the regime to power, in September of 1976, the junta issued a presidential message and prefaces to constitutional acts numbers 2, 3, and 4, in which the regime's view of counterinsurgency warfare was laid bare. Here, Marxism's "permanent aggression" had given rise to "unconventional war, in which territorial invasion is replaced by the attempt to control the state from within." This dangerous new war was total, and required the nation "to give power to the armed forces, since they are the only ones that have the organization and means to confront Marxism."[23] As in Brazil, a temporary threat from a shadowy enemy that fought on economic, social, political, and psychological as well military levels required the assumption of emergency powers by the military until the threat—as defined by the military—had subsided. While the rhetoric in the Chilean case is similar to enunciations in Brazil of national security doctrine, the conservative strain in Brazilian justifications for the trials seems deeper, and the corresponding actions are less severe.

Unlike its Brazilian counterpart, the Chilean military regime did not present its military court trials as evidence of an adherence to the rule of law when dealing with other governments and attempting to influence international opinion. The courts' procedures and actions were probably too far removed from international legal standards to bear much outside scrutiny. Instead, the Pinochet regime periodically revised its legal framework in an attempt to escape sanctions by the United Nations and foreign governments. For example, in September 1974 the regime enacted decree-laws that modified the government's emergency powers. These reforms were presented as improvements in the country's human rights situation. One of these, promulgated on September 11, 1974, modified the wartime state of siege to the category of internal defense, a newly created legal category that sounded less severe than "state of siege." According to Barros, the decree was merely a political maneuver in response to anticipated criticisms of the government in the United Nations General Assembly (Barros 1996, 170–72, quote p. 172).

Just as the Brazilian military regime reframed its military court trials to make them appear to be consistent with international norms of justice and standard legal procedures in civilian courts, the Chilean military regime relabeled its legal framework to make it appear less extreme than it actually was. In Chile's case, the maneuver was less effective than in Brazil because of the violence of the coup, the large exile community, and the denser international network of human rights organizations that existed in the 1970s compared with the 1960s (Keck and Sikkink 1998). However, for both regimes, the legal "spin" they put on their policies probably reassured some members of their domestic support coalitions and helped to create an image in which their violence was within the law and supportive of national unity while the violence of their enemies was illegal, illegitimate, and subversive.

The Fate of Political Prisoners in Chilean Military Justice

Most Chilean political prisoners who were put on trial were tried in military courts.[24] Chilean military courts in the 1973 to 1978 period were not the institutional equivalents of the Brazilian military courts. In normal times, the Chilean military operated courts in predetermined locations (Romero 1985, 436). However, after the coup, the new regime placed military commanders in charge of territorial units throughout the country. These commanders hastily created wartime military tribunals (*consejos de guerra*) consisting of seven military officers directly under their command. Most of these officers had no legal training. In some cases, civilian judges and lawyers formed part of the tribunals, but these were exceptions.[25]

The rights of defendants in these trials were far more circumscribed than they were in Brazil. Neither defendants nor their lawyers were allowed to cross-examine prosecution witnesses; evidence could be kept secret by military prosecutors; and there was no minimum time allowed for the defense to prepare its case. Most trials were conducted in a few days, and there was no right of appeal (Snyder 1995, 259, 265–66). These courts tried an estimated six thousand people in the first five years of military rule, sentencing approximately two hundred defendants to death (Snyder 1995, 266; Barros 2002, 139).

Of the total cases compiled by the Vicaría de la Solidaridad (Vicariate of Solidarity, an umbrella organization established by the Catholic Church and allied Protestant churches), 43 percent involved infractions of the 1972 Arms Control Law, while 55 percent concerned violations of the 1958 Law of State Security (the other 2 percent were for violations of the code of military justice or ordinary criminal law).[26] (As we have seen, these laws were slightly modified by the military regime, but their basic provisions antedated the advent of military rule.) While the Popular Unity government had used these laws to attempt to repress the right, the military regime used them to repress the left.

Like the Brazilian military regime, the Chilean military regime applied laws retroactively. The decree creating wartime military courts was issued on September 22, 1973, so constitutionally, only people charged with crimes occurring after that date should have been tried by them. But the Vicaría de la Solidaridad found cases in which defendants were charged in the wartime courts for crimes committed before September 22. In reality, the start and duration of the "war" declared by the regime was never made clear in legal terms. Some courts considered the war to have started under Allende, others on September 11, others on September 22. As the lawyers for the Vicaría put it, "in reality, the war did not exist." As in Brazil, very few political prisoners had engaged in armed combat with military or police personnel. Instead, "the war was a legal fiction that the military dictatorship established to put in play, with the appearance of legality, an entire repressive system, especially for those who exercised power in the government of Popular Unity."[27]

Table 5.1, based on a large sample of Chilean military court cases from 1973 to 1978, provides a marked contrast with the data on Brazilian military courts presented in chapter 4. (The samples, each including over two thousand defendants, are comparable in size.) In the Brazilian sample, acquittal rates were high, averaging 55.60 overall. Even the most punitive court, in Bahia, acquitted 36.84 percent of the defendants that it tried. Regional variation in the pattern of court verdicts was also very broad. The range went from the low of 36.84 acquitted in Bahia to 90.91 percent in Pará, or a range of 54.07. Only three of the twelve regional military courts acquitted fewer than half of all the defendants in the cases they tried. The most punitive and the most severe courts were located in peripheral areas, while courts in the core states of São Paulo and Rio de Janeiro acquitted defendants at about the average rate (see table 4.1.)

Table 5.1 shows a very different pattern of court behavior in Chile. The most striking finding is that the average acquittal rate, at 12.42 percent, is less than one quarter of the rate in Brazil. Political prisoners in Chilean military justice were thus far more likely to be convicted of crimes than their Brazilian counterparts. In Chile, six local military courts dealing with a total of 165 political prisoners did not acquit a single defendant. While three-quarters of the Brazilian courts acquitted more than 50 percent of their defendants, not one of the thirty-one regional military courts in Chile did the same.

The often extremely punitive nature of the Chilean military courts can be seen in several cases whose sentences were approved by the head of the military zone of San Antonio in late 1973 and 1974, Colonel Manuel Contreras Sepúlveda, who was later imprisoned in Chile for his role in the assassination of Allende's foreign minister, Orlando Letelier, in Washington, D.C. These cases provide important insights into Chilean military justice.

In one case the defendant was described as "an individual with the ideas of the left, a militant of the Socialist Party, a Marxist" who "provoked disorder in public acts and political meetings . . . shouting slogans aimed at provoking violence and frightening people." In what was essentially a conviction for crimes of thought and expression, the defendant was sentenced to three years in prison for violating various articles of the Law of State Security.[28] Another defendant, a taxi driver, was sentenced to 540 days (almost a year and a half) for insulting policemen while drunk—a violation of article 417 of the military justice code. The justification adds that the defendant was "also a socialist militant."[29] Yet another defendant received the same sentence for the same charge, insulting policemen, and also for saying in front of them that "the military who killed the president were assassins."[30] Another case was that of nine defendants who were convicted of crimes committed before the coup d'etat and sentenced to prison terms of four hundred to one thousand days. These defendants were accused of being members of the Socialist Party of Algarrobo, forming a Che Guevara group that propagated "doctrines that tend to destroy the constituted social order," and forming paramilitary groups with "the object of practicing self-defense and attack." The defendants were found guilty of violating both the Arms Control and State Security laws.[31]

Some cases were more serious. Six armed men who were caught by policemen five days after the coup and were suspected of planning to attack the police station were convicted of violating article 8 of the Arms Control Law. Two of them were sentenced to death the day after they were apprehended and were executed by firing squad, while four others received prison sentences of three to four years each. The only evidence that the men had planned to attack the police station were the confessions—probably extracted by means of torture—of two of the men (the ones later executed).[32]

These cases conform to an image of the Pinochet regime—largely deserved —as one that was unusually harsh and punitive. However, even in a region controlled by architects of state terror such as Manuel Contreras and Sergio Arellano Stark, the leader of the caravan of death, one can find the occasional acquittal. For example, in December 1973 a military court in Tejas Verdes convicted two de-

5.1 Acquittal rates in national security trials in regional military courts by location of court, Chile, 1973–1978

Court location	No. of defendants	No. of defendants acquitted	Acquittal rate (%)
Far North			
Antofogasta	211	24	11.37
Arica	57	11	19.30
Calama	34	3	8.82
Iquique	2	0	0.00
Pisagua	147	14	9.52
Regional Total	*451*	*52*	*11.53*
North			
Copiapó	43	2	4.65
La Serena	178	28	15.73
Regional Total	*221*	*30*	*13.57*
Middle Chile			
Angol	38	0	0.00
Cauquenes	26	2	7.69
Chillán	95	9	9.47
Concepción	108	10	9.26a
Curicó	9	0	0.00
Linares	152	33	21.71
Los Andes	37	2	5.41
Los Ángeles	94	23	24.47
Osorno	91	0	0.00
Quillota	1	0	0.00
Rancagua	82	38	46.34
San Felipe	82	9	10.98
San Fernando	14	2	14.29
Santiago	335	73	21.79
Talca	24	0	0.00
Talcahuano	135	22	16.30
Tejas Verdes (San Antonio)	56	4	7.14
Valparaíso	197	9	4.57
Victoria	5	1	20.00
Regional Total	*1,581*	*237*	*14.99*
South			
Puerto Montt	86	2	2.33
Temuco	91	3	3.30
Traiguén	38	1	2.63
Valdivia	131	4	3.05
Regional Total	*346*	*10*	*2.89*
Far South			
Punta Arenas	90	5	5.56
Total	*2,689*	*334*	*12.42a*

Note 1: In this table, Chile's twelve administrative units and Santiago have been grouped into five regions to facilitate comparison with the Brazilian data. The far north consists of administrative units 1 and 2; the north is administrative units 3 and 4; middle Chile consists of administrative units 5–8 plus greater Santiago; the south is administrative units 9 and 10; and the far south is administrative units 11 and 12.

Note 2: Map 3 is a selective depiction of this table. It shows the location of the nine most active courts from this sample, together with the thirteenth, fourteenth, and fifteenth most active (Punta Arenas, Puerto Montt, and Arica). These last three courts were chosen to show the range of locations of the military court trials.

Note 3: These data and the data in table 5.2 are from a sample of cases. For an explanation of the source of these data, see appendix 1.

aThis figure does not included defendants who were convicted but punished by only a fine or administrative measure (42), nor those who were convicted but given a suspended sentence (213). If these figures were added, the average acquittal/suspended sentence rate would be 21.90 percent.

fendants of subversive propaganda and sentenced them to four and a half years in prison. However, Brigadier General Arellano Stark, commander of the Second Division, overturned the court's conviction and had the prisoners released a year later. The details of the case deserve some attention.

The defendants were charged with propagating violent doctrines and violating article 4f of the State Security Law. The defendants were the secretary and treasurer of the Chilean-Soviet Cultural Institute of San Antonio. The institute contained books, magazines, pamphlets, tapes, and films with "a content tending to destroy or alter by violence the constituted social order." The defendants did not turn over the keys to the institute to the military at the time of the coup as they were required to do.

However, in his reversal of the original sentence, General Arellano Stark (or his legal advisor) found that the defendants, who lived in Santiago and only worked in the institute sporadically, could not be held responsible for the subversive propaganda that the institute contained. The institute was primarily dedicated to cultural work rather than political propaganda, and the defendants had no prior record of political agitation.[33]

On its face, this decision is rather extraordinary. While various interpretations are possible, a plausible conclusion is that like their Brazilian counterparts, the Chilean judges had some degree of class bias. Upper-class directors of cultural institutes who lived in Santiago might be considered imprudent for keeping a cache of subversive material in the provinces, but they were not the dangerous Socialist and Communist Party militants who influenced the "masses" and whom the regime saw as its immediate enemies. While lower-class, provincial taxi drivers and laborers were put in prison for several years for making offhand remarks to the police, the compilers and guardians of what was described as a major collection of subversive material were acquitted—not by the military court in the first instance, but by a senior military officer. The double standard, if that is what it was, shares a strong resemblance to the Brazilian military court judges' belief that society's natural class hierarchy should not be unduly disturbed in the administration of punishment.

Another important indicator of the way that political trials worked is the variation of acquittal rates from region to region. The range—the distance between the lowest and highest aggregate acquittal rates by region—is important because it suggests something about the consistency of military justice throughout the national territory by these military regimes. A reasonable assumption is that the range in Brazil—a vast, heterogenous country with a relatively decentralized, confederal state and a weakly organized working class and left—would be far higher than in Chile. Chile is a smaller and more homogenous country with a strong, centralized state, whose military regime initiated a far more violent wave of repression against a broadly based and popular left.

Surprisingly, this is not the case. The range of acquittal rates among the local courts in Chile is almost as large as in Brazil.[34] The Brazilian data show that in the north, the acquittal rate was 90.91, or almost 100 percent. The next highest rate, in the south, was 68.56 percent. This compares with the acquittal rate of 44.74 percent in the northeast, the region where courts were most severe. Overall, this produces an interregional range of 46.17 or an acquittal rate in one region that is more than twice as high as in another. If we discard the north as an outlier, the range is still high, at 23.82 (table 4.1).

In Chile, what emerges is a picture of a legal system that was more punitive but was not more standardized than its Brazilian counterpart. In Chile, courts in the various regions did not acquit defendants at similar rates—the south and far south were far more punitive toward defendants, with acquittal rates of only 2.89 and 5.56 percent, respectively, compared to an average of 14.16 for the other regions. The acquittal rate in middle Chile, where most political prisoners were prosecuted, was actually five times as high as in the south.[35] Although the number of southern cases in our sample is low and may therefore be misleading, the data suggest that differences between the regions as reflected in the trials were at least as great in Chile as they were in Brazil.

Regional patterns in the two countries differ on another dimension. As we have seen, in Brazil, courts in the periphery acquitted at much higher or lower rates than the average, while courts in heavily populated São Paulo and Rio acquitted at about the average rate. In the impoverished northeast, the courts were the most punitive. In Chile, the most heavily populated region had the highest acquittal rate, while courts in peripheral areas tended to be more severe. (In both countries military courts convicted more in poorer regions.)

Sentencing data from Brazilian and Chilean samples show some surprising similarities as well as differences. Table 5.2 shows that roughly 60 percent of defendants in the Chilean court sample received sentences of four years or less —only slightly lower than the nearly 63 percent who received sentences of one to four years in Brazil (table 4.6). In both countries, the bulk of those sentenced thus received relatively short prison terms. Given the more severe image of the Chilean military regime, this is surprising, even if we allow for the greater ferocity of repression there.[36]

5.2   Sentences of those convicted in national security trials in regional military courts, Chile, 1973–1978

Sentence	No. of defendants	Percentage
Suspended sentence/fine	258	12.78
Less than 1 year	199	9.86
1–4 years	757	37.49
Subtotal: 4 years or less	*1,214*	*60.13*
5–9 years	392	19.42
10–15 years	255	12.63
16–20 years	65	3.22
21–25 years	13	0.64
26–30 years	9	0.45
More than 30 years	6	0.30
Life	44	2.18
Death	21	1.04
Subtotal: 10 years or more	*413*	*20.46*
Total	*2,019*	*100.01*

Note: The percentages exceed 100 due to rounding. This data comes from a sample of 406 cases involving 2,689 defendants. From this original total I subtracted 334 defendants who were acquitted, 67 who were sentenced to exile from the country (*extrañamiento*), and 269 who were sentenced to *relegación*, a type of internal exile.

However, Chilean military justice did apply two sentences that were not applied in Brazil—life imprisonment and the death penalty. In Chile, around 20 percent of the defendants in the sample received sentences of ten years or more (table 5.2). In Brazil, only 12.40 percent received sentences of more than ten years (table 4.6).[37] These data suggest that while the majority of defendants in both countries received sentences of four years or less, the minority that received longer sentences of ten years or more was proportionally larger in Chile than it was in Brazil.

Public Contestation of the Political Trials

The human rights abuses of the Pinochet regime were met with a spirited reaction by the lawyers of the Vicaría de la Solidaridad, the umbrella organization established by the Catholic Church and allied Protestant churches. Roberto Garretón Merino, former chief of the Juridical Department of the Vicaría, thinks that this is very important. Because of legal actions, most typically the filing of a writ of habeas corpus, "each detained or disappeared [person] in Chile has a first and last name . . . each person preserved his dignity, in part."[38] (As we shall see, this is not true of Argentina.) Legal action thus established a record of the victims of repression without necessarily protecting them: the Supreme Court only accepted thirty of almost nine thousand habeas corpus petitions filed during the Pinochet regime.[39]

However, public contestation of the military regime's legality was tightly circumscribed. Whereas in Brazil, individual lawyers throughout the country took the cases of political prisoners, the Vicaría was virtually the only organization that was willing to furnish defense lawyers for political prisoners in Chile. Criticisms of legal decisions were generally not aired in the press. The civilian judiciary permitted fewer legal challenges to the military regime's repression than it did in Brazil. As we have seen, habeas corpus petitions were routinely granted in Brazilian courts until the passage of AI-5, more than four years after the beginning of the military regime. Also, legal challenges such as São Paulo prosecutor Hélio Bicudo's case against death squad leader Sérgio Fleury did occur within the civilian court system in Brazil.

There are some parallel cases in Chile. In 1979 Judge Servando Jordán required Manuel Contreras and two other members of the DINA to testify in court in a case involving the discovery of several bodies, presumably of people disappeared by the DINA, in the Maipo River delta area. However, the case was closed due to insufficient evidence.

Similarly, in 1983 appeals court judge Carlos Cerda investigated the disappearance of twelve Communist Party members in 1976 and charged thirty-eight members of the *carabineros* and air force, including General Gustavo Leigh, with responsibility for the murders. But the Supreme Court closed the case after several appeals, ruling that the defendants were protected by the 1978 amnesty law. The Supreme Court then censured Judge Cerda when he continued with his investigation after this decision.[40]

This last incident reveals that there were differences between military-judicial relations, and between the structure of the judiciary, in Brazil and Chile. In Chile, a centralized and extremely hierarchical judiciary strongly controlled by the conservative Supreme Court remained a pillar of authoritarian rule throughout the military dictatorship. It policed its own ranks, punishing renegade judges who pried into the human rights abuses of the regime. In Brazil, a more decentralized and pluralistic judiciary was largely supportive of military rule but permitted some dissent in the regime's early years and again in the 1970s.

Perhaps the case of Teodomiro Romeiro dos Santos, discussed in chapter 4, best captures the differences between public contestation of authoritarian legality in Brazil and Chile. When the regional military court sentenced Teodomiro to death, criticism of the decision—from members of Congress, prominent members of the clergy, and lawyers—was aired in the press. The public pressure was quite strong, and the Superior Military Court eventually commuted the sentence to life in prison.

In Chile, few of the elements that produced this outcome existed. Congress had been closed, church leaders had anointed the junta's leaders after the military coup, and the media did not look to the defense lawyers of political prisoners for quotes. Most crucially, an effective appeals process did not exist in the wartime military courts, and defendants sentenced to death were shot almost immediately after their trial, if they were tried at all. The death sentence was applied frequently in 1973–1974 without the outcry that can be seen in the Teodomiro case in Brazil. Chile thus went down a path of repression that Brazil did not. That point was probably reached even before the 1973 coup, when the consensus on the legal framework broke down under Allende, and the absence of civilian-military cooperation in the judicial sphere prevented the construction of a new one.

Military Usurpation of Judicial Authority

Chile represents a more radical process of organizational adaptation to the problem of how to legalize repression than its Brazilian predecessor. Why? This chapter has argued that a neglected factor is the prior history of military-judicial relations. The Chilean military was a more closed and insulated organization than its Brazilian counterpart. Paradoxically, the constitutional tradition of the military after the Ibáñez dictatorship may have decreased the military's interaction with judicial elites, and this separation of elites was reinforced by the judiciary's ideology concerning its apolitical role within the state. Chilean military officers lacked a repertoire of repression that integrated civilian and military elites (as in Brazilian military justice) and which they could trust. Chile's more rigid separation of powers—a feature that for most political scientists made it a more consolidated democracy—also inhibited the kind of flexible civil-military cooperation that characterized repression in Brazil. Instead, the Chilean military, principally the army, took it upon itself to usurp considerable judicial power after the coup of 1973, with brutal and tragic consequences.

Furthermore, elite consensus about the rules of the game were eroded to a far greater extent under the government of Salvador Allende than they were under João Goulart. A climate of emergency developed under Allende in which both partisans and opponents of the Popular Unity government felt that law was insufficient and increasingly irrelevant to the resolution of political conflicts. This contributed to the climate of radicalism that was taken advantage of by the military regime.

After the coup, the military constituted wartime military courts—exclusively military organizations—to try political prisoners. These courts convicted defendants far more quickly and at a far higher rate in Brazil and applied the death penalty, although average prison sentences were not substantially higher than the Brazilian ones. Acquittal rates varied considerably by region and were lowest in the south. The Vicaría de la Solidaridad was able to provide legal assistance to political prisoners and to document human rights abuses, but it was not able to contest the regime's repression to quite the same extent as the human rights community in Brazil, especially the Catholic Church-supported Justice and Peace Commission in São Paulo, which campaigned openly for amnesty for political prisoners in the 1970s.

While military courts dispensed summary judgments in Chile, the Supreme Court stood aside. The Chilean military seized judicial authority, whereas Brazilian military officers enlisted civilian cooperation in the creation of a modified but still largely traditional legal system. Unlike the Brazilians, the Chilean military regime also felt under threat from subversion throughout its rule and preserved its subsystem for dealing with political crime right up until the transition to democracy.

As in Brazil, Chilean military attitudes to "subversion" were shaped largely before the coup. Like their Brazilian counterparts, many Chilean military officers saw the political demands of the working-class and left political parties as threatening to a conservative vision of national identity (Smallman 2002, 26). Under Allende's Popular Unity government, the Chilean army had asked for and received the passage of an arms control law that allowed it to arrest and to try suspected members of the armed left. It was this law that furnished the most common charge against political prisoners after the coup. Like the 1963 prosecution of trade unionists in Brazil, the Arms Control Law in Chile signaled an active military role in combating the left even before the military takeover.

In the early phase of Chile's military rule, a violent assault on the support base of the Popular Unity government was covered by a very thin legal veneer. Most victims of repression in the early post-coup period were not processed in courts at all. Furthermore, the caravan of death showed how far the regime's inner circle was willing to stray from its own authoritarian legality in order to hold on to power. The Chilean rulers never lost their desire to retain the fig leaf of the rule of law, however, and after 1974, political repression became more selective. By the end of 1978, political prisoners faced peacetime military courts whose trials were slower and ensured more procedural rights for defendants than the wartime ones. (However, Chilean military tribunals in the first instance still lacked any integration with the civilian judiciary and were entirely military, located on military bases rather than in urban courthouses as in Brazil.) A 1978 self-amnesty and the (albeit dubious) popular ratification of an executive-centered constitution in 1980 further judicialized the repressive apparatus. The Pinochet regime's institutions of political justice therefore represent a greater deviation from previous traditions than Brazilian institutions, but without the all-out assault on judicial traditions of the Argentine dirty war—the subject of the next chapter.

6

Antilegalism in Argentina

Inter arma silent leges. (In time of war, the laws are silent.)

THE ATTEMPTS OF an unconstitutional dictatorship to cloak itself with legality and to prosecute opponents and dissidents for violations of national security may seem to be simply a façade for the exercise of uncontrolled power and violence. It might seem better to pass over this disturbing practice of dictatorships, assigning it to either the historical dustbin or to the specialized categorizations of comparative politics. However, an examination of the Argentine case helps us to realize that far from being ephiphenomenal and irrelevant to the real dynamics of power under authoritarianism, national security legality and political trials are one of the keys to understanding these regimes.

A closer inspection of the Brazilian and Chilean regimes reveals that they did not make up national security legality from scratch but rather borrowed existing statist and authoritarian institutions, laws, and organizations and used them for their own ends. In Brazil there was more borrowing and less innovation than in Chile, but in both cases regime leaders forged a consensus on a new authoritarian legality that mixed elements of the old and new. They built a working understanding between judicial and military elites, involving active cooperation in Brazil and wary acceptance of a division of labor in Chile. These efforts provided stability to these military regimes.

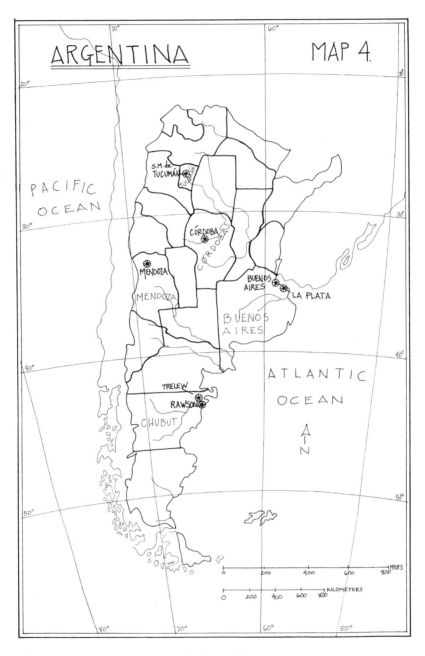

Map 4: Argentina, 1971–1983. Map by Lynne E. Perry.

In contrast, the Argentine regime, despite the rhetorical mildness of its proclaimed ambition of "national reorganization," was revolutionary in its disregard for and violation of preexisting legality. Instituted three years after the Chilean coup, it hardly involved courts in the administration of "justice" at all, and lacked a coherent vision of a new legal order. In Argentina from 1976 to 1983, civilian courts denied writs of habeas corpus and served as a cover for state terror, and military courts prosecuted a small number of people. But the most common repressive procedure was for military and police forces to apprehend people, take them to one of 365 secret detention centers, interrogate and torture them, and then disappear them without explanation or record. An estimated twenty thousand to thirty thousand people were killed in this way.[1] Approximately twenty-five thousand were detained, tortured, and subsequently released (Buchanan 1989, 54). The Argentine regime of 1976–1983 thus largely dispensed with any kind of legal strategy and engaged in total and merciless war on the alleged agents of subversion. In institutional terms, the Argentine regime was the most innovative and the most daring of the military regimes analyzed in this book. It was the only one of the three that accomplished the rare political feat of creating an institutional matrix that was truly new.

There are many explanations of the peculiar ferocity of the dirty war. Conservative discourse, neoliberal economic ideas, a conservative church, national security doctrine, and a divided middle class have all been offered as causal factors.[2] However, these factors existed, to a greater or lesser degree, in Brazil and Chile as well.[3]

This chapter advances a different explanation. It suggests that the failure of a prior attempt to create a judicial-military consensus on the treatment of subversion created an institutional vacuum that was eventually filled by the dirty war policies. This account emphasizes that factionalism within the armed forces was more intense in Argentina than in either Brazil or Chile, while military-judicial relations were more strained. There was more opposition in the judiciary to military notions of national security in Argentina than in either Brazil or Chile. Variables found in the other cases were combined in a different sequence to produce a distinctive outcome. First there was organizational innovation, then reversal, and finally the avoidance of that prior organizational solution, setting the military on an antilegalistic course.

Connections and Parallels between the Argentina Military Coup and Regime and Military Regimes in Chile and Brazil

Like *trabalhismo* in Brazil, the movement around Juan Domingo Perón—Peronism—transformed politics in Argentina. After a coup in 1943, then colonel Juan Domingo Perón became head of the National Labor Department, a post that he used to build the trade union support that propelled him into the presidency in elections held in February 1946 (McGuire 1997, 51). Reelected in 1951, Perón presided over "a greatly increased social and political presence for the working class within Argentine society" (James 1988, 25; see also Potash 1980). The political emergence of the working class was occurring at the same time in Brazil and Chile, but it was strongest in Argentina.

The armed forces removed Perón in a violent coup in 1955, in what its supporters called the liberating revolution. Perón retained substantial support, and Argentina descended into a spiral of violence that worsened over the years. While the military devolved power to civilians in 1958, it was never far from the center of power in these years and continued to develop its repressive capacities, trying suspected members of the nascent armed left in military courts in the early 1960s. The coup of June 27–28, 1966, was closely linked to the 1964 coup in Brazil. Both interventions were described as "revolutions" by the respective militaries. The Brazilian coup, quickly recognized by the United States, may have signaled to Argentine military officers that another intervention in politics would not be costly.

The subsequent military regime suffered from a progressive crisis of legitimacy and was not able to consolidate itself along Brazilian lines. Although it engaged in extensive constitutional and legal adjustments, issuing institutional acts like the Brazilians, these ultimately proved to be ineffective to counter growing opposition, including a rising armed left (James 1988, 235–48; Brennan 1994; O'Donnell 1988, 159–60). The military eventually handed over the reins of government to an elected president in 1973, and this was quickly followed by the return of Juan Perón and his restoration to power. Perón died the following year and was replaced by his widow Maria Estela Martínez de Perón, or Isabel Perón. There followed a period of increasing political polarization, ineffectual government, and escalating violence before the military stepped in yet again in March of 1976.

If the 1966 coup had been influenced by Brazil, the 1976 coup was more influenced by Chile. The Chilean coup had been highly repressive but the subsequent regime had withstood strong international criticisms and endured. As in the Brazilian and Chilean coups, the 1976 military intervention created uncertainty as to the duration of the new regime. As in Chile but not in Brazil, the new regime in Argentina started off in a highly repressive fashion. It closed Congress and went farther than the Chilean military by totally purging the Supreme Court. Before reviewing the regime's legal approach to repression, we will first survey the erosion of consensus that preceded the military regime.

The Dissolution of the National Penal Court

General Lanusse headed the last government of the 1966–1973 military regime. Under Lanusse, the National Penal Court (Cámara en lo Penal de la Nación) was created on May 28, 1971, to prosecute political opponents of the regime who were increasingly engaged in armed actions.[4] The dissolution of this court and the freeing of those convicted in it in 1973 contributed to the military's later adoption of dirty war tactics.

The National Penal Court, which consisted of three judges in each of three separate chambers (Potash 1996, 389), all located in Buenos Aires, was authorized to try defendants accused of certain specified crimes committed anywhere in the nation.[5] For its creators in the military regime, the National Penal Court bypassed the often slow and politically unreliable provincial court system by creating a speedy, specialized, centralized court staffed by a handful of judges with known pro-regime sympathies. In the two brief years of its existence, the so-called *cameron* (big court) or *cámara del terror* (court of terror) convicted at least three hundred people accused of various politically motivated crimes.[6] While civilian in nature, the National Penal Court served the same purpose that military courts did under the Brazilian and Chilean military regimes—the repression of the regime's opponents and dissidents in politically controlled venues.[7]

Not long after the creation of the National Penal Court, the Lanusse government passed Law 19,081, which allowed the military to investigate crimes that fell under the court's jurisdiction and to fight the armed left under state of siege conditions (Potash 1996, 390). The navy preferred using military courts against the terrorists but was overruled within the Lanusse government. Law 19,863 created special conditions for political prisoners. This was significant later, because many leaders of the 1976–1983 military regime believed that the segregation and special treatment of political prisoners under the prior regime of 1966–1973 had hardened the resolve of guerillas and strengthened the ties among them.

Remarkably, considering Argentina's subsequent history, the National Penal Court's structure and procedures made it a fairer venue, at least on paper, than either Brazilian or Chilean military courts. The court was civilian, and therefore formally outside the military chain of command, unlike military courts. (Under the 1853 Argentine constitution, civilians could not be prosecuted in military courts except during a state of siege.) All of the judges were thoroughly trained in the law—something that could not be said of Brazilian and Chilean military courts. Furthermore, as in Brazil, the death penalty was not applied.[8]

Also as in Brazil, prosecutions were handled by civilian lawyers, although the prosecutors' office, the Public Ministry, was civilian rather than military. The procedures were a mix of oral and written presentations, as they were in Brazil, rather than the purely written presentations of the Chilean trials, and were governed by the same rules that applied to ordinary federal courts. Cases were resolved at the same pace as cases in Brazilian military courts, typically lasting six months to a year. The trials were public, at least in principle. Defendants had the right to defense by a civilian lawyer, and the laws used to prosecute defendants were ordinary penal law, not military law. Defense lawyers had considerable scope for the defense of their clients.

Nevertheless, the National Penal Court was biased in ways similar to the bias of courts in Brazil and Chile. While the judges were civilian, they were directly appointed by the military president without the approval of the Senate. They were thus politically sympathetic and loyal to the military regime. Political prisoners could be held incommunicado for a period of ten days followed by five more days. Prisoners were often tortured during this time and their confessions accepted in the court as evidence; judges never investigated allegations of torture.[9] New laws on the books prohibiting "illicit association" with guerrillas and the expression of subversive ideas meant that defendants were often prosecuted for crimes of association—for example, meeting with suspected guerrillas —or opinion, for example, possessing books deemed to be Communist by the prosecution, or publishing articles sympathetic to the guerrillas. (Law 17,401, the Law for the Repression of Communism described in chapter 3, allowed the sort of prosecution described above.) The penalties for these crimes were often severe, and other vague laws gave ample latitude for conviction of the defendants. In many cases, as in Brazil and Chile, defendants practically had to prove that they were not "subversives" or "terrorists." And as in the other two countries, most defendants were not directly accused of crimes of violence, but rather of expressing ideas and engaging in actions that indirectly supported those engaged in violence.[10] This meant, in practice, that many people who were political activists criticizing the military regime were accused of terrorism.[11]

Furthermore, the structure of the court made defense lawyers' jobs difficult. While the crimes prosecuted in the court had occurred all over the country, and the prisoners were often in provincial prisons such as Rawson Prison in Chubut, the court was located only in Buenos Aires. Defense lawyers, who often took cases without charging a fee, were usually also located in Buenos Aires. They thus had to spend money traveling in order to prepare their cases.[12]

But the difficulties of defense attorneys went well beyond out-of-pocket expenses. The 1971 abduction of Nestor Martins, a well-known lawyer for political prisoners, sent a chilling message to the legal community and made finding defenders of the political prisoners more difficult. Defense lawyers often received anonymous threats and sometimes had to dodge assassination attempts. While the trials were formally public, few people beyond immediate family members of the defendants and their lawyers actually attended, because everyone who attended had his documents carefully checked, and an air of intimidation surrounded the court.

In the National Penal Court trials, the initial report that formed the basis of the prosecution was usually prepared by military intelligence or agents in the Division de Orden Político (Division of Political Order) of the Federal Police. (This division was similar to the DEOPS in Brazil, although it was a federal rather than a state agency.) This report was sometimes submitted to the judge without the defendant or his lawyer seeing it. The quality of the evidence presented in court by the prosecution was often poor, sometimes nothing more than a confession extracted under torture. Defense lawyers sometimes had insufficient time to mount a serious defense. Former defense lawyer Carlos A. González Gartland remembered that he had had only five days to prepare a defense in a case involving thousands of pages of documents.[13] Acquittals were apparently rare, although unfortunately the archives of the National Penal Court are not public, so a comparison of its cases with the Brazilian and Chilean military court cases analyzed in this book is impossible.[14]

The name "terror court" had a double meaning in the Argentina of that time. The court tried alleged terrorists—the regime did not call them "political prisoners" for obvious reasons. But the court was also greatly feared and criticized by all those who opposed the military regime. The name thus refers both to the defendants in the court and the feelings that it inspired in them and their supporters. Lawyers who defended political prisoners in the court included Raul Alfonsín, later president of Argentina. Rodolfo David Ortega Peña, a lawyer who defended many political prisoners in the National Penal Court, was killed by the Triple-A death squad in 1974.[15] Judges who served in the National Penal Court had a reputation for being hard-liners in the struggle against the armed left. They included one judge who served on the Supreme Court during the 1976–83 military regime, another (Jaime Smart) who went to the Ministry of Government (*gobierno*) in Buenos Aires province, and one who defended the junta leaders in the "big trial" of 1985. Judge Esteban Vergera, however, had a reputation for being liberal and reportedly intervened to prevent a prisoner in the hands of the police from being killed.[16]

Why was the National Penal Court created? Under the military regime of 1966–73, the Argentine Supreme Court, like the Brazilian Supreme Court, had a certain recognized if limited autonomy. Lawyers active during that period believed that the military did not press to try suspected guerrillas in military courts because they feared that the Supreme Court would find this expediency unconstitutional. Similarly, a significant part of the legal community was hostile to the regime and would have been expected to oppose the use of the military court option. However, the military was frustrated with the slow pace of political trials in regular courts and the tendency of these courts to acquit. They wanted to create a controlled venue in which they could place judges sympathetic to their conception of national security doctrine. In this way they could stage relatively quick trials that made a public spectacle of punishing the guerillas and their sympathizers. They also feared reprisals by guerrillas for convictions, and felt that by creating a single court with only nine judges in the federal capital, as opposed to the hundreds of judges scattered throughout the country previously deciding political cases, they could more easily protect the judges and influence them to convict more often.[17]

The Argentine solution to the legal dilemma of authoritarian regimes was thus in part a reaction to the independence and resistance of the existing judiciary. What was missing here that is present in the Brazilian case, and to a lesser extent the Chilean, is a consensus binding military and civilian judicial elites about the proper legal response to subversion. In Chile under Allende, the same kind of political polarization that existed in Argentina had eroded a prior consensus on the legitimacy of the judiciary in the wider society. But in contrast to Argentina, this polarization had not strongly affected the judiciary itself. The hierarchical judicial system in Chile's unitary system was solidly behind the opposition to Allende and then the military regime, whereas Argentina's more decentralized judiciary and politically engaged legal community was divided. So even when the Argentine armed forces changed the institutional matrix of the judiciary, a strong consensus on the proper legal response to the armed left eluded them.

A comparison with Brazil reveals another important difference in the Argentine case. In Brazil, the military was also unhappy with the liberality of the ordinary civilian courts in dealing with political trials. It took political trials away from these courts and placed them in military courts. This move was not strongly contested by the Brazilian judicial establishment or by civil society groups. The Brazilian military court system was also strongly integrated with the rest of the civilian judiciary.

In contrast, the creation of the Argentine National Penal Court was far more contested. The military regime created the court in order to appear to be respecting certain legal formalities in its repression, but instead this was interpreted by its opponents as a sign of the regime's arbitrariness. The court was severely criticized by regime opponents, some of whom argued that it was unconstitutional.[18] In general, the opposition saw it as a farce, a politically manipulated tribunal to punish people who were popular with at least some part of the citizenry. This was also the view of the military courts held by opponents of the military regimes in Brazil and Chile, but unlike in the latter two cases, in Argentina regime opponents were strong enough to eventually annul the authoritarian legality of the military regime. So where one sees the successful forging of military-judicial consensus in Brazil, and to a lesser extent in Chile, one sees its failure in Argentina. The National Penal Court was thus a temporary solution whose results were not enduring. It proved to be the last attempt of the Argentine military to deal with the armed left in a legalistic manner. After the dissolution of the court, the military decided to fight a war against "subversion."

In 1973, the Lanusse government completed its extrication project by arranging elections in which Juan Perón was forbidden to take part. This resulted in the March 11 election of a loyal Peronist, Hector Cámpora, under the slogan "Cámpora to the government, Perón to power." On the day of Cámpora's inauguration, May 25, there were tremendous popular celebrations of the end of seven years of military rule. That evening, crowds of tens of thousands of people gathered in front of the Devoto Prison in Buenos Aires and the Rawson Prison in Chubut and forced the release of over three hundred political prisoners.[19] The

National Congress subsequently authorized this fait accompli by passing an amnesty law for all political prisoners convicted under the military regime on May 27, 1973.[20] On the same day, the Congress also dissolved the National Penal Court, ending this brief period of judicial repression.[21] The court's employees were relocated to other parts of the judiciary. There was tremendous dissatisfaction within the military with this measure.[22] Cámpora ultimately served little time as president. He resigned on July 13, 1973, paving the way for new elections won by Juan Perón.

The end of a predominantly legalistic strategy of repressing dissent, however, gave way to an increase in clandestine state violence, as well as a corresponding increase in the violence of the armed left. Some of this violence centered around the activities of the now defunct National Penal Court. Former court secretary Bicenso was kidnapped in August 1973, and former judge Eduardo Manilla had his car fired upon in August 1974 but escaped unharmed.[23] Manilla's former colleague Jorge Quiroga was assassinated on April 26, 1974.[24] And the headquarters of the bar association (Asociación Gremial de los Abogados), which had provided defense lawyers to political prisoners in 1971–1973, was bombed in 1975 and partially destroyed.[25] Under Perón, the death squad Triple-A began its shadowy existence. Later, under Isabel Perón, the army developed harshly repressive policies in Tucumán Province in 1975 that basically sanctioned disappearances as a way of dealing with alleged subversives. This developed into a national policy after the military coup of March 24, 1976.

As we have seen, the military regimes of Brazil and the southern cone did not create authoritarian legality anew—they modified preexisting legislation to suit their ends. The Brazilian military regime used the 1953 national security law to prosecute opponents after its 1964 coup, and the Chileans used the 1958 Law of State Security and the 1972 Arms Control Law, both passed by previous governments. Similarly, when the Argentine junta took power in 1976 it encountered an already-existing state of siege, decreed on November 6, 1974, by the government of Isabel Perón. Similarly, Decree 2,772 of October 6, 1975, issued by the same government, ordered the armed forces to "execute military and security operations that are necessary to eliminate the actions of the subversive elements in the entire territory of the country" (Cheresky 1998, 81n1 on the 1974 state of siege, and 102n46 on the 1975 decree).

As in Chile, a climate of escalating confrontation, violence, and the erosion of consensus on the rule of law preceded the military coup in Argentina. Some voices spoke out to urge that the antisubversive struggle be carried out within legal bounds. For example, Senator Francisco Cerro spoke in the Senate in September of 1975 and protested a kidnapping in Tucumán province, declaring that "It is the concern of all responsible sectors in the country that the antisubversive war be fought inside of the legal parameters and by the security forces and national defense forces that are prepared for it constitutionally and legally."[26] Similarly, on September 30, 1975, Senator Hipólito Solari Yrigoyen denounced human rights abuses by security forces and paramilitary groups, and in particular the Triple-A, in various parts of the country.[27] And in a speech to Congress that she gave just three months before the military coup, President Isabel Perón asked the representatives to renew the state of siege because "the agents of subversion and chaos, with false ideological and political pretexts, harass the organized community and the national government purposefully and permanently, looking for their annihilation and destruction. This aggression . . . includes the most varied forms of subversion."[28] Congress approved the measure. However, there were protests from senators such as Senator Eduardo César Angeloz,[29] who complained that the state of siege was unconstitutional because indefinite, and that it did not authorize authorities to violate the constitutional rights of citizens as they had been doing.

Other representatives in Congress tried courageously to stop the descent into violence. Deputy Nilda Celia Garré condemned the government for doing nothing to stop a wave of violence in the province of Córdoba in late February of 1976,[30] and Deputy Osvaldo Alvarez Guerrero demanded that the government provide detailed information as to the identity, profession, and political antecedents of victims of violence, together with information as to whether the victim was killed by terrorists or government security forces. This demand for a basic system of accounting of the dead—a necessary if not sufficient element of the rule of law—was aimed at countering the executive's descent into a policy of clandestine violence. Deputy Alvarez Guerrero pleaded, "At this moment . . . it is necessary to be conscious of the fact that human lives still have value in our country, and we must do all we can so that public opinion knows in detail, objectively, the results of political terrorism, the operational characteristics of the distinct subversive organizations, and the results of the organic repression of the legal institutions in each case."[31] But this plea was overtaken by events. A week later the military staged its coup, and the political violence was covered by an even heavier and darker shroud of secrecy than before.

The 1976 Coup and the Dirty War

The Argentine junta created by the coup made a far more radical break with legality than the Brazilian or Chilean military regimes. On the first day of the coup, the Supreme Court, the Attorney General's office, and the provincial high courts were purged. At the same time, "all other members of the judiciary were suspended from duty. All judges, whether newly appointed or confirmed in their posts, had to swear to uphold the articles and objectives of the 'process' instigated by the Military Junta" (Argentine National Commission on the Disappeared 1986, 386). Regime leaders were open about their need to circumvent legal restrictions. Looking back, General Tomas Sanchez de Bustamente said in 1980, "There are judicial norms and standards which do not apply in this instance . . . everything has to be enveloped in a cloud of silence."[32]

In this repression, defense lawyers of political prisoners were targeted. About 90 defense lawyers linked to the thousands of people detained by the coup makers were kidnapped and presumed killed between March and December of 1976 alone (Argentine National Commission on the Disappeared 1986, 413). More than one hundred lawyers were imprisoned during the same period, and a larger number went into exile. Overall, according to one estimate, 132 lawyers were killed by the security forces between 1976 and 1983.[33] (In contrast, there are no reports of killings of defense lawyers under military rule in Brazil and Chile.) One victim was Guillermo Raul Diaz Lestrem, a judicial functionary who had dissolved the National Penal Court in 1973. He was taken to the infamous Navy Mechanics' School (ESMA) and murdered; his body was found in Palermo Park in 1978.[34]

Opponents of the military regime were shocked by the ferocity of this new round of state violence. Many of them came to appreciate—albeit belatedly and often bitterly—the limited rule-boundedness of the previous military regime of 1966–1973. Former political prisoner Manuel Gaggero said in an interview in 1997:[35]

> I was a prisoner . . . when they passed the law imposing the death penalty after the execution of Aramburu in 1970. I remember a *compañero* saying to me that they were going to apply this to us, because we were prisoners. And I remember saying no, it can't be, they are not going to apply it retroactively. Everyone said no, what could happen is they will release us, kill us, and claim that we had been trying to escape, make up a false escape. And I said

no, this could happen in Guatemala, but not in Argentina. Argentina has a military that is going to respect legal forms and is more civilized. And I was wrong, unfortunately. And our whole generation was wrong just as I was wrong.

The evidence strongly suggests that the turn toward a policy of widespread disappearances by the military in 1976 was, at least in part, inspired by the military's frustration at the failure of their earlier more judicial strategy of repression under the Lanusse government. While many members of the military, or at least those who considered themselves to be hard-line, were pleased by the performance of the National Penal Court during its brief period of existence, they were dismayed that the court's work was so quickly overturned after the end of the military regime. The disappearances were therefore to some extent the result of the military's weak hold on power. Under more consolidated regimes such as Brazil's and Chile's, legal strategies of repression could be carried out with more confidence in their durability. Another factor in the Argentine regime's decision seems to have been a desire to avoid the costs of public repression, costs demonstrated in the case of Chile after the 1973 coup.

This interpretation is confirmed in an essay by Carlos Acuña and Catalina Smulovitz in which they state that in September 1975 the army decided "that the coming repression was to be predominantly clandestine. Furthermore, it was to be used not only to neutralize but also to physically exterminate all militant opposition, regardless of whether suspected opponents were involved in armed struggle. This decision was reached in order to foreclose the possibility that subsequent civilian governments might later release opponents to the regime who could then return to generate a counteroffensive, as had been the case in the 1973 democratic opening (Acuña and Smulovitz 1997, 98). Similarly, Emilio Dellasoppa writes that the dirty war was strongly influenced by the military's "conviction of the inefficiency of democratic institutions and the judiciary to satisfactorily resolve the problem posed by the existence of guerrilla organizations. The conviction that putting subversive elements in prison created the problem of their permanent ideological consolidation and radicalization, as well as not guaranteeing the 'staunching of the contagion' brought the armed forces to the belief that annihilation was the desired solution" (Dellasoppa 1998, 371).

A confidential State Department cable from the U.S. Embassy in Buenos Aires to Washington, D.C. (dated September 1980) provides a further glimpse into the views that prevailed within the Argentine military. The cable discusses in great detail why the Argentine government was not pursuing a legalistic strategy of repressing its opponents and recommends that the U.S. government encourage the Argentines to adopt alternatives to the tactic of disappearances. It states: "we believe that the establishment of an effective system of military justice may be the best answer. If the military could be shaken out of their belief that death is the only reasonable punishment for terrorists, the armed forces might see advantages in using the military courts. The Brazilians relied on them during their successful bout with terrorists. This example might help convince the Argentines that they should seriously consider this alternative." It then attributes the Argentine military government's practice of disappearances to its belief that courts "would simply let the terrorists go" and to the fact that "the military does not have full confidence in the future."[36] The State Department analyst also suggested that Argentine military officers were reluctant to take responsibility for signing sentences against the armed left for fear of retaliation: "there is virtually no Argentine officer who wants to have his name on record as ordering the execution of a terrorist"; and that under the system of disappearances, "the military are responsible as an institution but the individual is free from accountability" (Guest 1990, 434).

Lewis confirms the interpretation offered here, explaining that General Videla, chief of the army general staff in 1976 and one of the regime's leaders, argued before the coup that the best way to restore "order" quickly and decisively was to wage a radical war on the guerrillas, without legal restrictions, and that anything less "would drag out the war against subversion with no certainty of victory." With a policy of disappearances, "There would be no more amnesties like Cámpora's in the future" (Lewis 2002, 120, 157).

Argentine military officers themselves corroborate this interpretation. Retired General Héctor Rodríguez Espada wrote in the *Revista militar*, the official magazine of the Argentine armed forces, in 1997: "The irresponsible amnesty approved unanimously by both houses of the legislature, liberating all the condemned subversives, the dissolution of the court that judged them [the Cámara en lo Penal de la Nación] and the abolition of the legislation that permitted this to be done, *represented the defection of the judicial power, such that the armed forces were left obliged to resolve the war without its assistance*, preventing them from doing so fully within the law, as had been done up to that moment" (emphasis added).

Rodríguez Espada continues: "Moreover this circumstance led the same elected government, at first without the knowledge of the armed forces and later with their express opposition, to organize paramilitary elements (the Triple A). This did not prevent the fact that, once the war was terminated and the country returned to institutional normalcy, thanks to the defeat of terrorist subversion, the judicial power raised an archangel with a flaming sword and released, without shame or remorse, a very particular and politicized 'justice'" (1997, 25).

In the same article Rodríguez Espada continues his attack on the judiciary, specifically its alleged betrayal of the armed forces' project when some of its members cooperated in the "big trial" against nine junta leaders in 1985. He writes, "the submissive, partial, and arbitrary performance of members of the judiciary who worked in the service of a political power whose self-interested and open objective was to denigrate and disqualify the armed forces and its members before society and history . . . this intention was realized and the author, with explicit pessimism, does not see—for the moment—that the true assessment of the responsibilities of the institutions will be made. . . . many men who exercised and still exercise power . . . approved of and encouraged the form and procedures that the military employed in the face of the subversive organizations" (1997, 19).

This attack on the judiciary reflects a sense of betrayal within the Argentine officer corps, a feeling that the military was unjustly scapegoated for repressive policies that were supported and even carried out by many civilians. Jaime Malamud-Goti argues that this sentiment is partially justified, as civilian participants in the repression such as intelligence officers and policemen were often overlooked in the politics of post-authoritarian transitional justice, while military personnel were not (Malamud-Goti 1996).

Nevertheless, many former military officers in Argentina seem to have concluded that it was a tremendous error to have abandoned a legalistic strategy in 1976. Former naval captain Carlos Raimondi, for example, declared that "It was an error not to reestablish the Cámara in 1976."[37] He said that organizing trials on a large scale was considered within the military but that "there were many hatreds" and in the end, each military commander was left to orchestrate the war against the guerrillas in his sector as he saw fit. Raimondi ruefully admitted that a "Chilean solution"—the use of military courts—would have been better for the Argentine military, and that the Chilean organizational solution helps account for Pinochet's longevity in power even after the democratic transition of 1990.[38]

Argentina thus represents a distinctive path of state repression that, under the military regime of 1976–1983, largely bypassed the courts (military or otherwise) as a venue for repressing dissidents and opposition. One source alludes to some 350 defendants convicted in military courts in this period (Nino 1996, 80), but the vast majority of the state's repressive actions against individuals were completely extrajudicial. The judiciary was not so much subordinated as made irrelevant. The Argentine case comes closest to George Orwell's nightmare of the future, *1984*, in which people are arbitrarily executed without a crime having been committed and without courts being involved.[39]

Framing the Disappearances

Juan Corradi writes that "a striking feature of Argentine terror was the duplicity with which it was administered and suffered. . . . Something like a dual state existed in the country during the years of intense repression: one state within which two systems operated, one serving as a mask for the other. One operated under the remnants of the constitution. . . . The other operated under individual measures in which expediency, arbitrariness, and considerations of military security overrode all law" (1985, 119–21).

The language with which the Argentine military regime legitimated its dirty war is particularly notorious and more violent and uncompromising than the language of the Chilean military regime and certainly its Brazilian counterpart. At the same time, the Argentine regime, like its Brazilian and Chilean predecessors, also lacked a complete legitimating ideology—a fact noted by Juan Linz— and often legitimated itself in terms of an eventual return to liberal democracy.[40]

The initial proclamation of the new regime issued a "firm summons to the . . . citizenry" in which "there is a battle post for each citizen" in the "rigorous task of eradicating, once and for all, the vices which afflict the nation." This document, delivered on the radio the day after the military takeover and then released to the public, also declares that the junta "will continue fighting, without quarter, all forms of subversion, both open and clandestine, and will eradicate all forms of demagoguery"; furthermore, the new regime would not tolerate "any opposition to the process of restoration which has been initiated" (translated and reprinted in Loveman and Davies Jr. 1989, 197–98). There are many other notorious statements of this nature, including the analogy between disease and subversion that can also be seen in the transcripts of the Brazilian military court trials. For example, Rear Admiral César Guzzetti, writing in *La opinión* on October 3, 1976, declared that "the social body of the country is contaminated by an illness that in corroding its entrails produces antibodies. These antibodies must not be considered in the same way as [the original] microbe. As the government controls and destroys the guerrilla, the action of the antibody will disappear. . . . This is just the natural reaction of a sick body."[41]

On the other hand, the regime issued declarations such as this one by President Videla: "The passion for liberty makes the army one of the firmest defenders of authentic representative democracy, with full realization of our republican and federal principles, as the only political system compatible with the dignity of the nation's being" (quoted in Cheresky 1988, 84n14). Like their Brazilian and Chilean counterparts, the Argentine military regime's leaders saw themselves as guardians of an emergency regime that would cleanse the body politic and eventually restore a liberal democracy.

It is not true that the Argentine military regime completely dispensed with legal maneuvers. However, these legal covers for repression were draconian and largely irrelevant to the practices of the regime. For example, special military courts (Consejos de Guerra Especiales Estables) were established to try all defendants charged with violating the Law of Repression of Sabotage (Law 21,264 of March 24, 1976). In these courts, defendants only had the right to a summary judgment, and were not allowed to be defended by civilian lawyers. The trials were held in secret, and the defendant had the right only to defense by a designated military official who was generally not a lawyer. The defendants had no right to know the evidence presented against them (Cheresky 1988, 81 text and n. 3). These procedures were more biased against defendants than the "wartime" military courts in Chile, and certainly more than the military courts in Brazil.

The new military regime modified the penal code to introduce the death penalty. Old laws were changed to increase sentences for political crimes. For example, perturbation of public order, which had previously been a minor offense deserving of a fine or thirty days in prison, became a federal crime punishable by up to eight years in prison. A new law also allowed security forces to shoot suspects caught in flagrante who refused to be apprehended at the first command of the authorities. Another law approved sentences of two to four years in prison for workers who refused to work diligently after a strike had been declared illegal (Cheresky 1988, 82).

Similarly, under National Executive Power (Poder Ejecutivo Nacional, PEN), political prisoners could be detained indefinitely without being formally charged with any crime (Cheresky 1988, 83n10). The PEN provisions had been used during states of siege declared by previous Argentine presidents, including Isabel Perón. Under PEN, anyone deemed by the executive to be a threat to the peace and security of the nation could be incarcerated indefinitely without charge and without access to a lawyer. A large number of people were detained in this way, including students and labor leaders, some for as long as eight or nine years if they had been apprehended before the coup, during the government of Isabel Perón. PEN prisoners were supposed to have the option of exile, but many former PEN prisoners say that they were denied this choice. In addition, the torture of PEN prisoners was apparently common (Marchak 1999, 128).

According to CONADEP (Comisión Nacional sobre la Desaparición de Personas, or National Commission on the Disappearance of Persons), the commission that produced the *Nunca más* report after the end of military rule, 5,182 prisoners were held under PEN during the military regime. The total number of people who were incarcerated for long periods was 8,625. Of these, 4,029 were detained for less than a year, 2,296 for one to three years, 1,172 for three to five years, 668 for five to seven years, and 431 for seven to nine years. CONADEP found 157 cases of PEN prisoners who were disappeared after being released from detention.[42]

However, these numbers are overshadowed by the number of disappeared, which is estimated at twenty thousand to thirty thousand. The policy of disappearances, in which bodies were destroyed, was advantageous to the regime for several reasons. First, it allowed the regime to plausibly deny its practice of murdering opponents. This enabled it to maintain an image of respectability abroad, at least for a time, and to avoid the isolation of the Chilean military regime, whose public executions in 1973 had evoked heavy criticisms at the United Nations and in other venues. Disappearances also prolonged the terror of the population, spreading fear, silence, obedience, and defenselessness, atomizing and paralyzing the populace. Finally, disappearances avoided the uncertainty of legalistic repression that would have subjected people to trials; instead, it bypassed the legal system and rendered the latter incapable of response.[43] Like the Brazilian military regime, the Argentine regime did not formally carry out the death sentence that it had allowed through its amendment to the penal code. Instead, as the CONADEP team writes, "There were thousands of deaths. None of these came about through an ordinary or military trial, none was the result of a sentence. Technically speaking, they were murders. . . . [T]he regime which considered it necessary to change our legal tradition by introducing capital punishment, never used it as such. Instead, it organized a collective crime, a veritable mass extermination" (Argentine National Commission on the Disappeared 1986, 209).

In Hannah Arendt's words, disappearances kill not only people but the "juridical person in man." They are part of a system that is outside the law. Under a system of disappearances, concentration camps outside the normal penal system receive victims who are outside the judicial system, people who were never charged with a definite crime nor sentenced to a predictable penalty. "The murderer leaves behind him a corpse, and although he tries to efface the traces of his own identity, he has no power to erase the identity of his victim from the memory of the surviving world" writes Arendt. "The operation of the secret police, on the contrary, miraculously sees to it that the victim never existed at all" (1958, 434–35, see also 447).

The disappearances contributed to the Argentine regime's strongly dualistic character. More dramatically than in Brazil and Chile, the regime was divided between a public and a clandestine wing. This led the regime to deny the policy of disappearances, as when President Videla declared, "I roundly deny that there exist in Argentina concentration camps or prisoners in military establishments [being held] beyond the time that is indispensable to interrogate a captured person in a procedure and before going to an established prison."[44] In the same period, during an appearance on U.S. television, Videla admitted that some people had disappeared in Argentina due to the "excesses" of the security forces, but claimed that most of the disappeared were guerrillas who had voluntarily gone into hiding in order to combat the government clandestinely, or who had been killed by their comrades for treason.[45]

While such denials and obfuscations also occurred in Chile, the public nature of the executions at the beginning of the regime made them less plausible. In Brazil, denials by regime leaders of torture, disappearances, and the existence of political prisoners were also common, but the dirty war in Brazil was waged on a relatively small scale.

The Fate of Political Prisoners in the System

The fate of political prisoners under the Argentine "process of national reorganization" or *proceso* reflects the decentralized and fragmented institutional configuration of the regime. Authority was dispersed along service lines. The country was divided into zones controlled by commanders of the different branches of the armed forces. According to Arceneaux (2001, 13), "Control by the Military Junta over the repressive activities of the corps commanders was more formal than real." The government constantly claimed discretionary executive powers as a result of the state of siege, which remained in effect until October 28, 1983. Discretionary powers filtered down the hierarchy, giving lower-level personnel a sense of impunity. The antisubversive laws were vague and open-ended—for example, Law 21,528 authorized the arrest of anyone with a "rebellious position." Commanders of each zone basically had the latitude to wage the war against subversion in whatever manner they chose.[46]

It is striking that according to *Nunca más*, 62 percent of the victims of disappearances were abducted from their own homes. A further 24.6 percent were kidnapped on the street, and only 7 and 6 percent, respectively, were captured at work or school. Only 0.4 percent of the disappeared had been legally detained in military, penal, or police establishments, suggesting that legal recognition conferred protection on detainees, and that conversely, clandestine abduction provided a cover for execution by the authorities (Argentine National Commission on the Disappeared 1986, 11).

Disappearances usually started when a group of about five or six people burst into a home. The intruders were usually heavily armed and sometimes wore uniforms. These assaults usually took place at night or early in the morning near the end of the week, so that the relatives of those abducted would be unable to take any action over the weekend. As with those prosecuted by military courts in Brazil, the majority of victims were young males. *Nunca más* reports that 69.13 percent of the disappeared were between the ages of sixteen and thirty, and 70 percent were male (Argentine National Commission on the Disappeared 1986, 285).

Another striking fact reflects the distinctiveness of the Argentine path of political justice. Of the 371 political prisoners freed by the 1973 amnesty, 61, or 16 percent, were listed as disappeared by the 1976–1983 military regime.[47] Thus a former political prisoner's probability of being disappeared was more than 160 times that of a member of the general population, which was roughly one in a thousand, or 0.1 percent.[48] It is hard to know whether former political prisoners were deliberately targeted by the leaders of the *proceso* or whether many former political prisoners remained engaged in political militancy and were randomly caught up in the police-military dragnet along with many others. The former explanation seems more likely than the latter. What the numbers suggest is that for military officers, the dirty war was a corrective to a judicial solution that in their view had not worked. For them, the dirty war was partly about "getting it right the second time around." The war that had put prisoners in the dock in the National Penal Court was subsequently fought by other means, using tactics that made "justice"—this time—irreversible.

Public Contestation of the Repression

Opposition to the military regime's repression was more atomized in Argentina than in either Chile or Brazil. However, international networks were probably more important in reinforcing the actions of the small number of groups that challenged the regime's explanations of its actions.

Alison Brysk divides the Argentine opposition into four types of groups. First were the civil libertarian groups, the most important of which were the Liga Argentina por los Derechos del Hombre (Argentine League for the Rights of Man), the Asamblea Permanente por los Derechos Humanos (APDH, Permanent Assembly for Human Rights), and the Centro de Estudios Legales y Sociales (CELS, or Center for Legal and Social Studies). A second type of group coordinated the actions of family members of the killed and disappeared; the most important of these were the Madres de Plaza de Mayo (Mothers of the Plaza de Mayo), the Abuelas de Plaza de Mayo (Grandmothers of the Plaza de Mayo), and the Familiares de Detenidos y Desaparecidos por Razones Políticas (Family Members of those Detained and Disappeared for Political Reasons). Third, there were religious movements such as SERPAJ (Servicio Paz y Justicia, or Peace and Justice Service), the Movimiento Ecuménico por los Derechos Humanos (Ecumenical Movement for Human Rights) and the Movimiento Judío por los Derechos Humanos (Jewish Movement for Human Rights). Finally, international groups were important: the OAS Human Rights Commission, the Washington DC–based Center for Law and Social Policy, the Geneva-based International Commission of Jurists, Amnesty International, the New York-based Lawyers' Committee on Human Rights, and others.[49]

The record keeping of these groups became vitally important after the fall of the military regime and furnished the raw data for the CONADEP report. The protests of the Madres de Plaza de Mayo were also vital in symbolizing resistance to the atrocities of the regime and hope for a better society in the future. Nevertheless, unlike in Brazil, opposition groups in Argentina could not engage in very much public, effective debate of the regime's policies. Contestation had to wait until the fall of the regime, and then it came with a vengeance.

Military Rejection of Judicial Authority

The Argentine dirty war represents another road not taken by the Brazilian military regime. While the latter used military courts as an instrument for the prosecution of civilian opponents and dissidents (and its Chilean counterpart used a variation of the Brazilian approach), the Argentine military embarked on a much more radical war against subversion that dispensed with legal formalities almost entirely. In Argentina, disappearances became a full-scale program and an official policy.

If Chile's organizational solution to the problem of subversion reflected a lack of prior cooperation between military and judicial elites, Argentina's solution can be traced instead to the failure of prior attempts to cooperate. Under the presidency of General Lanusse in the early 1970s, a special civilian court tried and convicted many political prisoners to the apparent satisfaction of the regime and its supporters. But the abolition of this court and the freeing of the prisoners in 1973 persuaded many military officers that judicial solutions to the problem of subversion were untenable and that a more radical solution had to be tried.

Scholars of Argentina might be skeptical that the abolition of a specific court could have had such a large influence on a complex process such as the dirty war. After all, institutions were routinely purged and abolished with each pendulum swing of Argentina's post–World War II political history. My contention is that generalized institutional instability does not necessarily invalidate the causal mechanism posited here, because only specific institutions affect particular policy areas, and the entire ensemble of state institutions are not relevant to any given issue.

In the treatment of opposition and dissent under authoritarian regimes, courts are crucial. The existence of courts that the military considers reliable— whether civilian or military—is a factor in military officers' assessments of the costs and benefits of judicialized repression. The abolition of the National Penal Court and the annulment of its results seem to have been a turning point at which a majority of top military officers rejected further experimentation with judicialized repression and embraced armed confrontation of the presumed opposition without any form of legal mediation.

This is not to say that the Argentine military regime of 1976–1983 did not engage in some of the same kinds of legal manipulations that characterized the Brazilian and Chilean regimes. However, these legal maneuvers were usually more draconian than those of the other two regimes in granting even fewer procedural rights to defendants. They were also less relevant to the overall repressive policies of the regime because these policies were dominated so overwhelmingly by the practice of disappearance.

Ultimately, the Argentine organizational solution to the problem of legalizing repression was more duplicitous than the solutions in Brazil and Chile. The Argentine regime had the most dualistic character in that the gap between formal legality and the actual practices of the regime was widest; disappearances were clandestine, extraofficial, and denied by regime leaders, even as formal legality still acknowledged some (minimal) rights for political prisoners.

Just as prior attempts to forge a consensus across military and judicial lines about the proper legal response to subversion influenced each military regime's repressive policies, the repressive policies themselves generated resistance. That resistance could only be significant in legal terms if courts allowed a minimum of procedural guarantees to defendants and their lawyers. I return now to the only system of authoritarian legality among the three cases where this was true —the Brazilian military courts.

7

Defense Lawyers in Brazil's Military Courts

REDEFINING FREE SPEECH, SUBVERSION, TERRORISM, AND CRIME

May not a perversion of the law be a trifle better than a
disregard for all law?

James Bryce, *South America:*
Observations and Impressions (1916)

BRAZIL'S RELATIVELY CONSERVATIVE authoritarian legality led to a series of
political trials that preserved more elements of traditional legal procedures and
doctrine than did the repressive tactics of the later Chilean and Argentine military regimes. It was only in Brazilian political trials that defense lawyers were
able to gradually roll back some of the most draconian interpretations of national security law. Brazilian defense lawyers successfully won the recognition
of certain individual rights from the military court judges, including the right
to express certain political beliefs, to criticize government officials, to possess (if
not distribute) "subversive" materials, and the right to disseminate such materials to small, elite audiences. I argue here that Brazil's defense lawyers shifted
the boundaries of national security legality in the courts.

The Roles and Resources of the Defense Lawyers

Brazilian national security law, like national security law in Chile and Argentina,
was notoriously broad and vague. In political trials judges were forced to interpret
the concrete meaning of terms such as "subversion," "offense against authority,"

140

"subversive propaganda," "psychosocial subversion," and the like. Military court judges had to decide which thoughts and actions were actually proscribed by national security laws and which were not. These decisions involved complex political, ideological, and legal judgments. In making them, judges transformed formal or paper laws into an evolving system of norms. This system of norms redrew boundaries between licit and illicit behavior and ideas, creating a new, more repressive legal system, but one that was not as severe or as discontinuous with the past as those of the other regimes in the region, particularly in Chile. Brazilian military courts were more likely than their Chilean counterparts to acquit certain categories of defendants, especially priests and defendants accused of recently created national security crimes. Perhaps most importantly, the boundaries shifted, in part because the perceived threats to the regime diminished in the 1970s, but also because the arguments of defense lawyers and critics of national security legality hit home.

A civilian-military consensus about the trials and the judgments made in them posed formidable obstacles to defense lawyers in Brazil's military courts. The defense faced judges who generally believed that the country was in a dire political emergency that required an extraordinary judicial response. The judges were not constrained by the need to be consistent in their rulings, and they deliberately considered the political ideas of the accused. Furthermore, the existence of an armed left made them relatively intolerant of criticisms of the regime, because they saw such criticisms—even if unaccompanied by any actions—as potential psychosocial subversion that was antinational.

On the other hand, legally recognized detainees were spared extrajudicial execution, and the workings of the military courts, while procedurally stacked against the defense, were closer to ordinary criminal justice than were most systems of military justice, including that of Chile. Furthermore, repudiations of oppositional political views and expressions of remorse were taken seriously by the judges and tended to result in leniency. Defense lawyers were able to take these slight opportunities and use them to their advantage.

Most defendants accused of political crimes in Brazil's military courts did not make impassioned defenses of their political views before the judges. This kind of political defense involved the defendant describing his revolutionary beliefs and denouncing the military regime. (Vinicius Oliveira Brandt, whose case was discussed in the introduction, was one of the few defendants who did make such a defense.) These kinds of defenses were punished harshly, usually with the maximum sentence, because the judges viewed them as proof of the dangerousness and incorrigibility of the defendant, even if he or she had not participated in violent actions.[1]

Defense lawyers usually persuaded their clients to avoid political defenses and make one of two other kinds of defenses. The juridical defense involved the defendant abjuring any belief in so-called subversive ideas and denying that he or she had committed any violation of the national security laws. This latter contention was made either by negating the material facts of the case or arguing that they did occur but did not actually constitute crimes. This last type of argument is particularly important for our purposes, because in making them, defense lawyers sometimes persuaded judges to reinterpret national security laws in such a way as to recategorize as legal certain kinds of behavior once deemed to be illegal.

Other frequent arguments by the defense were absence of knowledge, that is, the defendant had unwittingly helped a subversive group, not knowing the activities of his friends or acquaintances; errors in charges, in which the alleged crimes were not covered by the cited legislation; errors in laws, in which portions of national security laws were said to be unconstitutional; invalid proof, especially when a confession had been extracted under torture; inadequate or contradictory proof or absence of proof; and double jeopardy, in which the lawyer's client was already being tried for the same crime in another case (Vannucchi Leme de Matos 2002, 88–89).

The mixed defense was a combination of a purely juridical defense and a political one. The defendant might defend some of his or her ideas and actions, but deny that they were subversive.[2] Or the defendant might appeal more directly to the political sympathies of the judges, claiming that he or she had abandoned political activity, was remorseful, and/or disagreed with revolutionary ideas.

Lawyers were especially likely to use purely juridical defenses at the higher levels of the military justice system. In a sample of cases, Marco Aurélio Vannucchi Leme de Matos found that lawyers made extralegal arguments in 28.71 percent of cases in regional military courts, and only 4.31 percent of cases in the Superior Military Court (STM) (2002, 91).

Defense lawyers were crucial in mitigating the effects of repression on political prisoners for two reasons. First, they spread the word of the detention of prisoners. Sought out by family members and loved ones of the victims of repression, they informed newspapers, the Vatican, Brazilian church leaders, Amnesty International, and other domestic and international entities that detainees had been apprehended by the security forces. Even though informing the public did not accomplish anything in juridical terms, it created some guarantees for the prisoners by letting authorities know that others knew whom they were holding.[3]

Defense lawyers' connections to civil society groups gave them additional resources in the struggle against the repressive tactics of the military regime. Because certain groups, especially those connected to the Catholic Church, retained a certain ability to criticize the regime, lawyers could help these groups to propagate a particular view of certain cases, or the actions of the regime in general. These connections could be used to reduce sentences on appeal, as when Teodomiro Romeiro dos Santos's death sentence was commuted to a prison sentence in 1971.

Second, the defense lawyers, by mounting juridical defenses of the kind described above, found ambiguities and loopholes in the national security laws and argued for favorable interpretations in ways that sometimes achieved benefits for their clients. The defense lawyers for political prisoners, who numbered only a few dozen across the country, gave "juridical first aid" in a system that was biased against defendants.[4]

A common obstacle to an adequate defense was the fact that lawyers did not have access to prisoners in the first phase of detention, and by the time they did, their client had often "confessed" under torture and signed a document incriminating himself and others. Despite this handicap, lawyers worked carefully within the military justice system to do what was possible for the defendant. The lawyers, usually young to middle-aged men, served to give moral support and link the defendants, usually young men and sometimes women, to the outside world. The lawyers overcame intimidation and threats from the security forces and often worked for little or no compensation (their clients usually had little ability to pay). They appear in the main to have been motivated by ideological and religious convictions, although most were careful not to have a known affiliation with any particular political party. "The defense lawyer was the priest, confessor, friend, and lawyer" of the defendants, said Idebal Piveta, a former defense lawyer. "It was a thoroughly dangerous form of lawyering . . . but it was our way of working to try to establish the rule of law."[5]

The military justice system did give the lawyers some room to maneuver in the system.[6] The acquittal rate reflects this. Most lawyers felt that the STM was more open to well-argued defenses than the lower-level courts, and in fact the evidence suggests that the STM had a higher acquittal rate, and lower average sentence, than did the lower courts (Pereira 1998, 46).

In the first instance, defense lawyers' legal strategies were shaped by the courts. The political trials were not really the triadic conflicts of classic courtroom drama and legal theory, adversarial proceedings before independent and neutral judges.[7] Instead, their proceedings were dyadic and inquisitorial, with the defense on one side, and the prosecution and the judges together on the other. Four out of five judges were active-duty military officers, making them members of one side of the military regime's antisubversive campaign. The civilian judges in the military courts were generally known for their pro-regime views. The judges' presumption therefore was usually that the prosecution's case had merit. Furthermore, the judges could actively question witnesses. Judges were thus at the same time active participants in the construction of the case against the defendant, arbiters of the court's proceedings, and signatories of the final verdict and sentence in the case.

This delicate situation presented special challenges to defense lawyers. If they were too aggressive in the defense of their clients, they risked alienating the judges. If they were too passive, they might allow the judges to taint the defendants and create the legal justification for a stiff punishment. The situation therefore called for tact, guile, finesse, and knowledge of the personal and political predilections of the judges, especially the civilian judges. Some lawyers appealed to judges to apply the national security laws according to dictates of government—this was an appeal to the aspirations of some judges for a new "revolutionary" legality. Others appealed to the conservative image that some judges held of themselves as defenders of the traditional rule of law, urging them to fulfill the liberal function of an independent judiciary (Vannucchi Leme de Matos 2002, 93–95).

As might be imagined, flattery was often an effective instrument with which to disarm the judges. One defense lawyer wrote in his brief to a regional military court: "It appears to be indisputable at this stage of Brazilian life that military justice does not have to regret the opportunities it has provided to innumerable young people involved in the illegal contestation of the regime. Of those who were treated with an indulgent judgment, very few returned to illegal activities. Therefore, this indicates that the position adopted by the military courts was the best path to the defense of national security. It was certainly more effective then rigorous repression, even when used in conformity with the law."[8]

Prominent defense attorney Heleno Fragoso echoed these sentiments by stating "it was thought that military justice would function with revolutionary criteria, applying the law with an implacable severity. This is not what happened.

... [Instead,] we always had the law applied according to criteria of justice, and not to attend to the supposed conveniences of national security, mistaken for the security of the dominant political power" (quoted in Almeida 1986/87, 25).

Defense Lawyers' Achievements

The work of the lawyers gradually pushed military justice toward greater liberalism. This achievement was most clearly manifest by the mid to late 1970s, but it was partially obscured because national security law became more severe and less liberal in the late 1960s. Overall, however, lawyers achieved important victories in several areas of national security law. These include court judgments that acknowledged the right to express certain political beliefs; the right to criticize certain government officials and policies; the need for the prosecution to demonstrate dissemination and not just possession of subversive propaganda in order to obtain a conviction for that particular crime; and the idea that the expression of subversive ideas to small, elite audiences did not violate national security law. Each of these achievements will be dealt with in turn.

Questioning the Crime of Certain Beliefs

A series of cases in military justice established the right of defendants to their own political views. For example, an important case decided by the Superior Military Court (STM) in 1966 upheld the principle that Communism itself was not a crime. The case involved two leaders of a textile workers union who had been arrested in 1964 for having subversive literature, including pamphlets and biographies of Lenin and the Brazilian Communist leader Luís Carlos Prestes. One of the trade unionists was a member of the Brazilian Communist Party (Partido Comunista Brasileiro, or PCB), and had been convicted of this crime by the lower court in 1985. The STM ruled that the defendant's membership in the PCB did not in itself constitute a crime, because "the documents do not demonstrate that he wanted to or sought to subvert the order of the nation."[9] The STM therefore rejected the attempts by advocates of the Brazilian "revolution" to criminalize Communism.

This principle was not consistently upheld by the courts in subsequent years, particularly after the hardening of the national security laws in the late 1960s. Defendants were later convicted for membership in banned organizations, including the Communist Party, and even for the expression of "Communist" beliefs. But the liberal notion that a democratic society could not criminalize political organizations merely for the views that its members expressed was upheld in other cases. For example, in a case decided in 1973, the brief submitted by the prosecution—not the defense—stated, "The fact of being communist is not a crime."[10] This statement could have reflected the fact that the left splintered and went underground in the 1960s, and the regime's bête noire became not Communism but a conglomeration of small groups of "subversives" and "terrorists." But it also reflects the successive pleadings of defense lawyers in the military courts, forcing the judges to recognize a right to certain political beliefs.

In another case, a twenty-two-year-old accounting student was accused of writing subversive graffiti in public places in Inhapim, Minas Gerais, in the early hours of September 23, 1969. The phrases that he allegedly wrote included "Down with Pig Society," "Down with Oppression—Liberty," "Down with Oppression —Long Live the Struggle," and "Long Live the Struggle." Interestingly, the DOPS report alleged that the accused boy had been influenced in his actions by the wife of an army captain who happened to be the regional military commander. The captain's wife, according to the DOPS report, was "considered by innumerable people to be a woman who has expressed ideas contrary to the objectives of the March 1964 revolution and who insists on telling the people around her of her ideas and viewpoints." In the trial, this woman testified that she did not have dissident ideas and that she had not known about the graffiti until after it had happened.

The regional military decision of August 23, 1971, acquitted the defendant on a vote of four to one, reasoning that the graffiti "was not clear enough to produce incitement to war or the subversion of the political-social order, nor incite against or offend any entity that exercises public authority or any public official"; the verdict went on to characterize the slogans as "insignificant and even inexpressive" and ruled that they could not even be interpreted as the work of "someone in solidarity with any type of subversive propaganda." The acquittal was upheld by the STM on November 22, 1971.[11]

In a case decided in 1969, Rio de Janeiro journalist and doctor Helio Pellegrino was acquitted of incitement to subversion for writing articles in the newspaper *Correio da Manhã* that condemned the 1964 coup and praised Ché Guevara. The fact that such articles were published reveals a difference between the Brazilian military regime and its Chilean and Argentine counterparts. The case also resulted in acquittal on the grounds that the defendant was not a member of a subversive organization. He was also defended by illustrious names in

Brazilian letters, the playwright Nelson Rodrigues and the poet Carlos Drummond de Andrade. The defense brief, written by Heleno Fragoso, quoted the "unimpeachable" Nelson Rodrigues (who was a public supporter of the military regime) as saying that his friend was "anti-Communist and anti-Marxist" and mentions that Pellegrino had voted for the right-wing UDN party (União Democrático Nacional) in the 1960 presidential election. This kind of defense of a client's political ideas and actions was standard among defense lawyers in the political trials. Pellegrino's lawyer Fragoso also defended his client's article that criticized United States involvement in Vietnam, writing that "This does not constitute a crime. A respectable portion of North American public opinion— if not the majority of that people—vehemently oppose the prosecution of the conflict." Fragoso ended his brief by declaring that his client's newspaper articles did not incite people to overthrow the government and that "we are not dealing with a terrorist, but a man of thought."[12] The sentence of the regional military court declared, "Brazilian justice has never condemned anyone, no matter who they were, for a crime of opinion. The very constitution guarantees liberty of thought and the equality of all before the law. . . . Brazil always applied and observed the principle of legality of [the treatment of] crime and sentences" which was not the case in the Soviet Union or Nazi Germany.[13]

This statement is rather extraordinary, first for its defensive disclaimer that Brazil under the military was unlike Stalin's Soviet Union and Hitler's Germany —a rather weak claim to distinction, in light of the company—and second for its self-congratulatory tone, despite the fact that this was a verdict in the case of a man prosecuted for stating his political opinions in newspaper articles. The regime was clearly harassing people for crimes of opinion. However, in this and many other cases, defense lawyers eventually won recognition of the right to freedom of expression in the courts.

The Right to Criticize Government Officials

National security law was sometimes stretched very far and became a means for local and national politicians to prosecute their critics and opponents. In this way, political trials facilitated the building of local support for the military regime along lines of political clientage and were also weapons that national politicians could use against their antagonists. However, defense lawyers were able to successfully argue in military courts that this type of criticism constituted subversion. They pointed out that these kinds of criticism were not directed at the military regime as a whole, but only at certain individuals who happened to occupy positions of authority, and this reality was acknowledged by the judges. The lawyers won many acquittals in these cases.

For example, the owner of the Rio de Janeiro newspaper *Correio da Manhã*, Niomar Moniz Sodré Bittencourt, was prosecuted in 1968 for allegedly offending then president Costa e Silva in editorials published in her newspaper. However, she was acquitted by the regional military court and the STM upheld the acquittal. One of the STM judges wrote, "one does not find in the proceedings against the accused . . . elements that indicate that she sought to attack any aspect of national security."[14]

In a later case, a fifty-five-year-old man in the interior of São Paulo was arrested and charged with "adverse psychological warfare" after publicly calling the notorious political police agent Sérgio Fleury a death squad leader and drug trafficker. The defense lawyer in the case presented a mixed political and judicial defense, getting his client to recant these views and ascribe them to a momentary lapse of judgment brought on by strong emotions. The regional military court acquitted the defendant in 1975 and the STM upheld the acquittal in 1976.[15] The STM ruled that "certain statements . . . offered in public . . . that affect the authorities . . . can, as in this case, constitute personal injury without . . . [amounting to] attacks against the security of the state."[16]

There were many other similar acquittals over the years. In a 1971 case, a man in the interior of Pernambuco who publicly called his mayor and state representative "shameless goats, thieves, and con men" was charged in military court with "political and social nonconformism." The accused denied making the remarks and his defense lawyer asked for an acquittal. Even the prosecutor's office refused to press for a conviction, and the defendant was acquitted at the regional court level and by the STM in 1972 on the grounds that national security law did not apply when offensive remarks were personal and did not "affect public authority in its attributions."[17]

In a similar case involving a 1968 incident, a man in the state of São Paulo was accused of an "offense against authority" for saying in public that his mayor had bribed an electoral judge. The regional military court took the charge seriously, and the penalty attached to the charge was six months to two years. The judges wrote, "attacks made on municipal authorities must be examined in criminal proceedings, taking into consideration that the political-administrative foundation of the nation rests in the local governments." They also added that in cases of injury, calumny, and defamation, the court had to balance the protection of human dignity and liberty with the possible abuse of these protections.[18]

In the case, the defense lawyer submitted a letter from a prominent member of the national attorney general's office arguing that the alleged crime did not constitute subversion.[19] The defendant, who was a supporter of the opposition candidate for mayor and had been accused by supporters of the pro-military regime candidate, also prudently denied that he had made the alleged statements.[20] The regional military court felt that there was enough ambiguity about the evidence to acquit the defendant, implying that if he had actually made the statements, he might have been convicted. The STM was more liberal, in that it noted that the remarks were allegedly made in a bar in a discussion with the defendant's political enemies, and that the charges were marked by a "lack of a specific crime."[21]

In these and many other cases defense lawyers successfully wrung from the courts the admission that to be violations of national security, offenses against government officials had to be subversive offenses, and that there could be no subversive offense without subversive intent. In the words of one defense lawyer, "the national security law must be applied with the maximum prudence . . . so that it does not become distorted either in its application or its effects, because in that case the country could be transformed into an immense concentration camp or a tropical Siberia."[22]

According to defense lawyer Heleno Fragoso, this effort was particularly fruitful at the level of the STM. The STM "rejected all the attempts to place within national security law offenses against the authorities that had nothing to do with the security of the state" (1980, 29). This is not to say that military Brazil was a model of political pluralism and tolerance. Far from it—prosecutors regularly charged people with crimes of association and opinion for all but the last six years of military rule. But defense lawyers were able to use the law to prevent some of its worst abuses. They successfully pushed the courts into upholding the traditional liberal distinction between attacks on the state and social order and legitimate criticisms of the performance of elected officials and other political authorities.

The Need to Show Dissemination of Subversive Propaganda

As with the national security laws against offenses against authority, the laws against subversive propaganda were a potentially enormous restriction on the freedom of speech in Brazil. However, the military courts were inconsistent in applying these laws and adjusted their rulings to changing political conditions. As in the cases involving offenses against authority, defense lawyers were eventually able to liberalize the interpretation of the laws so that the prosecution had to demonstrate the widespread dissemination of the propaganda and not just its possession.

The first period of the regime, from 1964 to the end of 1968, was notable for the lack of severe repression of antiregime propaganda. Political criticism in the press and in the cultural and artistic sphere was persistent, and there were mass demonstrations against the regime.[23] Tolerance of dissent and opposition declined considerably during the so-called "years of lead" (*anos de chumbo*) following the end of 1968, and the regime cracked down through press censorship, the closing and intimidation of Congress, repression of public demonstrations and marches, and the widespread use of torture.[24] Tolerance rose again slowly under the presidency of Ernesto Geisel from 1974 until 1979, and again under the Figueiredo government that ended with the return to civilian rule in 1985.

A case decided in 1966 exemplifies one approach to the issue of subversive propaganda that was broadened over time. In the STM case discussed earlier involving two leaders of a textile workers union, pamphlets and biographies of Lenin and the Brazilian Communist leader Luís Carlos Prestes found in the possession of the defendants in 1964 were deemed by the lower court to constitute subversive propaganda in 1965. But the STM ruled on appeal that the mere possession of subversive propaganda did not constitute a crime under article 11 of the 1953 national security law, and acquitted the trade unionists. The ruling, signed by the fifteen STM judges (ten of whom were military officers), argued that even when defendants were found with subversive propaganda, the courts could not assume that they intended to distribute it.[25]

Despite this ruling, the STM failed to uphold its own declared principle in a similar case decided only a few months later.[26] This shows the arbitrariness of the political trials. However, defense lawyers had enough room to maneuver, and military justice was flexible enough, for judgments to begin to lean in a more liberal direction in the mid to late 1970s, when the climate of political emergency had waned.

The pressure on the military courts to deal harshly with cases of subversive propaganda increased markedly after the rise of the armed left, the passage of AI-5, and the kidnapping (and eventual release) of the American ambassador Charles Elbrick in September of 1969. Furthermore, the courts had the means to do so, due to the passage of Decree-Law 314 in 1967 and a series of new national security laws (particularly Decree-Law 510 of March 20, 1969, and Decree-Law 898 of September 29, 1969) passed in response to the events above.

Prosecutors used Decree-Law 314 to charge four female college students with subversive propaganda in 1970. The students had been caught in 1969 in Santo André, São Paulo, with 2,400 pamphlets in their Volkswagen van. The pamphlets said, among other things, "down with the government," "down with the dictatorship," and "the organized and united people will overthrow the dictatorship." Despite the absence of any evidence tying these students to the armed left or evidence of distribution of the pamphlets as opposed to possession, the lower regional military court convicted the students and sentenced them to six months in prison each. On appeal, the STM upheld the sentence.[27]

This ruling contrasts sharply with a case of alleged subversive propaganda decided by the STM much later in 1976, after the threat of the armed left had been defeated. In this case, a twenty-year-old man in São Paulo was alleged to have circulated articles and pamphlets among colleagues at work in 1975. His manager seized one of the articles and took it to his superiors, who turned it over to the political police. After being detained for almost a month, the unfortunate youth was prosecuted for subversive propaganda under Decree-Law 898 of 1969. The case rested on material found in the man's possession, including pamphlets with titles such as "Critique of the Capitalist Structure" and "Characteristics of the Soviet Regime." The case appeared to be so weak that the Military Public Ministry prosecutor who handled it asked for an acquittal, but was required under the rules of military justice to bring it to court and then appeal the case to the STM, after the regional military court did acquit.

In its ruling, the STM invoked several important principles. First, the defendant had shown remorse. Second, there was no evidence that he was a member of an illegal organization. Third, most of the material had been legally acquired at bookstores. Finally and most crucially, the defendant did not disseminate the material on a mass scale, instead restricting his audience to colleagues at his place of work. The defendant's actions thus did not constitute subversive propaganda.[28]

These cases illustrate that over time, defense lawyers in Brazil's political trials were able to successfully argue that national security laws protected the possession, if not the widespread distribution, of subversive material. The laws themselves were vague on this point, but the defense was able to make active and widespread dissemination of material the litmus test for conviction. This test was generally consistently applied in the courts by the mid 1970s.

Expressions of Subversive Ideas to Small, Elite Audiences Are Not National Security Crimes

In 1969, Alberto João Rocha, a twenty-two-year-old student at the School of Agronomy of Amazonia in northern Brazil, turned in a term paper with the innocuous title, "A Study of the Current Situation of Mechanization of Agriculture in Brazil." The result of a team research project, the paper praised Communist China's agricultural policies and concluded that solutions to Brazil's agrarian problems could be found if Brazil imitated the Chinese model. It declared that Brazil needed a "socialist revolution" that initiated a "strong dictatorship of the proletariat" with the "support of the worker/peasant masses."

Alberto's professors were not amused. The paper's arguments directly opposed the policies of the military regime, which was promoting its own version of capitalist "modernization" in the countryside. The professors gave Alberto a grade of 6.8 out of 10—a relatively low if not disastrous mark by Brazilian standards—and refused to discuss their grading with him.

Alberto decided to fight back. With the support of some of his fellow students, he wrote an open letter to his professors, deploring their "extremism and despotism." The school's administrators, disturbed by this challenge to their authority, opened an investigation into the incident. The investigation led to a report, dated December 2, 1969, whose conclusions were harsh. Alberto was accused of indiscipline and a lack of respect for his professors. More seriously, he was alleged to have "concepts and goals of a subversive ideological tone." Furthermore, the report concluded, Alberto's written advocacy of a socialist revolution and a dictatorship of the proletariat "directly clash with the traditions of the Brazilian people and nation, as well as constitute a grave violation of existing law."

The Agronomy School promptly expelled the student. But his problems did not end there. A conflict that began inside the school became a matter of national security. In 1970, a prosecutor charged Alberto with violating Decree-Law 898 of 1969. Specifically, the prosecutor alleged that Alberto's term paper and open letter to the professors had incited "subversion of the political-social order" and the "collective disobedience of laws." The open letter constituted subversive propaganda by "injuring, slandering, or defaming" public officials, while the term paper did so by advocating "the violent struggle between social classes."[29]

In the subsequent trial, which took place in a military court in Belém, Pará, Alberto's lawyer Idebal Piveta argued that his client had a right to think and express himself freely in an institution of higher learning. Alberto's paper had dealt with "purely technical-sociological concepts, without leaving the terrain of theory or cogitation"; it did not urge anyone to disturb the social and political order, and therefore did not constitute subversive propaganda. The prosecution, for its part, referred to Decree-Law 898 of 1969: its article 3, paragraph 2 clearly prohibited anyone from "influencing or provoking opinions, emotions, attitudes, or behaviors of groups of foreigners, enemies, neutrals, or friends, against the achievement of national objectives." Alberto's paper and open letter, they argued, had done just that, by criticizing the government's agricultural policies, and by turning students against their professors. Those professors, because they taught in a public university, were also government officials.[30]

The judges in the military court weighed the arguments. In the document they produced, probably written by the single civilian judge, they expressed ambivalence about the conflicting claims at stake in the trial. On one hand, like many other military court judges, they upheld the right to freedom of speech: "In our country, thank God," they wrote, "ideas are not punished, even when they are offensive or senseless." On the other hand, they found it necessary to contest the ideas expressed in Alberto's term paper, which had been submitted as evidence by the prosecution. They disagreed with his praise of the agrarian policies in China and Russia, pointed to the Brazilian government's success in stimulating the mechanization of agriculture, and argued that in China, unlike Brazil, people *were* prosecuted for their ideas. The judges thus appeared to be in something of a tangle. They were clearly taking Alberto's ideas into consideration while judging his crime, but they also praised themselves for recognizing his right to freedom of expression. Despite the latter, they seemed to link Alberto's defiance of authority to his ideas, and they considered both together.

The judges voted to convict. Concluding that Alberto possessed the "profound spirit of an agitator," they found him guilty of defaming and slandering public functionaries, his professors, and thus of committing one form of the many types of subversive propaganda defined in the law. But they found him innocent of inciting the subversion of the political-social order and the collective disobedience of laws.[31] The judges' unanimous verdict and sentence—one year in prison—was announced on August 4, 1970.[32]

Alberto's lawyer appealed the conviction to the STM. In his brief, he stated once again that Alberto's open letter to his professors did not constitute subversive propaganda because it did not circulate outside the school and did not encourage behavior that would put the security of the country at risk. Furthermore, argued the lawyer, ten students signed the open letter, and one person should not be condemned for a collective act. Finally, his client had already suffered by being expelled from university.

This time, the court ruled in Alberto's favor. The STM overturned the lower court conviction and acquitted the student on September 22, 1972. Nearly three years after writing his term paper praising Chinese agriculture, Alberto João Rocha was no longer a political criminal. The decisive issue in the case seems to have been the nature of the readership of his term paper and petition: professors and students in an elite university setting. While communication in this small, elite venue did not constitute subversion, pamphlets and broadsides addressed to "the masses" did.

This distinction was questionable in sociological terms, in that it hinged on an elitist distinction between well-educated individuals, who could responsibly consume subversive material, and allegedly ignorant and gullible members of the masses, who could not. Nevertheless, it was a wedge that defense lawyers were able to use to elicit acquittals in the political trials, and this line of reasoning can be seen in many other cases.

For example, the STM acquitted a thirty-three-year-old filmmaker in 1972 on grounds similar to the one above. João do Nascimento made a film called *Gray Dawn* (*Manhã Cinza*) that was exhibited at the Museum of Modern Art in São Paulo in 1969. The film was confiscated and sent to the censors (Serviço de Censura), who found that it "disposed the people against the constituted authorities" and therefore violated article 16 of Decree-Law 898 of 1969. The political police agents who interrogated Nascimento even responded to his protestations that the film was not subversive with the statement, "You are not being accused, you made this subversive film!"[33] In this as in many other instances, the political police did not observe the formality of presuming the defendant's innocence.

The filmmaker was prosecuted in a military court in Rio de Janeiro and acquitted in a 3–2 vote. Upon reviewing the case, the STM ruled that although the film was subversive, it had only been seen by a small, elite audience of about ten people at the museum, and thus did not constitute subversive propaganda. The STM upheld the acquittal and ordered the return of the film to Nascimento.[34]

Defense lawyers were also able to win the acquittal of book publishers who ran afoul of the national security laws. In 1970 five people who published two separate editions of a book by Soviet author Afanasiev entitled *Fundamentals of*

Philosophy were prosecuted on a variety of charges. In the words of the police report, the book "advocated class struggle, revolutionary war, [and] the dictatorship of the proletariat, all in a clear and, we would say almost popular language. The book is evidently subversive, capable of broadly and maliciously influencing the student population; it infringes the national security law because it does not just divulge, but it enthusiastically exalts Marxism Leninism, that is: an ideology that contradicts the principles of the Brazilian constitution."[35]

The political police (DOPS) had moved aggressively, seizing the book from book shops all over Rio de Janeiro. DOPS agents alleged that Enio Silveira, one of the publishers of the book, bought a newspaper called *The Working Class*, recommended closer cultural ties with the Soviet Union, participated in a congress of solidarity with Cuba, had his political rights suspended for ten days in 1965, and was investigated in a police-military inquiry (IPM) investigating the Brazilian Communist Party in 1964.[36]

Enio Silveira's lawyer Heleno Fragoso dryly argued in his brief that the contents of *The Fundamentals of Philosophy* were "freely debated in the universities of countries where freedom of thought is allowed" and declared that the book is "essentially philosophical, and has awakened the attention of the zealous authorities of our political police simply because it refers to a method of thinking developed by Marx, a proper name that has compromised the exhibition of a film of three old and spiritual brothers. . . ."[37]

The judges agreed with Fragoso. Both the regional military court and the STM voted to acquit all the defendants. The STM reasoned that the book's publication had already been authorized by a judicial sentence in 1965, and the fact that the defendants published other books indicated a lack of criminal intent, and instead mere pecuniary motives. However, the trump card in the judges' reasoning was that the book targeted an erudite audience, not a popular one; and that "pamphlets and bulletins freely distributed are more pernicious than works that are expensively acquired."[38] In other words, books for the elite were not subversive, but pamphlets with the same content handed out at factories and poor neighborhoods were. Here, the judges were reimposing Brazil's traditional social hierarchy on questions of politics, and defense lawyers used this traditionalism to win acquittal for their clients. The right to freedom of expression was upheld in military court judgments, even if the effect of these rulings was mitigated by the fact that the courts did not investigate or punish severe human rights abuses by the security forces that did inhibit freedom of speech.[39]

The Significance of Defense Lawyers' Achievements

In Brazil, defense lawyers stretched the boundaries of permissible activity and speech within national security law and served to lay the foundations for a proto-civil society, one that demanded fuller respect for human rights These lawyers not only changed the application of national security law, they served as interlocutors between regime authorities and the (mostly young, sometimes armed) opponents of the regime, serving as a kind of "loyal opposition" to the regime when that role was extremely limited for elected officials in the national Congress. Finally, the lawyers advised and counseled the young men and women who dissented from and attacked the regime, playing a part in their reevaluation of armed struggle and the evolution of the armed left into a group of legal political parties based in grassroots social movements.

Neither in Chile from 1973 to 1978 (under wartime military justice) nor in Argentina from 1976 to 1983 did the type of jurisprudence described here exist. In Argentina there were extrajudicial disappearances and hardly any trials. In Chile, wartime military courts operated rapidly (usually in a matter of days) and without appeal from 1973 to 1978, preventing the type of reconsideration that took place in Brazilian military justice.[40] In these two countries, political defense lawyers were "communities of memory," recording and protesting vainly against the machinations of an authoritarian legal order based on violence and intimidation.[41] In Brazil, defense lawyers were also this but something more. They were active shapers of national security legality.

To compare Brazil's military regime with the more violent and less judicialized regimes in the southern cone is not to attempt to rehabilitate it. By no stretch of the imagination was it a genuinely constitutional regime with anything approaching a rule of law. It was clearly a dictatorship. A high degree of arbitrariness governed the treatment of political prisoners, and there was little separation of powers, allowing the executive to change the rules of the game at will. However, to fully appreciate the achievements of the defense lawyers, we have to recognize the existence of a very limited "judicial space" within the regime.[42] In other words, judgments in the political trials were not entirely capricious and arbitrary. There was a shared understanding of the meaning of national security laws within the courts that changed over time as the political threats to the regime subsided, and the arguments of defense lawyers were accepted.

A corollary of my argument is that the legal orientation of military regimes may affect patterns of repression. Authoritarian legal orientations are not pure casuistry—although plenty of casuistry exists—that merely justify expedient decisions about the application of violence. Legal orientations can have a feedback effect on security forces. If a regime declares that domestic national security law applies to the treatment of political prisoners, for example, the general pattern is likely to be torture and a decision to prosecute or release, as in Brazil. If, on the other hand, regime leaders announce that domestic law does not apply to the "war" against subversion, as in Argentina from 1976 to 1983, then the general pattern is more likely to be the torture and disappearance of political prisoners.[43]

This brings up a difficult question: What is the general pattern of repression and what are exceptions? How many exceptions change an assessment of the general pattern? Many would argue that the military regimes of Argentina, Chile, and Brazil were essentially similar in their mixture of violence and authoritarian legality, and they were similar in many respects. For example, in its campaign against a rural guerrilla in the state of Pará from 1972 to 1974, the Brazilian army tortured and disappeared its victims in a manner equal to the behavior of the Argentine armed forces in its dirty war.[44]

Yet, as I showed in chapter 2, the ratio of those prosecuted in military courts to those killed extrajudicially is about 23:1 in Brazil and 1:71 in Argentina, whereas in Chile the ratio is close to parity, or about 1.5:1.[45] Whether these numbers are significant, and whether they reflect a qualitative difference between the regimes, are difficult questions of interpretation. We can say yes to both without accepting the conclusions of supporters of Brazil's military regime that the dictatorship "was not that bad" and that its campaign of violence, brutality, and intimidation was somehow justified.

What did Brazil's defense lawyers in political trials ultimately achieve? This reckoning is also a complex one. Between 1964 and 1979, defense lawyers were able to win the acquittal of a series of political defendants. In different legal judgments that were not consistently upheld but were nevertheless significant, the courts recognized that mere belief in Communism was not in itself a crime; that criticism of specific government policies was not unpatriotic or subversive; that possession of subversive propaganda was not illegal without evidence of the propaganda's dissemination; and that expressions of subversive ideas to limited, elite audiences were not violations of national security law.

However, the very characteristics of the military justice system that made it flexible and amenable to changes in interpretation—thus offering some relief to political prisoners—were also beneficial to the regime. They allowed the regime to collect information about opinions in society, facilitated cooperation within and between the legal and military establishments, and allowed the regime to modify its rule incrementally. (A controlled Congress fulfilled much the same function.) While flexible and malleable on the margins, the institutions of the Brazilian legal order were also "sticky" with respect to their essential features. The hybrid civil-military nature of the system and its broad sharing of responsibilities across an array of officials, including civilian prosecutors and judges as well as military officers, gave many figures in the state apparatus a vested interest in the continuation of the near status quo. The defense lawyers' actions produced concrete results in sparing political prisoners from treatment that could have been worse. They created a record that enabled the lawyers and their supporters to accurately and thoroughly condemn the legality of the authoritarian regime. But they created little foundation for an overhaul of the legal system under democracy. The Brazilian self-amnesty of 1979 closed the book on the political trials and the authoritarian manipulation of the law far more conclusively than a similar Chilean amnesty of 1978 or the attempted self-amnesty in Argentina in 1983. It is to transitional justice, or the popular response to authoritarian political justice, that I now turn.

8

Transitional Justice and the Legacies

of Authoritarian Legality

What is not resolved will always return.

Nilmário Miranda and Roberto Valadão, *Relatório final da comissão
externa destinada a atuar junto aos familiares dos mortos e
desaparecidos políticos após 1964, na localização dos seus restos mortais*

IF THE DIFFERENT modes of political justice analyzed in this book had simply been abolished after the end of military rule in each country, their significance would be relatively minor. They would then be of interest to historians
and almost no one else. However, the democratic transitions that occurred in
Argentina, Brazil, and Chile in the 1980s preserved, to varying degrees, elements
of the legal systems under which opponents of military rule had been prosecuted. Furthermore, the military and judicial elites responsible for the repression retained considerable corporate cohesion and autonomy and perpetuated
their own interpretations of the recent past.

To be sure, the end of military rule in each country did bring significant
changes. In each case there was a struggle to implement transitional justice,
measures taken at the beginning of a new democracy to punish perpetrators of
past human rights abuses; to establish a new, official history that condemns the
authoritarian past; and to commit the new regime to the rule of law.[1] Key periods in the forging of transitional justice in our cases are 1983–1987 in Argentina,
1984–1988 in Brazil, and 1988–1991 in Chile.

8.1   A comparison of outcomes in transitional justice: Argentina, Chile, and Brazil

Issue	Brazil	Chile	Argentina
Military's self-amnesty overturned	no	selective[a]	yes
Civilians excluded from military justice	no	no	yes
Purges of the judiciary	no	no	yes
Constitution promulgated by military regime retained	no; new constitution passed in 1988	yes; some reforms in 1990	no; 1854 constitution reinstated, then replaced in 1994
Trials of authoritarian regime leaders	no	no	yes
Trials of other perpetrators	no	some	some
Official truth commission	no	yes	yes
Indemnification of victims	yes[b]	yes	yes
Purges of police/military	no	no	yes

[a]Some judges interpreted the amnesty to allow the investigation (but not the prosecution) of human rights abuses; furthermore, some judges ruled that disappearances were an ongoing crime and therefore not covered by the amnesty.

[b]Indemnification was paid to family members of the killed and disappeared in 1996–1998, in the fourth civilian government after military rule.

Two of the most important institutions of transitional justice, widely implemented around the world in post-authoritarian situations, are an official government commission to investigate and report about past human rights abuses (a "truth commission") and trials of perpetrators.[2] If we use the creation of these institutions as a yardstick, our cases exhibit strikingly different outcomes. In Argentina the first post-authoritarian government established a truth commission and tried leaders of the military regime, as well as other perpetrators of human rights abuses. In Chile, the new civilian government set up a truth commission but did not try military regime leaders, although some trials of human rights abusers subsequently took place. In Brazil, the outcome was starkly minimalist: no truth commission, and no trials.[3] These outcomes were shaped by both the nature of authoritarian legality and the constraints produced by the different democratic transitions in each case. (See table 8.1.)

However, truth commissions and trials were not the only transitional justice issues faced in these countries. Whether and how to reform the judiciary and the military were also pressing concerns. Again, our cases exhibit wide variation. In Argentina, both the judiciary and military were purged and constrained in new ways in an unstable pattern of reforms that two observers characterize as a "progressive-regressive cycle" (Roniger and Sznajder 1999, 55–78, esp. 55). In

Chile, a largely unreconstructed and insulated military endured alongside a judiciary undergoing a gradual, continuous, and significant transformation. And in Brazil, conservative judicial and military organizations remained largely unreformed despite democracy.

Different patterns of transitional justice have thus produced different authoritarian legacies in Brazil and the southern cone. For purposes of this chapter, authoritarian legacies are institutional configurations that "survive democratic transition and intervene in the quality and practice of post-authoritarian democracies."[4] The capacity of military and judicial elites to prevent the dismantling of their prerogatives after the end of military rule varied—it was lowest in Argentina, highest in Brazil, and mixed in Chile.[5] Because of this, the authoritarian legacies in each case are also different.

Transitional Justice Outcomes

Brazil

Brazil's military regime was the longest lasting and most entrenched of the three analyzed here. Its level of lethal violence was far lower than in the other two cases and had declined to close to zero ten years before the transition, a far longer stretch of time than in Argentina and Chile.[6] In addition, as in Chile, the military regime had managed the economy much more skillfully than its Argentine counterparts, enhancing its legitimacy. Furthermore, everyday violence in Brazil was more pervasive than in Argentina or Chile. The Brazilian homicide rate, for example, was more than four times the rate in Argentina and seven times that of Chile.[7] This diminished the relative political significance of the military regime's repression in Brazil.[8] All of these factors facilitated the military regime's management of a "slow, gradual, and sure" transition that culminated in the indirect election of a civilian president in 1985.

The transition involved both concessions to the opposition and authoritarian assertions of executive privilege. The regime issued a broad amnesty in 1979 that shielded all members of the security forces from prosecution for human rights abuses, while at the same time freeing almost all political prisoners and permitting political exiles to return home. Competitive, multiparty political competition was restored at the state level in 1982. Furthermore, unlike its Argentine and Chilean counterparts, regime change in Brazil did not involve the emergence of a coherent, disciplined, programmatic oppositional party. The Workers' Party (Partido dos Trabalhadores, or PT), which later became such a party, was too small in the early and mid-1980s to make a difference at the level of national politics.

The first new civilian president after military rule, José Sarney, unlike his counterparts Raúl Alfonsín in Argentina and Patricio Aylwin in Chile, was not a critic of the military regime. Instead, he had been an ardent supporter of it and a member of the regime's political party, ARENA, and later the PDS (Partido Democrático Social, or Democratic Social Party).[9] The political career of Sarney reflected the tremendous continuity in personnel and policies of Brazil's democratic transition (Zaverucha 2000). Despite the massive demonstrations of the *diretas-já* (direct elections now) campaign of 1984, Brazil's movement to civilian government was an elite-dominated, highly controlled process in which both the military and the judiciary retained almost all of their prerogatives.

Given these factors, it is not surprising that Brazil's democratic transition lacked both a truth commission and trials. This outcome is well known, but what is less recognized is how the military and judiciary actively defended the status quo in Brazil, thus shaping a transition in which a feigned amnesia—combined with overt pride in the authoritarian past—was the order of the day. We must trace the evolution of the military regime to understand this outcome.

As we have seen in chapter 4, the Brazilian military regime did not engage in large-scale purges of the judiciary, and political prosecutions took place without radical innovations or breaks with traditional military and judicial practice. Military court jurisdiction had been merely expanded to include civilians in 1965, and existing national security laws were gradually modified with a series of decree-laws and constitutional modifications in the late 1960s. However, beginning in the 1970s, judicial (and even some military) dissent against the national security laws began to develop within the system. For example, the Brazilian Bar Association became a prominent critic of national security laws. Even supporters of the military coup began to voice a desire for a return to constitutional and legal normality.[10]

During Brazil's transition, large-scale prosecutions of civilians in the military courts were ended in 1979, when AI-5 was abolished. However, in a maneuver little noticed at the time, the Geisel government in 1977 changed the court jurisdiction in cases of crimes committed by members of the military police.[11] After the 1977 change, civilian courts were no longer responsible for trying such crimes; instead, they went to state military courts (Mesquita Neto 1997, 8). Convictions for crimes against civilians are extraordinarily difficult to achieve in state military courts, in part because most judges are military police officers. Here we see an example of regime transition leading to an increase, rather than a decrease, in the prerogatives of the armed forces.

Although military prerogatives remained high during the Brazilian transition, the military regime came in for substantial criticism, most notably in *Brasil: Nunca mais* (1985), a best-selling book produced by the Archdiocese of São Paulo that documented torture under the authoritarian regime.[12] In contrast, the judiciary's image remained fairly positive. The actions of the bar association, the involvement of lawyers in the justice and peace commission that lobbied for an amnesty for political prisoners and protested human rights abuses in the 1970s, and the celebrity of a small group of lawyers who had defended political prisoners all helped to create a public image of the Brazilian legal establishment as antiauthoritarian. Even though large number of civilian prosecutors and judges had participated in the political trials, the democratic transition saw little blame placed on the Brazilian judiciary for its performance under authoritarian rule.[13]

Consequently, when calls for reform of the judiciary did come in Brazil, they aimed at increasing the individual independence of judges, not decreasing it. As in Chile but unlike Argentina, there were no purges of the judiciary after Brazil's 1985 democratic transition. The main achievement of reforms was to restore the judiciary to the status quo that had existed prior to the military regime by guaranteeing once again the irremovability of judges. The result was that judicial reformers "swept aside the balancing constraint of accountability" (Prillaman 2000, 82).

Significant action in the area of transitional justice only occurred in Brazil after the inauguration of President Fernando Henrique Cardoso in 1995. Cardoso was the first elected president after military rule who had genuinely opposed the dictatorship. Under his leadership, the Brazilian Congress authorized the creation of a commission to examine the claims of state-sponsored killings and disappearances under the dictatorship. The commission began its work in 1996, eventually examining the cases of 360 people, and voting to indemnify 284 of them on the grounds that they had been killed by state security forces (see Miranda and Tibúrcio 1999, 16). However, the results of the commission's work were never officially published by the government as in Argentina and Chile (Miranda and Tibúrcio 1999). The government seemed afraid to publicize this modest and belated response to past human rights abuses.[14] This timid approach to the issue did not change with the inauguration of the Lula government in 2003.[15]

Leonardo Avritzer captures the paradox of the Brazilian transition, in which the same legal institutions that mitigated the authoritarian repression became a roadblock to subsequent efforts to deepen democracy. He writes: "restoring the rule of law is, perhaps surprisingly, easier in the countries in which the legal system did not have any autonomy during the authoritarian period (Chile and Argentina) than in countries that passed through a semi-legal form of authoritarianism and experienced greater legal continuity between authoritarianism and democracy (Brazil and Mexico). This is so because in the cases in which authoritarianism changed the structure of the rule of law, it is almost impossible to enforce retroactively the rule of law in relation to the period previous to democratization" (Avritzer 2002, 105).

This is not to say that there were not significant developments in the field of transitional justice in Brazil. One example of change is the post-authoritarian governments' handling of historical documents. Alone among our three cases, in Brazil, some of the archives of the authoritarian repressive apparatus—such as the political police (DEOPS) archives in various states—were opened to the public. In addition, an innovative law of habeas data established the right of all Brazilian citizens to request the release of government files compiled against them.[16] Similarly, innovative efforts within civil society attempted to repudiate the authoritarian past, memorialize the victims of repression, and revalorize human rights and the rule of law.[17]

Nevertheless, at the level of the national state, transitional justice in Brazil was largely symbolic, and the judiciary and military continued to function under democracy largely as they had under military rule. For example, in 1996 —eleven years after the formal end of the authoritarian regime—the Brazilian army was proudly displaying not one but five copies of Mario Pessoa's *Law of National Security* (*O direito da segurança nacional*) in the bookstore of its Rio de Janeiro headquarters.[18] The book, cited earlier, is an elaborate justification of the military regime's authoritarian legality written in 1971—the very height of the regime's repression. Much of the specific legislation that it praises was repealed in the late 1970s and early 1980s. Its presence in a shop open to the public speaks to the continuities within the Brazilian military.

Another indication of the unreformed nature of the military was revealed in October of 2004. Responding to the publication of photographs of a political prisoner of the 1970s, the commander of the army General Francisco Roberto de Albuquerque authorized a press release describing the military's repression under military rule as a legitimate response to the violence of the armed left.

Despite the furor aroused by this statement, the general kept his post while the civilian minister of defense, José Viegas, was forced to resign. General Albuquerque's posture contrasts sharply with that of counterparts in Chile and Argentina, who have publicly apologized for the armed forces' human rights abuses under military rule.[19]

The Brazilian judiciary, like the military, remains a highly insulated, privileged corporate group under democracy. Brazil's judicial salaries are some of the highest in the world, while the courts' efficiency in terms of cases decided is relatively low.[20] The military justice system, responsible for the prosecution of thousands for nothing more than crimes of association and opinion in the 1960s and 1970s, has largely escaped any serious criticism, in contrast to the pointed critiques of its counterpart in Chile.[21] Instead, the military and judicial elites in the military court system have aggressively perpetrated the myth, at state expense, that under military rule, military justice was an impartial and wise dispenser of legal judgment.[22]

For example, in 1994 a military court official wrote in a government publication, "The actions, not only of the STM, but equally of the innumerable judgments of the military courts in the first instance, will demonstrate that the judicial power, as a whole, without doubt, owes much to the numerous proceedings of military justice, in the worrying moments of the 1960s . . . until the reestablishment of the rule of law."[23]

In Brazil, an enduring consensus across judicial and military lines has largely prevented reform of the judicial and military organizations. Military and judicial elites fused by Brazil's hybrid military justice system had both an interest and the means to propagate a fairy tale about the benevolence and fairness of Brazil's military courts during the dictatorship. The relatively small scale of lethal violence helped these apologists to claim that the military courts had approximated the high standards of an ideal type of the rule of law. The fiction was convenient in maintaining the status quo, despite the demands for change of the democratic era.

Argentina

Of our three cases, the most intense transitional justice efforts were made in Argentina. The Argentine military regime collapsed in the wake of a severe economic recession and defeat in the Falklands/Malvinas War of 1982, leading to elections and the victory of the Radical Party candidate Raúl Alfonsín, a former human rights lawyer, in October 1983. Alfonsín ran against the military's "final document" of April 1983, which had attempted to prevent any attempts at transitional justice by the new government. After gaining 52 percent of the votes cast, Alfonsín attempted to address some of the legacies of the violence of the past.

Shortly after taking office in December 1983, President Alfonsín established a truth commission named after its chairman, Ernesto Sabato. This commission interviewed survivors of the military regime's detention camps, family members of the disappeared, members of the military and police, and virtually anyone else willing to provide information, compiling over fifty thousand pages of testimony on seven thousand different cases. It produced a report whose title, *Nunca más* (*Never Again*), echoed the Nuremberg trials (see Comisión Nacional sobre la Desaparición de Personas 1984b; Argentine National Commission on the Disappeared 1986; and Nino 1996, 79). The report garnered tremendous international and domestic attention, not just for its substantive response to human rights abuses in Argentina but for its formation and procedures. Thereafter, actions in the area of transitional justice in Argentina went well beyond what occurred in Chile and Brazil.

The Argentine military's defeat in war made it much weaker than its Brazilian and Chilean counterparts. Military self-amnesties were upheld in the latter two countries, but in Argentina the Congress annulled the military's amnesty in 1983.[24] Later, it stripped military courts of jurisdiction over civilians, leaving the military fewer judicial prerogatives vis-à-vis civilians than it had enjoyed before the 1976 coup.[25] Nine top leaders of the former regime were put on trial, and five were convicted and sent to prison. Hundreds of military officers were also prosecuted (Nino 1996, 60–73). Again unlike Brazil and Chile, the new president carried out a purge of the judiciary, replacing all the judges of the Supreme Court and some federal judges. Later, a judicial council (Consejo Superior de la Magistratura) was created, subjecting the judiciary to some external control and ostensibly improving the administration of the courts. In Argentina, transitional justice also included reparations. Compensation was paid both to family members of the disappeared and people illegally detained during the dictatorship.

While the dirty war was not a primary reason for the breakdown of the military regime, its flagrant violation of legal norms eroded military prestige and power and allowed civilian reformers to launch a program based on this perception. Popular mobilization was also important in the Argentine case. As the military withdrew from power in 1983, human rights groups marched in the streets of Buenos Aires to demand an accounting of the fate of the disappeared (Avritzer 2002, 4). The executive was able to capitalize on these protests and introduce reform measures, using the rift between the military and the judiciary to its advantage. President Alfonsín was able to entrust young judges and prosecutors elevated by his judicial purges with the prosecution of military officers.[26]

However, despite the moral fervor of Argentine efforts, not all of the initial achievements of transitional justice endured. Uprisings by junior military officers put pressure on the Alfonsín government to stop its efforts to address past human rights abuses. President Alfonsín eventually passed Full Stop and Due Obedience laws (in 1986 and 1987, respectively) that ended most prosecutions for human rights abuses under military rule, undercutting the symbolism of the conviction of the top regime leaders.[27]

President Alfonsín was replaced in 1989 by his elected successor Carlos Menem. Shortly after his inauguration, President Menem pardoned the more than four hundred military officers then being prosecuted, effectively short-circuiting the trials. In 1990 he pardoned those who had already been convicted, including the former military regime leaders.[28] Furthermore, President Menem politicized the courts, especially in 1989 when he expanded the Supreme Court from five to nine justices, and appointed four of his cronies to the new seats. Argentine courts in the 1990s suffered from a lack of independence from the executive, with serious additional problems of corruption and inefficiency (Prillaman 2000, 126–29).

In 1998 the Argentine Congress repealed the Full Stop and Due Obedience laws, a measure reinforced by Judge Gabriel Cavallo when he declared the laws unconstitutional in 2001 (Jelin 2003). Transitional justice in Argentina experienced yet another twist after the election of President Nestor Kirchner in 2003. One of the new president's first actions was to fire fifty-two senior military officers, "the biggest purge [of the military] since democracy was restored in Argentina in 1983."[29] Kirchner also revoked a decree impeding the extradition of Argentines to face charges abroad. Furthermore, in the first year of Kirchner's presidency, ninety-seven military personnel were charged with human rights violations and detained by the Argentine justice system.[30]

Argentina's transitional justice efforts were therefore far more radical than Brazil's. The lack of integration of and consensus between judicial and military elites was exploited by civilian politicians who were able to divide and rule both corporate groups. The truth commission and the trials shattered the wall of silence around the dirty war disappearances and punctured the military's impunity. Elected presidents moved aggressively to slash military prerogatives, prestige, and resources, while purging the judiciary and maintaining its subordination to the executive. Argentina's transitional justice has not been entirely successful in that it is subject to the progressive-regressive cycle alluded to earlier, in which measures taken by one government are undone by its successor. But it has not been restricted by the immobilism that we find in the Brazilian case.

Chile

Transitional justice efforts in Argentina were facilitated by the fact that the prior regime was short lived and failed to institutionalize an alternative, authoritarian legal system; the transition was thus marked by legal discontinuity. This was not the case in Chile.[31] Chile reflects the greatest amount of legal continuity of our three cases. Not only did its 1978 amnesty law cover most of the incidents of authoritarian violence, but its 1980 constitution provided the framework for the transition and is still in force today.

As discussed in chapter 5, the Chilean military regime succeeded in largely judicializing its repression with the shift to peacetime military courts in 1978 and the passage of a referendum approving the new constitution in 1980. However, its previous mode of political justice had been far more abrupt and radical than that of the Brazilian regime. If in Argentina wholly extrajudicial repression was the norm, Chilean repression from 1973 to 1978 was a military usurpation of judicial power, with the complicity of the legal establishment.

As in Argentina, this abuse of power generated widespread criticism of the performance of the judiciary in the aftermath of the dictatorship. In both cases, divisions between the military and the judiciary created by the form of authoritarian legality gave civilian reformers some leverage with which to promote change. In Argentina, Alfonsín's advisors were able to reform both the military and the judiciary. In Chile, given the power of the military in the transition, only the judiciary was an available target. In the words of one commentator, the Chilean judiciary was three different animals. Before the 1973 coup, it had been a sacred cow, aloof and impenetrable. Under Pinochet, it had been a lamb, meekly consenting to the repression. After the end of military rule, it was a scapegoat.[32]

Chile's democratic transition was induced by the failure of President Pinochet to win another eight-year term in a 1988 plebiscite. The subsequent 1989 election was won by Patricio Aylwin, the candidate of a multiparty coalition known as the Concertación.[33] Aylwin had supported the 1973 coup but had emerged as a prominent critic of the military regime, and in particular the 1980 Constitution.[34]

The Chilean transition, however, was highly constrained by the legal strait-jacket devised by the military regime. Most of the latter's 3,600 decrees were retained and political prisoners were still incarcerated when President Aylwin took office, although most were gradually released over the course of the next year. Furthermore, the jurisdiction of military justice remained broad after the transition; civilians could be and were prosecuted in military courts in ways that they were not prior to military rule. Nevertheless, jurisdiction over political crimes was transferred back to civilian courts after the transition.

Unlike both Argentina and Brazil, prior convictions for political crimes in military courts were not annulled in post-transition Chile. Employers could in theory ask for the criminal record of potential employees, and political prisoners' records of conviction in military courts would appear on these documents. While discrimination on this basis in the private sector was possible, it was rare in practice in the public sector, where many former political prisoners can be found.[35] However, in this respect, authoritarian legality was not overturned in Chile, but instead became the foundation of the new regime.

Furthermore, the military used the period between President Pinochet's loss in the 1988 plebiscite and the 1990 inauguration of Aylwin to reinforce and even increase its prerogatives and autonomy. For example, the military negotiated for itself an unsupervised and guaranteed budget, and maintained its autonomy in promoting officers up the chain of command.[36] Because of the latter guarantee, Chilean presidents were in the embarrassing predicament of lacking a basic prerogative of most democratic heads of state: the right to replace the heads of the armed forces.

The most significant achievement of the Aylwin administration in the area of transitional justice was the creation of the National Commission on Truth and Reconciliation, headed by former senator Raúl Rettig. Like President Alfonsín in Argentina, President Aylwin established the commission early in his administration, in this case just six weeks after his inauguration. Unlike the Sabato Commission, the Rettig Commission included supporters of the Pinochet regime, reflecting the greater strength of the leaders of the old regime in the Chilean transition.

For evidence, the Rettig Commission relied heavily on the archives of the Vicaría de la Solidaridad, compiled by defense lawyers for political prisoners, but also interviewed family members of the killed and disappeared. Its report, published in Februrary 1991, was an indictment of the systematic abuse of human rights under the Pinochet regime. However, it did not receive the public attention of *Nunca más* in Argentina. This is in part because of the highly constrained nature of the Chilean transition,[37] and also because of the assassination of one of the architects of the military regime's constitution, Jaime Guzmán, in the weeks after the release of the report (Hayner 2000, 37).

If the military has retained most of its prerogatives in post-authoritarian Chile, this is not the case with the judiciary. The Concertación governments have engaged in serious efforts in this area. Many advisors to President Aylwin believed that Chile's civilian judiciary, especially the Supreme Court, had been unacceptably complicit in the human rights abuses of the Pinochet regime (Boeninger 1998, 445). This view was also strongly expressed in the Rettig Commission's report (Chilean National Commission on Truth and Reconciliation 1993, vol. 1, 117–26). The judiciary was also not strongly defended by the military itself. However, the new government was tied down by the military's 1978 self-amnesty. Its leaders concluded that they could not realistically hope to cleanse the judiciary of all those judges who had collaborated with and covered up repression, nor reduce military prerogatives and autonomy. But they could reform the procedures and architecture of the judiciary, which is what they did.

Reform achievements include the creation of a judicial council (Consejo Superior de la Magistratura), as in Argentina, and a judicial academy to train judges and set criteria for promotions, thereby weakening the power of the Supreme Court. Other reforms were the passage of a new penal code in 2000, which began a process of separating the prosecutorial and adjudicating functions of judges; the creation of a new national public prosecutor's office; and the substitution of purely written procedures in trials for oral arguments. The latter three changes were intended to reduce the inquisitorial nature of trials as well as to make them speedier and more adversarial, thus strengthening the rights of defendants in the system. Other, less spectacular, but perhaps equally important reforms were the building of ten new courthouses and the creation of an arbitration program for commercial disputes. The government also expanded access to the civilian courts by increasing the number of positions at free government legal clinics, staffed by law school students and graduates, and creating a public defenders' office (Defensoria Penal Pública). Finally, in 1997, presidential appointments to the Supreme Court were made contingent on the approval of the Senate.[38]

Significantly, military justice was completely exempt from these reforms, and its jurisdiction and procedures were not affected in any way. This reflects the very different status of these two corporate groups in democratic Chile. Most members of the judicial elite were pulled into the process of democratic reform, while military officers remained part of the autonomous "state within the state" that is recognizable in earlier stages of Chilean political development.

Furthermore, some Chilean human rights groups and judges were creative in pushing the boundaries of the 1978 amnesty. The journalist Patricia Verdugo published a book about the caravan of death (discussed in chapter 5) that led to the prosecution of General Arellano Stark, who waived his right to immunity granted by the amnesty. In 1996 a human rights group brought a suit on behalf of Spanish citizens disappeared, killed, or tortured by the Pinochet regime to Spain's high court (Audiencia Nacional). The suit eventually resulted in Judge Baltazar Garzón's request to extradite former president Pinochet when he visited London in 1998 (Barahona de Brito, González-Enríquez, and Aguilar 2001, 47–48), leading to Pinchet's arrest. When Pinochet was eventually released by the British and returned to Chile in 2000, he was stripped of his parliamentary immunity and investigated in Chilean courts. In the end he was not charged with crimes, due to the allegedly frail state of his mental health. However, in August of 2004, the Supreme Court took away Pinochet's immunity from prosecution, and the former dictator was investigated once again.[39]

These incremental but cumulatively substantial measures mirrored the Chilean military regime's "middle way" between the institutional gradualism of Brazilian authoritarianism and the radical rupture of the Argentine dirty war. They represent some progress, despite inauspicious beginnings. The prior history of authoritarian legality helps explain this outcome. The military and the judiciary, more separate than they had been in Brazil, remained relatively separate under democracy. The post-transitional government was not able to launch the full-scale program of President Alfonsín; it left the military untouched. But the judiciary was both a target and a tool of its significant reforms.

Legacies of Authoritarian Legality

The political trials of military Brazil and Chile, and Argentina in 1971–1973, amounted to a double violation of both the rule of law and political prisoners. The latter were often tortured and then charged and sentenced by courts as if the torture had never taken place. The courts' official transcripts were thus at the very least incomplete, so that after the end of military rule, one of the essential acts of affirmation of many victims was to simply describe and denounce their torture.

However, conflicts over transitional justice also revolved around how to reform the military and the judiciary so that the repression would not occur again. Since the organizational relationship between the military and the judiciary had been very different in Argentina, Brazil, and Chile, so were the prospects of reform. In Argentina, the rift between the organizations was wide. The military had basically ignored the judiciary in its authoritarian repression, and the post-transition executive was able to purge the judiciary and use it to prosecute the military. In Chile, the relations were closer. Both organizations had been part of the repression under military rule and stood fast in resisting calls for the prosecution of human rights abuses. But they were separate enough that civilian politicians could single out the judiciary for reform after the transition.

In Brazil, in contrast, strongly judicialized political repression was sanctified by a hybrid military court system that fused judicial and military elites in a single organization and maintained a high degree of consensus across the two corporate bodies. After the transition, elites ensconced in the military justice system, as well as the broader judiciary and military, defended their records under authoritarian rule and resisted reforms that might have affected their organizations. Transitional justice in Brazil was minimal. There was no truth commission as in the other two countries, no trials of regime leaders or significant reform of the military as in Argentina, and no significant modification of the judiciary as in Chile.

The Brazilian case thus suggests a paradox. Conservative legal systems that are adapted to authoritarian rule may restrain security forces and offer some possibilities for the defense of human rights, as was argued in chapter 7. However, they also create entrenched bureaucratic interests and an "official story" that can serve as an immense barrier to efforts at reform after the end of authoritarian rule. In Brazil even more than in Argentina and Chile, the legacy of authoritarian legality has cast its shadow over democracy.

9

The Sword and the Robe

MILITARY-JUDICIAL RELATIONS IN AUTHORITARIAN
AND DEMOCRATIC REGIMES

> With the sole exception of Nazi atrocities, the phenomenon
> of complicity in oppressive legal systems . . . has seldom been
> studied.
>
> Robert Cover, *Justice Accused:*
> *Antislavery and the Judicial Process*

THIS BOOK HAS dwelt almost exclusively, up to now, on the Brazilian and southern cone military regimes. Much of the context and characteristics of these regimes are specific to a particular place and time. Latin America has long been correctly seen as a distinctive part of the developing world, with states that are generally older than those in Africa, Asia, and the Middle East. The region has been subject to U.S. hegemony and interventions to a greater degree than elsewhere, its populist movements of the mid-twentieth century are rightly seen as unlike those of other regions, and its militaries and judiciaries developed in regionally specific ways also.[1] Furthermore, Brazil, Chile, and Argentina are quite different from the other countries of Latin America. With the exception of Mexico and Uruguay, the rest of Latin America is less urban and industrialized and has weaker states.

All of these factors make it dangerous to transfer any generalization derived from the Brazilian and southern cone cases to another part of the world or another historical time period. However, I argue in this chapter that the nexus between military and judicial elites can help to explain the judicialization of repression and its absence elsewhere. In particular, the pattern seen in Brazil and the southern cone appears to hold in other cases: a radical approach to the law and the deployment of extrajudicial violence is more likely in regimes where relations between the military and judiciary are strained or distant. On the other hand, more conservative, incremental approaches to the law and judicialized repression are more common in regimes with a high degree of judicial-military cooperation, integration, and consensus.

It is easy to see why this pattern might apply to military regimes.[2] When militaries control the executive and seek to judicialize their repression, they are likely to rely on some elements of the traditional judiciary to do so. This is important, because the most ubiquitous type of authoritarian regime in the twentieth century was the military dictatorship.[3] Even today, when military regimes are less common, the threat of military coup remains a political factor in many countries.[4]

However, the real innovation in twentieth-century authoritarianism was the dictatorship of a political party (Brooker 2000, 4). Especially in the interwar years, new authoritarian regimes with powerful new ideologies emerged in Europe. In this chapter, I argue that the framework developed here can help to explain the authoritarian legality of some of these regimes. A focus on military and judicial elites sheds light on the legal dimension of regime repression in three well-known dictatorships: the Nazi regime in Germany (1933–1945), the Franco dictatorship in Spain (1939–1975), and the Salazarist regime in Portugal (1926–1974). Each of these regimes is similar to one of our three cases in its approach to legality: the Nazis to the Argentine *proceso*, Franco's Spain to Pinochet's Chile, and Salazar's Portugal to the Brazilian regime.[5]

A comparison of these cases has many potential pitfalls, not least because of the widely differing life spans of these dictatorships, ranging from seven years in Argentina to forty-eight years in the Portuguese case. The longer-running regimes, especially, were subject to complicated transformations. Furthermore, each of the European regimes—which were part of an authoritarian wave that predated the Brazilian and southern cone cases by forty years—clearly has important idiosyncrasies.[6] For example, Nazi repression had a strong ethnic and racial dimension lacking in most of the other cases, and the Nazi regime was engaged in a total war for half of its existence. The Franco regime emerged from a full-blown and heavily internationalized civil war absent in the other cases. Salazar's Portugal was smaller and more rural than any other regime analyzed here and was the only one that managed a long-standing and extensive colonial empire.

Such differences undoubtedly affect patterns of regime repression. Nevertheless, by matching the Brazilian and southern cone cases with better-known and more intensively studied European precursors, I show how an emphasis on judicial-military relations can help analyze authoritarian legality more generally. I distinguish between these basic patterns of military-judicial relations: cooperation and integration; usurpation of judicial authority by the military; and rejection of judicial authority by the military. While such an exercise cannot identify all the conditions influencing outcomes, it can show that similar patterns of judicial-military relations can have similar effects across cases. In the final section, I examine the post-9/11 United States in order to apply the framework to a democratic regime.

Nazi Germany

The Nazi regime in Germany was radical in its approach to the law and, especially in the last few years of its rule, resorted heavily to the extrajudicial extermination of large numbers of people. Therefore, it is placed in the lower right-hand corner of figure 9.1 as probably the most extreme example of political injustice in the twentieth century. As in Argentina, the Nazi case is marked by a low level of integration and consensus between military and judicial elites and purges of both corporate groups. The German case goes well beyond the Argentine in that the Nazi party hierarchy led by Adolph Hitler eventually circumvented not only the judiciary (as in Argentina) but the military as well. The extermination policy that came to be known as the Final Solution was carried out largely by the SS rather than the army or another conventional branch of the armed forces.

Less well known than the Final Solution is the Nazis' use of courts. A large number of political trials took place in the People's Court (Volksgerichtshof, or VGH) in Nazi Germany between 1934 and 1945. The People's Court was a special court created by the Nazis to try cases of treason and terrorism. However, the Nazis created a large area of extrajudicial repression alongside and completely beyond the purview of the People's Court. It was not uncommon, after 1936, for the Gestapo to rearrest people acquitted in the People's Court and send them to concentration camps (Köch 1989, 3–6). And after November of 1942, Jews were not subject to the court or any other kind of legal procedure. At that time the Ministry of Justice confidentially instructed state officials that "courts

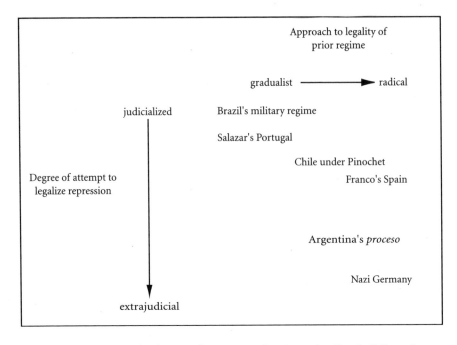

Figure 9.1: Variation in legal approaches to repression: Argentina, Brazil, Chile, and other cases

will forego the carrying out of regular criminal procedures against Jews, who henceforth shall be turned over to the police" (Miller 1995, 52).

The grotesque perversion of justice represented by the People's Court was created by what Miller calls the Nazi regime's "legal atheism" and its specific measures to distort and manipulate the law for its own ends. For example, roughly one-fifth of the legal profession was purged under Hitler: Jewish, socialist, and democratic members were removed (Müller 1991, 296). Furthermore, the 1933 Law for the Restoration of the Professional Civil Service allowed the executive branch to dismiss judges for any reason—an effective instrument for keeping those who had not been purged in line, and one also used by the southern cone military regimes. In 1939, Nazi prosecutors were allowed to appeal acquittals.[7] The Nazi regime encouraged jurists to prioritize the political needs of the regime and to attempt to see the spirit, not the letter, of the law, leading to artful constructions of laws that completely gutted them of specificity and justified extreme harshness by the state.[8] And special courts could reduce the uncertainty of trusting political cases to the ordinary judiciary. In this way the People's Court gained almost complete jurisdiction over crimes of terrorism and treason, while over time treason itself was defined in ever-expanding ways. The court's judges were handpicked for their devotion to National Socialism and their expertise in espionage and national security.

However, the political trials in the People's Court were also shaped by the politics of the pre-Nazi Weimar regime and the Second Reich (1871–1918). The legal bases of VGH judgments were two long-standing definitions of treason. H. W. Koch writes "neither the legal basis for, nor the legal procedure of, the VGH differed significantly from treason trials of the past" (1989, 3) The prohibition on the right of appeal in treason trials was promulgated in 1922, eleven years before the Nazis took power. The artful interpretations of the spirit rather than the letter of the law favored by the Nazi regime reflected an authoritarian and predemocratic legal ideology prevalent among German jurists since at least the late nineteenth century (Müller 1991, 296). Criminal trials under the Second Reich had been inquisitorial and heavily biased in favor of the state. For example, the prosecutor addressed the court while located on the same level as the judge, while the defense attorney sat at a lower level with the accused. The bench and bar posed little opposition to Hitler when he assumed power in 1933.[9]

For Koch, the roots of the People's Court "lay in the Weimar Republic, when the judiciary had become politicized" (1989, x). The widespread belief that Germany had lost World War I due to treason and revolution (it had been "stabbed in the back") was shared by many in the judiciary. In 1924, Hitler in *Mein Kampf* had advocated the creation of a special court to try tens of thousands of people responsible for the treachery (Müller 1991, 140). Even in a regime as ruthless and as ambitious as the Third Reich, political justice was shaped by conditions inherited from previous political regimes. Nazi legality was a distorted and intensified version of existing tendencies within the law, rather than an entirely new creation. For that reason, it proved to be highly resistant to feeble attempts at denazification after World War II. While under Allied occupation the political trials described above came to an end, Müller shows how the mentalities and decisions of many judges did not. Even in 1985, the German parliament could not bring itself to take the symbolic action of declaring convictions in the People's Court and special courts under Nazi rule null and void (Müller 1991, 284–92).

Of the Latin American cases, Argentina comes closest to the Nazi experience. As in Argentina, the lack of a consensus within and between judicial and military elites contributed to the extrajudicial horrors of the Nazi regime. As Gordon Craig shows in his study of the Prussian army, Hitler was able to purge and Nazify the army and to effectively subject military officers to his control (Craig 1955, see in particular 468–503). But even this subjugated army was not completely reliable as an instrument of repression from the Nazis' point of view, and neither was the judiciary.

When it came time to implement the Final Solution, the main tasks were not entrusted to either courts or the army. Even a court that executed half the defendants that came before it, such as the People's Court, was too restrained for the Nazi leadership's plan, and even an army that had already proved its willingness to massacre civilians was deemed unprepared for the systematic mass slaughter that was perpetrated. Instead, the responsibility was entrusted to the Economic and Administrative Main Office (Wirtschafts und Verwaltungshauptant, WVHA) of a special political-military body, the SS. The SS was controlled by the Armed Forces High Command or OKW (Oberkommando der Wehrmacht), directly under Hitler. The concentration and labor camps of the SS in Germany and the occupied territories, managed by the WVHA from 1942 to 1945, imprisoned roughly ten million people, killing millions of them.[10] As bad as the People's Court was, the number of victims of its lethal "justice" (thirteen thousand) was small compared to the camps run by the SS.[11] Nazi political repression was thus largely extrajudicial and radical with respect to preexisting legality.

It was thus not trust and consensus between judicial and military elites that led to the Nazis' particularly perverse form of dual state, but its absence, and in particular a reluctance on the part of Hitler and his inner circle—including military officers—to entrust the highest political goals of the regime to either judges or fellow generals. For example, Hitler himself assumed command of the army between 1941 and 1945. And only an inner circle of Nazi party officials was allowed to direct and profit from the horror of the death camps.

Franco's Spain

If Argentine repression bears some resemblance to that of Nazi Germany, Chile's repression looks more like that of Franco's Spain (1939–1975). As in Chile, Franco's forces were involved in a rollback military action, in this instance trying to undo the extensive mass mobilization of Republican rule. Similarly, the initial repression was quite violent, it was led by a highly insulated military that had declared martial law throughout the whole national territory, and it was only partially judicialized. However, despite Franco's declaration that his regime was "based on bayonets and blood,"[12] the regime judicialized its repression over time, as did the Pinochet regime in Chile.

During the Spanish civil war of 1936–1939, military courts (*consejos de guerra*) tried people for political crimes. These military courts operated during a ferocious conflict marked by the "red terror" of the Republicans and the "white terror" of the Nationalists.[13] Shortly after the July 17, 1936, military rebellion that began the war, on July 28 the forces of General Francisco Franco y Bahamonde declared martial law throughout Spain. All civilian and military crimes were thenceforth regulated by the Military Code. Civilian jurists were supposed to play an auxiliary role in military court trials, but apparently this was done only when conservative jurists were available and military commanders were willing to employ them.

The military court trials took place in a climate of intense reprisals and repression. Executions without any sort of judicial procedure were common. From July 1936 until roughly July 1937, mass killings occurred all over Spain, conducted by the army, the Civil Guard, the Falangists, and right-wing militias.[14] In Payne's words, "the various elements on the Nationalist side were, in effect, free to kill almost whomever they chose, as long as it could be said that the victim had supported the [Republicans'] Popular Front" (Payne 1967, 416). Peasants and workers found with trade union cards, people suspected of having voted for the Republicans, Freemasons, officeholders in the Republic, or people with "red" or even liberal political views were shot after two-minute hearings by military courts, or no hearings at all. The mass executions even bothered the German attaché, a Nazi, who met with General Franco twice—to no avail—to urge him to stop them.[15]

As in Chile, the uncoordinated and largely extrajudicial violence of this early period was later replaced by a more centralized, judicialized type of repression. This occurred during the course of 1937. On October 31 of that year, the new chief of internal security, public order, and frontier inspection decreed that executions could not take place without a military court passing a sentence. This does not seem to have slowed down the rate of executions, but it did provide a legal cover for the killings. On February 9, 1939, less than two months before the end of the war, the Franco forces promulgated the Law of Political Responsibilities to regulate and civilianize the prosecution of political crimes. This extended the liability for political crimes back to October 1, 1934 (almost two years before the military rebellion that initiated the Franco regime) and included as a political crime "grave passivity." This meant that people who had lived in Republican zones and who had not been members of the government or leftist groups, but who could not demonstrate that they had actively fought against the Republicans were liable for prosecution. Special Courts of Political

Responsibilities were established, composed roughly equally of army officers, civilian judges and Falangist representatives (Payne 1967, 418).

Spanish political justice under Franco was extremely violent; on a per capita basis it was much more violent than Pinochet's Chile. According to official figures of the Spanish Ministry of Justice, 192,684 people were executed or died in prison in Spain between April 1939 and June 30, 1944. (Gallo gives the figure of those executed as around 100,000. The total population of Spain in 1935 was 24 million.) This included 6,000 schoolteachers and 100 out of 430 university professors. The total dead in the civil war is estimated at 560,000, including combatants, victims of bombing raids, those executed, and those who died in prison. Gallo calls Spanish justice in the immediate aftermath of the war "a ruthless machine for dealing death" and lists as some of its features confessions extracted by torture and perfunctory trials. Like the leaders of other authoritarian regimes, the Spanish nationalists were capable of ignoring their own legality when it suited them, as when a defendant was officially reprieved, released by authorities, but then picked up again and shot.[16]

As in Chile, Spanish political trials began as a settling of scores by the new regime and then evolved into a mechanism of social control. While less active in later years, Francoist courts still executed opponents up to the last days of the regime in 1975. Once again, institutional pathways proved hard to reverse—political trials continued throughout the course of the regime, although at a much less intense level than they had in the 1930s. In addition, state institutions were not on a synchronous path—inquisitorial political trials of the early 1970s coexisted with the liberalization of other state institutions. As with other cases of authoritarian legality, the political trials were not stopped until the demise of the regime. This occurred in Spain in a transition negotiated by key figures both within and without the regime.

The course of Spanish legal repression involved a changing relationship between military and judicial elites. In the early days of the regime during the civil war, integration of and cooperation between both sets of elites were practically nonexistent. Courts had largely stopped functioning during the war, and the military took it upon itself to mete out punishments, with or without hastily conducted legal proceedings. As in Chile, the military usurped judicial authority; this phase of the repression resembles Chilean wartime military justice between 1973 and 1978 (even though, in Chile, there was no real war taking place at that time). Subsequently, after the civil war's end in 1939, Spanish authoritarian legality incorporated civilian judges into the special courts, making it roughly comparable to peacetime military justice in Chile from 1978 to 1990. Again, judicial-military consensus was a key component of this judicialization of repression.

Salazarist Portugal

Another important example of authoritarian legality is that of the Salazar regime (1926–1974) in Portugal.[17] Unlike Nazi and Francoist repression, Salazarist repression can be characterized as dictatorial, aimed primarily at containing, rather than exterminating, declared opponents of the regime.[18] This puts it in the top left corner of figure 9.1, closest to the case of Brazil.

Unlike General Franco in neighboring Spain, Salazar was a civilian. While Franco obtained power through force in a civil war, Salazar was granted power by military officers several years after a coup in 1926. While the Nazis and the Franquistas in Spain enjoyed staging theatrical demonstrations of mass support, the Salazar regime—like the 1964–1985 military regime in Brazil—was content with a depoliticized, passively acquiescent population.[19] And like the Brazilian military regime's repression, Salazarist repression came in two distinct waves, the first at the beginning of the regime in 1926 and the second in the middle of its rule, between the electoral campaigns of 1949 and 1958.

In 1933 the Salazar regime created special military tribunals to judge political crimes. Subversion of the "fundamental principles of society" was one of those offenses (Cruz 1988, 87). As in other cases, the roots of these political prosecutions lay in the immediate past, in this case in the conflict between the Communist left and the fascist right in the interwar years. Defendants in political trials could be imprisoned prior to sentencing under the law. The Policia de Defesa Política e Social (Police for Political and Social Defense, or PVDE) was in charge of all phases of the political trials and could determine whether a defendant could remain at liberty during his or her trial or be imprisoned. The PVDE was not overly scrupulous about the law; between 1932 and 1945, 36 percent of the political prisoners that it held in special prisons were incarcerated for more time than their sentences stipulated (Cruz 1988, 88). This is similar to the way in which the Brazilian military regime frequently violated its own laws restricting the detention of political prisoners to a fixed period of time.

In 1945 the special military courts for dealing with political crimes were abolished and replaced with the Plenary Criminal Courts (Tribunais Criminais Plenários, or TCPs), special civilian courts located in Lisbon and Porto. Unlike the military courts, these courts were presided over by judges trained in the law. At the same time, the PVDE was reorganized and renamed the PIDE (Polícia Internacional de Defesa do Estado, or International Police for the Defense of the State).[20] A 1956 decree gave the PIDE the authority to detain politically "dangerous" individuals for six months to three years, renewable for up to another three years (Cruz 1988, 92). After the early 1960s, the PIDE also ran notoriously harsh special prisons for political prisoners in the colonies of Angola and Cape Verde. This gave huge administrative discretion to the PIDE, allowing its officials to run a virtual state within a state, without court power to intervene. Deaths during interrogation by the political police sometimes occurred, and even writs of habeas corpus issued by the Supreme Court were sometimes disrespected by the PIDE. In this sense Portuguese repression was somewhat less judicialized than Brazilian repression under military rule. Furthermore, defendants' right to a lawyer were not guaranteed in political trials. As in Brazil, defendants were routinely convicted solely on the basis of confessions extracted by torture.

Despite the lack of accountability of the Portuguese repressive apparatus, Salazarist political justice was not radical in comparison to prior legality. According to Manuel Braga da Cruz, the repression was "paternalistic" and not aimed at the extermination of opponents. The main target was the Communist Party. As in Brazil from 1964 to 1985, the death penalty was not used (the special courts did not issue death sentences) and sentences were comparatively light (only 9 percent of those convicted in political trials between 1932 and 1945 were sentenced to more than five years in prison).[21]

Salazarist authoritarian legality ended dramatically with the collapse of the regime in the 1974 revolution. (The dictator himself had died several years earlier.) As in Brazil, the personnel of the special courts were not subject to a widespread purge but merely transferred to other parts of the bureaucracy. While the institutions responsible for political trials changed in Portugal, the intensity and scope of political trials rose and fell in line with the political contingencies faced by the regime. Once the machinery of political prosecution was established, it was not dismantled until the regime itself was overthrown by revolution.

The Portuguese case illustrates the effect of a relatively high degree of integration of and consensus between military and judicial elites. As with some of the other cases, political repression became more judicialized and more civilian over time. For most of the regime, political trials were presided over by civilian judges in special courts rather than by military officers themselves. While this institutional configuration was different from military courts in Brazil, in both systems civilian judges trained in the law were pivotal to the administration of a highly legalistic form of repression, unlike the repression of the other two types of authoritarian legality.

Figure 9.1 shows the placement of all three European authoritarian regimes within the matrix presented in the introduction, along with the original cases of Brazil, Chile, and Argentina. The analysis here is illustrative rather than systematic; in it, I suggest that the distinctive pattern of authoritarian legality found in the three Latin American cases can be found elsewhere in the nondemocratic world. Clearly, the European cases are more complicated than my presentations of them here. In particular, the rulers of the executive branch were members of distinctive parties and groups that had their own relationships with the military and judiciary. This complicates our analysis, requiring us to examine the three-way dynamic between each set of elites. Nevertheless, the similarities between the cases are intriguing.

While more cases would have to be analyzed to fully test the framework offered here, it seems likely that gradual and judicialized authoritarian legality —the type represented by military Brazil and Salazarist Portugal—is the most common legal form among authoritarian regimes. This is because few authoritarian rulers even aspire to the ruthlessness of the Nazis or Spanish fascists, let alone achieve it. Most authoritarian regimes muddle along with slightly modified versions of previously created legal systems. Perhaps most interestingly for our own time, democratic regimes may also modify their legal systems in order to deal with political emergencies, which brings us to the case of the United States after September 11, 2001.

The United States after 9/11

Citizens in the United States in the twenty-first century live under a political regime that bears little resemblance to the authoritarian regimes of Brazil and the southern cone. Nevertheless, it is not necessarily inappropriate to compare legal measures taken against presumed political enemies in authoritarian regimes with those adopted in democracies. Differences across regime types should be demonstrated, not assumed. As Franz Neumann points out, modern liberal states have used force to destroy local bases of power that threatened central authorities at various points in their histories (1957, 22). Furthermore, democratic governments have certainly engaged in political trials, especially in wartime. For example, Steven Barkan points out that some two thousand political dissidents were prosecuted in the United States during World War I, mainly for violating laws that forbade most forms of criticism of U.S. involvement in the war (1985, 1).

The attacks in New York City and Washington, D.C., of September 11, 2001, constituted a political emergency that the government of President George W. Bush used to declare a "war" on terrorism and initiate the invasion and occupation of Afghanistan in 2001 and Iraq in 2003. Since 9/11, the United States has moved down and to the right in the matrix in figure 9.1, toward a more radical approach to preexisting legality and toward a greater recourse to extrajudicial measures to deal with perceived threats. A key question is whether this movement is temporary, the effect of a single government, or whether it will become a more long-term attribute of the U.S. state.

The Bush administration accelerated important domestic changes that had already been taking place in the realms of intelligence gathering, policing, the control of immigration, and the legal adjudication of politically motivated crime. These developments combined to place the national security community in the United States in a situation in many ways comparable—despite the very different political environment in which it operated—to those of the Brazilian, Chilean, and Argentine military regimes of the 1960s and 1970s. They also appeared—at least initially—to enjoy very broad support among military and judicial elites in the United States, as well as members of Congress.

Among the parallels between the two sets of situations are the following. First, President Bush signed an emergency order on November 13, 2001, that established military commissions to try noncitizens accused of terrorism. As in Brazil and Chile, the executive in the United States decreed that a terrorist "war" necessitated the use of a special court system, controlled by the executive and insulated from the civilian judiciary. Unlike Brazil and Chile, in the U.S. case this system did not consist of preexisting military courts but was a relatively little-used institution—the military commission or tribunal—that was in many ways more severe than ordinary military justice.[22]

Second, the Bush administration created a new legal regime to deal with suspected terrorists. For citizens, it invented the designation "enemy combatant" and claimed the right to apply this label to anyone it suspected of terrorist activity. These suspects were then indefinitely detained in military facilities, without access to a lawyer and without charges being brought.[23] As for noncitizen terrorist suspects, the Department of Defense decided in early 2002 to call them "unlawful combatants" and place them outside the purview of both U.S. justice and the Third Geneva Convention dealing with prisoners of war. Captured in Afghanistan and incarcerated on the Guantánamo naval base in Cuba, these detainees are subject to the jurisdiction of the military commissions created by President Bush's 2001 order.[24]

These two features of the legal response to the terrorist attacks constitute an extraordinary change in traditional U.S. legality as it relates to political crime. As in Brazil and the southern cone, the policies have produced a debate between their supporters, who feel that they are measured responses to a severe threat, and their critics, who fear the erosion of constitutional rights by the executive.[25]

There are other similarities between the situation in the contemporary United States and the political conflicts in Brazil and the southern cone of the 1960s and 1970s. For example, the use of torture to extract information from terrorist suspects has been condoned by U.S. officials and even advocated by some observers. The White House legal counsel issued a memo not long after 9/11 that said that detainees captured in Afghanistan and held by the United States were not subject to the Geneva Conventions or U.S. law. According to the journalist Seymour Hersh, it was in this climate that Defense Secretary Donald Rumsfeld created a clandestine program in which detainees in Afghanistan, Guantánamo, and later Iraq were interrogated under torture, in the first and third locations sometimes to death.[26] The U.S. government also relied on governments, such as those of Egypt, Morocco, and Saudi Arabia, to supply information extracted from detainees under torture.[27] And a prominent legal scholar even suggested the issuance of "torture writs" to allow judicial authorities to use torture in specific cases.[28] Most notoriously, photographs of the torture of prisoners by American soldiers in Abu Ghraib prison became public in April 2004.[29] It is important to point out that unlike authoritarian Chile and Brazil, in the United States these human rights abuses were thoroughly covered by the press and led to prosecutions of some of the perpetrators among the lower ranks of the military.[30]

Beyond the legal sphere, the "war on terror" has led to important legal and bureaucratic changes to facilitate the centralization of information and prioritize the repression of terrorism. The USA PATRIOT Act, hastily passed by Congress in the wake of 9/11, expanded the powers of law enforcement agencies to monitor and act against suspected terrorist organizations and individuals, building on the 1996 Anti-Terrorism law.[31] Weeks after the attacks, the administration began to dismantle the wall between the Federal Bureau of Investigation (FBI) and the Central Intelligence Agency (CIA), potentially erasing the restrictions against domestic operations of the CIA. The Bush administration also created the Department of Homeland Security, the biggest reorganization of the federal government in fifty years. The new security posture has led to a crackdown on civil society groups alleged to have connections to terrorists, even quite indirect ones.[32] Because the 9/11 attackers were foreign Muslims, the war on terror has been accompanied by an upsurge of patriotic, nationalist, and religious sentiment. Finally, the search for terrorists and their allies has reached into the armed forces themselves, as military personnel have been detained and accused of aiding terrorists.[33] Again, these developments invite comparisons to the policies of the Brazilian and southern cone military regimes.

The military commissions established to try the Guantánamo detainees are in many respects more draconian than Brazilian military courts under military rule. As described in the order, they are to be constituted ad hoc by the Secretary of Defense; in other words, the executive branch would directly control their composition and procedures. The identities of judges and prosecutors are apparently to be kept secret, as with the "faceless courts" sometimes used in Latin America. Defendants would not be allowed any right of appeal to a civilian court, either in the United States or abroad. (Appeals could only be made to panels named by the Secretary of Defense.) Judges in the tribunals were given the leeway to close the trials to the press and public for almost any reason.[34] In all these respects the courts afford fewer procedural rights to defendants and more zealously guard executive privilege than the Brazilian military courts of 1964–1979.

In other respects, the U.S. military commissions will be depressingly familiar to readers of chapters 4 and 5 of this book. The commissions are authorized to sentence defendants to death with a unanimous vote of their members.[35] Federal officials, including President Bush, have publicly suggested that some of the defendants are guilty. Lawyers complain of an inability to adequately represent their clients. Charges in the commissions are likely to involve membership in particular organizations as much as specific actions. And evidence presented by prosecutors is likely to include statements made under duress or even torture.[36]

The creation of the military commissions constitutes a major reform of the judiciary, accomplished by presidential decree. In this special court system, there is little separation between executive power, on one hand, and judicial power, on the other. In classic military style, defendants are first and foremost "enemy combatants," and only secondarily bearers of rights as in the civilian court system. The 2001 emergency order therefore represents a potentially serious breach of the U.S. constitutional tradition and a significant militarization of the judiciary. Together with the unshackling of many legal restraints on law enforcement and intelligence agencies, this act invokes emergency war powers in day-to-day security operations inside the United States, operations that are, or at least up to now have been, essentially civilian in nature.[37]

The assertion that this increase in power holds no danger to U.S. democracy because of the country's "culture of nonjudgmentalism," as argued by Alan Wolfe, is just not credible.[38] The United States is a more tolerant and multicultural country than it was, for example, during World War II, but this tolerance does not always extend to Muslim foreigners, nor to Americans who protest against U.S. military action abroad. In 2004 a law enforcement official was quoted as saying "You can make an easy kind of link that, if you have a protest group protesting a war where the cause that's being fought against is international terrorism, you might have terrorism at this protest. You can almost argue that a protest against that is a terrorist act. I've heard terrorism described as anything that is violent or has an economic impact. Terrorism isn't just bombs going off and killing people."[39] Older residents of Brazil, Argentina, and Chile will be familiar with this logic.

The U.S. military seems serious that the "war on terrorism" is a war, even though it is not a conventional interstate conflict and it has a nebulous and shifting array of declared enemies that includes United States citizens, United States resident aliens, and noncitizens alike. If this is the case, then it suggests that the U.S. executive branch is claiming huge, unprecedented new prerogatives to monitor, detain, and punish people all over the globe, in ways that clearly strike at the heart of democratic rights in its own country. If, as Andrew Arato writes, "Constitutionalist self-limitation of elected power . . . [is] the one truly American achievement" in the political realm, then it is not clear that this achievement will entirely survive the onslaught of the "war on terrorism."[40] U.S. law professor Laurence Tribe invoked a southern cone military regime when he talked about the treatment of citizens accused of being "enemy combatants." He said that in these cases the government is "asserting power akin to that exercised in dictatorships like Argentina, when they just 'disappeared' people from their homes with no access to counsel, no list of the detained or executed."[41]

A review of the historical record of the use of military courts in Brazil and Chile alerts us to the fact that such courts are often a convenient tool of executives anxious to avoid compromise, dialogue, and the give-and-take of democracy. The expansion of military court jurisdiction, invoked in response to specific, seemingly unique emergencies, is often gradually ratcheted upward to encompass more people and circumstances. Over time, its pro-prosecutorial bias allows investigators, prosecutors, and judges to get sloppy about evidence and procedures, violating rights and giving the executive branch the benefit of every doubt. The result is the emergence of an unaccountable state within a state. The preemptory manner in which the 2001 order was decreed is itself disturbing.

However, considerable conflict over the executive branch's legal response to terrorism has occurred and will continue to grow. A small band of commentators in the news media criticized the order to create the military commissions.[42] Some of this criticism may have had an effect, because in addition to modifying the original order, the Bush administration placed the accused terrorists Richard Reid and Zacarias Moussaoui, as well as the "American Taliban" John Walker Lindh, on trial in civilian, federal courts. Perhaps more importantly, judicial elites—law professors, legal commentators, and some prosecutors and judges—have begun to criticize the executive's claims to be able to indefinitely detain prisoners, both citizens and non-citizens.[43] One such critic characterized the architects of the federal government's detention policies as "executive power absolutists."[44]

The most significant conflicts over these issues will involve judicial elites, on one side, and the military and civilian proponents of militarized law on the other, with groups of activists across the ideological spectrum also playing an important role. Already, judges have ruled against the executive branch in several high-profile cases. For example, in October 2003, a federal judge ruled that accused 9/11 terrorist Zacarias Moussaoui should not face the death penalty because the government would not allow his defense lawyers to question al Qaeda prisoners. In this case, the right of defense to have the same access to witness testimony and other forms of evidence was upheld by the court. The government lawyers had claimed that the right had to be restricted in the interests of national security.[45]

More sweepingly, in June of 2004 the U.S. Supreme Court partially rejected the Bush administration's positions in three cases involving the rights of detainees held in the war on terrorism. The most important, and the biggest reversal for the government, was *Hamdi v. Rumsfeld*. In it, the court ruled that a U.S. citizen held as an "enemy combatant" in the United States has a right to a hearing to determine the legality of his incarceration. While the court did not rule that a U.S. citizen could not be tried by a military tribunal, it did uphold the right of detainees to a notice of the charges against them, an opportunity to contest those charges, and the right to appear before an ostensibly neutral authority. In *Rasul v. Bush* and *Al Odah v. United States*, the court ruled that prisoners being held in Guantánamo Bay had the right to present legal objections to their detentions in federal courts.[46]

Other important rulings followed the Supreme Court decisions. In late January 2005 a U.S. district court judge ruled that Guantánamo detainees may challenge their incarceration in U.S. courts, because the military tribunals handling their cases violate the U.S. Constitution. And in late February 2005 another federal judge ruled that President Bush had no constitutional power to indefinitely imprison "enemy combatant" José Padilla and the government either had to charge or release him.[47] While both of these judgments have been appealed, they suggest that the extraordinary powers claimed by the executive after 9/11 will be at least partially and incrementally rolled back by the U.S. judiciary.

The case of the United States is an important one for an understanding of political justice. If we can recognize the occasional existence of a limited "judicial space" and some procedural rights for defendants under an authoritarian regime, as we have in this book in the Brazilian case, we must also be alert to the possibility of the development of authoritarian legality in a democracy. Put another way, democracies can modify their legal systems in ways that undermine their rule of law characteristics, fortifying arbitrary executive power and unshackling military and security forces. The important point to note is that when that occurs, it is judicial-military conflict—not consensus—that can serve as a mechanism by which individual rights are protected.

The open question about the U.S. case is therefore to what extent judicial elites will eventually challenge the prerogatives claimed by the executive branch and rule that some powers—such as the right to indefinitely detain citizens deemed to be "enemy combatants," or to try noncitizen terrorist suspects in the special military commissions—are unconstitutional.[48] After both World Wars I and II, the U.S. judiciary rolled back some of the emergency powers claimed by the executive during those conflicts. Such a scaling back of executive privilege has begun to take place during the "war on terrorism," but it is also far too early to make a definitive judgment on how the "war" will reshape the legal treatment of opposition and dissent in the United States.[49] This is an extremely important conflict in which both the unique constitutional tradition and extraordinary protection of basic rights in the United States are at stake.

The Dynamics of Military-Judicial Relations
under Different Regimes

A comparison of the Brazilian and southern cone cases with European dictatorships suggests that the framework developed to explain variation in the legality of the former—one that emphasizes the degree of integration of and consensus among military and judicial elites—may shed light on the legality of other authoritarian regimes. It may illuminate the legal choices and practices, not just of military regimes, but of the type of classic party dictatorship that emerged in the twentieth century. The U.S. case suggests that the framework may have to be modified when applied to democracies. In the United States, unlike under the military regimes of Brazil and the southern cone, military-judicial consensus and integration have not been a moderating force in the legal response to terrorism, because they have reduced rather than enlarged the space in which defense lawyers and civil society groups can defend the rights of suspects.

It appears that in democratic regimes, military-judicial conflict, rather than cooperation, can serve to constrain the executive's legal strategy, opening up space for the defense of constitutional guarantees. In authoritarian regimes, the military often has the power and autonomy to engage in extrajudicial repression. If there is too much military-judicial conflict and military officers see the judiciary as an obstacle to their mission, they resort to direct repression. In such a system, judicial-military integration and consensus provide a rule-bound system in which "trustworthy" courts can favor the regime, while preserving some physical guarantees for political prisoners. Where civilian control of the military is more secure, as in many democratic regimes, conflict within and between military and judicial elites over national security law may instead have the beneficial effect of preserving individual rights that might otherwise be suppressed. The dynamics of political justice therefore may be very different depending on the nature of the political regime.

10

The Puzzle of Authoritarian Legality

WHY DO AUTHORITARIAN regimes bother with legal maneuvers, changes to the law, complicated and time-consuming formal procedures, and trials? If they come to power by force, why don't they continue to rule by force and force alone, dropping all pretenses to legality? Given that most of them do not, and instead attempt to judicialize their repression, why do some regimes achieve this judicialization more extensively and effectively than others? Similarly, why are some more radical in their approach to previous legality than others? Finally, what difference does variation in authoritarian legality make for the scope and intensity of repression?

Existing approaches to these questions are not wholly satisfactory. For example, variations in authoritarian legality under military regimes cannot be adequately explained as resulting from the strength of the opposition facing the regimes. Similarly, broad generalizations about differences in political culture do not appear to easily fit the cases analyzed here. Instead, this book suggests that the beginnings of robust answers to these questions can be found in institutions and history. Specifically, the cases of Brazil, Chile, and Argentina show that attempts by judicial and military organizations to impose institutional solutions to the problem of organizing repression succeed and bind them together, or fail and drive them apart. The degree of military and judicial consensus, integration, and cooperation is a key neglected variable in unlocking the puzzle of variation in authoritarian legality.

This book therefore suggests a two-part answer to the question, why do authoritarian regimes bother to judicialize repression? First, all other things being equal, there are advantages to authoritarian regimes in legitimating their rule with some kind of appeal to the law. Legal manipulations and political trials are useful to a regime because they can demobilize popular oppositional movements efficiently, reducing the need to exercise force; garner legitimacy for the regime by showing that it "plays fair" in dealing with opponents; create positive political images for the regime and negative ones for the opposition; under some circumstances, help one faction gain power over another within the regime; and stabilize the repression by providing information and a predictable set of rules around which opponents and government officials' expectations can coalesce.

The second part of the answer is that authoritarian regimes judicialize repression because they can. Given that judicialization has advantages for authoritarian regimes, those that judicialize repression are able to rely on "trustworthy" courts—courts, either civilian or military, that will produce verdicts in line with the regime's conception of legality and not challenge the fundamentals of regime rule. However, such trustworthy courts have to be produced by trial and error, over time. That is not easy, and the courts must be flexible enough to adapt to new exigencies of regime rule. Traditional legal establishments may also resist these new exigencies. Sometimes the attempts to create trustworthy courts succeed, building up a consensus across military and judicial elites, and at other times they fail. When regimes resort to extrajudicial violence and an all-out assault on traditional legality, it is often because they have failed to manipulate the law and courts to their advantage. Behind a dirty war probably lies an organizational failure—the collapse of a trustworthy court that was ready to prosecute regime opponents under authoritarian laws. Regimes therefore resort to widespread terror and force when they lack the organizational means to institute more judicialized forms of repression.

In identifying this mechanism, this book does not claim to have constructed a universal theory of political development, nor does it deny the many idiosyncrasies of the Argentine, Brazilian, and Chilean military regimes. In isolating two state organizations—the military and the judiciary—and studying their relationship, we inevitably lose sight of other factors that may also be vitally important in understanding authoritarian legality, such as ideology; ethnic, racial, gender, and class divisions; and broader legal cultures. Nevertheless, in the literature on authoritarian regimes, regime dynamics are sometimes reduced to the struggle between regime leaders and their opponents. I have attempted to go beyond such a perspective in this book.

When analysts have examined intra-regime and inter-elite relations, they have often kept their focus broad. For example, Guillermo O'Donnell recognized that the Brazilian and southern cone military regimes were distinctive because of the nature of their alliance between the military and members of technical and administrative elites as well as the transnationalized capitalist class (1973). He recognized that the effectiveness of these new authoritarian regimes was in part the product of an increase in the overall capacities of the state to administer society, or what Michael Mann calls infrastructural power (1993, 59–63). I have attempted to build on these insights by showing how such infrastructural power was constructed in the judicial realm, shifting the focus from the macropolitical level to the long-term micromechanisms that operated between two sets of "middle managers" of the state apparatus: judicial elites, particularly judges, prosecutors, and law professors; and military officers. As we have seen, even apparently similar regimes can be based on quite different institutional arrangements and understandings between these two elite groups, built up over years of conflict, compromise, and trial and error. These arrangements and understandings have serious consequences for the victims of authoritarian repression, and many of their characteristics predate the creation of the authoritarian regime itself.

Similar Origins, Different Legalities

Carl Friedrich claims that under Roman dictatorship four conditions limited the power of the dictator, and that these limitations are relevant to the consideration of emergency government in the modern era. The conditions are that the appointment of the dictator take a constitutional form; the dictator must not have the power to declare or terminate the state of emergency; dictatorial power can be exercised for only a precise, limited time, and the limit cannot be indefinitely extended; and the ultimate goal of constitutional emergency powers must be the return to the constitutional order.[1]

The military regimes in Brazil and the southern cone analyzed in this book did not meet any of these four conditions. First, they all came to power through unconstitutional means as coups that deposed a legitimately elected president. Second, the coup leaders took it upon themselves to declare the extent and duration of the emergency, drastically limiting the power of other branches and levels of government in order to preserve ample discretionary powers for the military president—not elected by popular vote—and his advisors. Third, the regimes kept extending the time period of their exceptional rule, and finally, none returned to the prior constitution.[2] These regimes were therefore similar in constitutional terms; each was a "rule by law" rather than a "rule of law," meaning that the sovereign could exempt itself from rules and exercise power directly by force (Maravall and Przeworski 2003, 3).

However, as we have seen, the regimes differed widely in how such discretion was wielded. They exhibit considerable variation in what I have called their modes of political justice. Where judicial-military consensus, cooperation, and integration were high, regime repression was largely judicialized, and the legal system was modified conservatively and incrementally. Where the military broke with judicial elites, repression was a radical, largely extrajudicial assault on traditional legal procedures. Where the military and judiciary were quite separate, and cooperation limited, repression took a form that was midway between these two poles.

This book has explained such variation with a historical-institutional argument that traces how each military regime's basic legal approach grew out of the politics of previous regimes in each country. Inter-elite relations mattered because they affected patterns of repression and thus the parameters within which non-elites could resist authoritarian rule. Distinctive institutional approaches to opposition and dissent could be discerned in Brazil, Chile, and Argentina in the decades prior to the military dictatorships of the 1960s and 1970s. Military rejection of judicial constraint, military usurpation of judicial authority, and military integration and cooperation with at least some judicial elites are the basic patterns that can be seen in Argentina, Chile, and Brazil, respectively. These different patterns in each case influenced key decisions after military coups that laid the foundations for new systems of authoritarian legality.

A high degree of organizational integration and consensus between military and judicial elites can be found in Brazil, where the military regime was the most conservative and gradualist, and where there was the least amount of extrajudicial political repression of the three cases. In contrast, the Argentine military regime's political justice involved widespread extrajudicial violence. Its military and judicial elites had a low degree of integration and consensus and were both marked by factionalism, purges, and mutual mistrust between the two corporate bodies. Chile lies between the Brazilian and Argentine cases both in the extent of its extrajudicial violence and departure from preexisting legal norms, on one hand, and the degree of its judicial-military integration and consensus, on the other.

My argument is therefore that institutional trial and error matters to the form of authoritarian legality. Brazil's hybrid military justice system, forged well before the military regime, was brought into service by regime leaders to prosecute civilians in 1965. The courts imposed record-keeping requirements on the security forces that did not abolish arbitrary behavior but made lethal violence less likely than in systems without such procedures. The prior existence of this system meant that even when regime repression hardened in late 1968, a large-scale dirty war did not ensue. Instead, suspected members of the armed left were prosecuted in the military courts and relatively few were killed.

In Chile the separation between military and judicial elites prior to the coup was greater than in Brazil, so that rather than fully cooperate with the judiciary, the military, once in power, largely usurped judicial authority and declared its right to try civilians in "wartime" military courts. Trials in these courts, unlike their Brazilian counterparts, were rapid, purely military, and not subject to appeal. Like Brazilian military justice, Chile's military courts produced acceptable results from the point of view of regime leaders. The Supreme Court did not challenge these results, leading to the endurance of this legal system and its subsequent modification into a peacetime military justice system in 1978.

In Argentina, prior institutional failure helps explain the radical and extrajudicial dirty war. The National Penal Court was a special court created under military rule in 1971 to prosecute political prisoners. It convicted hundreds of defendants over a two-year period, but it was abolished in 1973 when the Peronists returned to power, and all of the prisoners who had been convicted were amnestied and released. Military officers saw this failure to judicialize repression as requiring new tactics, and dirty war practices subsequently escalated. When the military seized power again in 1976, the dirty war became national policy.

This argument suggests that variations in authoritarian legality cannot be ascribed purely to ideological or attitudinal differences among military officers or judicial elites in each country. Expressions of an exterminationist dirty war mentality by military and judicial elites can be found in the historical record in all three countries. Instead, this study suggests that institutional constraints on the security forces at moments of political conflict shaped the authoritarian legality of each regime.

The form of authoritarian legality matters to political prisoners as well as to the security forces. I argue that the Brazilian system gave defense lawyers for political prisoners and supportive civil society organizations the greatest room to defend individual rights as well as protest authoritarian legality. Within Brazil's hybrid military courts and gradualist and conservative legal system, judges were generally reluctant to convict certain categories of defendants, such as clerics. They were also less likely to convict defendants accused of certain types of crimes than others. Defendants accused of newer crimes created by the most recent national security legislation and crimes such as offenses against authority that did not necessarily involve "subversive" intent were convicted at lower rates than defendants accused of traditional crimes involving violence, such as armed robbery. Furthermore, defense lawyers were able to move the boundaries of legal interpretation over time, rolling back some of the most repressive interpretations of national security law. For example, by the late 1970s a judge even acquitted a defendant because of evidence that he had been tortured while in detention, a concession to human rights norms that had been routinely violated by judges in previous eras.

A further point is that political trials "worked" for the regimes that used them. That is, they stabilized expectations on both sides of the repression-opposition divide, gave the security forces greater flexibility in dealing with opponents, helped to marginalize and de-legitimate the opposition, purchased some credibility for the regimes both at home and abroad, and provided regime leaders with information about both the opposition and the security forces, thus facilitating the adaptation and readjustment of repressive policies. It is also plausible that the political trials in both Brazil and Chile helped to consolidate and prolong authoritarian rule. It may not be a coincidence that the shortest-lived military regime of the three examined here, the Argentine, was also the one that engaged in the most extrajudicial repression.

Otto Kirchheimer wrote, "Justice in political matters is the most ephemeral of all divisions of justice; a turn of history may undo its work" (Kirchheimer 1961, 429). While political justice may be undone quickly when political circumstances change, legacies of authoritarian legality appear to have endured far beyond the moment of democratic transition in Brazil and the southern cone. This book suggests that there is no real escape from the challenge of building the rule of law in post-authoritarian democracies. Each form of authoritarian legality leaves a distinctive legacy that has to be surmounted by democratic reformers. In Argentina, the law was skirted, violated, and broken, and the rule of law had to be reconstituted. In Brazil, the law was manipulated, bent, and abused, and had to be reformed. The first challenge was probably met better than the second, in part because in Argentina there was broad consensus that reform was necessary. Brazil experienced the least transitional justice after democratic transition of all three cases, in part because the gradualist and conservative authoritarian legality of its military regime involved the participation of much of the legal and military establishments and continued to be legitimized under democracy. Thus Brazil did not witness the kind of reformist backlash that occurred in Argentina and Chile, in which coalitions with significant political support were able to overturn key aspects of authoritarian legality and reform the judiciary, the military, or both. This book therefore suggests a paradox. Conservative legal systems such as the Brazilian may prevent some violence on the part of the security forces, but they are likely to be far more intractable once authoritarian rule ends.

The counterargument to the position taken here is that military-judicial integration and consensus did *not* affect the legal forms of repression in these military regimes. This is certainly a hypothesis that should be seriously considered. Within this perspective, courts do not impose meaningful restrictions on the actions of security forces in authoritarian regimes; police-military action is autonomous and decisive, and legal decisions are primarily ex post facto justifications for state violence. Security forces do what they want; the courts are mere appendages of the police and prisons and not vice versa.[3]

This book has argued against such a view. One does not have to subscribe to the whole panorama of liberal pieties about the law to recognize that even military leaders who come to power through force of arms might be willing to grant some—often very limited—autonomy to courts, and that courts and the systems of rules that they interpret can therefore influence the behavior of security forces even under authoritarian rule.[4] The legal orientation of authoritarian regimes has some effect on security forces; extrajudicial repression—in both authoritarian and democratic regimes—tends to be more violent when it is less accountable and less regulated. Judicialized repression tends to be more constrained, even when judiciaries are not genuinely independent of the executive, because they impose record-keeping requirements and some degree of transparency on the state's proceedings.

Despite military rulers' frequent resort to revolutionary rhetoric, their approach to prior legality is often gradualist and conservative—they do not intend nor do they attempt to rebuild legal systems from scratch. Similarly, they often judicialize regime repression to some degree. Furthermore, this matters.

Where repression is judicialized, regime opponents are likely to have a few more rights and a little more space in which to contest regime prerogatives.

In the cases of Nazi Germany, Franco's Spain, and Salazarist Portugal, as in the Latin American cases, a lack of cooperation and integration between judicial and military elites led to more extrajudicial repression, and its presence led to the opposite. However, we need to modify our framework somewhat when dealing with authoritarian regimes that are not dominated by the military. In these types of nonmilitary authoritarian regimes, the rulers of the executive branch emerge more clearly as separate actors, creating a three-way dynamic between the executive and military and judicial elites.

The post-9/11 United States suggests another way in which the framework developed for Brazil and the southern cone might have to be altered if applied to other cases. In democratic regimes, military-judicial conflict, rather than co-operation, can serve to restrain the arbitrary exercise of executive power and open up space for the defense of individual rights.

In authoritarian regimes, the military often has the ability to resort to extrajudicial repression. If military officers feel that judicial opposition poses too great an obstacle to their anti-insurgency operations, they are likely to circumvent the courts. Where such defection is an ever-present danger, judicial-military integration and consensus provide a rule-bound system in which "trustworthy" courts can favor the regime, while preserving some physical guarantees for political prisoners.

However, where civilian control of the military is more secure, as in many democratic regimes, military escape from judicial constraint is far less likely. In such a setting, it is conflict within and between military and judicial elites—not cooperation—that is likely to best protect the individual liberties of those targeted by national security law. The dynamics of political justice may consequently vary significantly by regime type.

The Rule of Law, Authoritarian Legality, and Emergency Rule

This book has undoubtedly raised more questions than it has answered. However, such questions deserve to be researched and debated, because the political and legal issues covered in the preceding pages are likely to remain important for many years to come. The legal response of both authoritarian and democratic regimes to political emergencies and the ability of new democracies to escape the negative legacies of authoritarian legality are important for at least three reasons.

First, the legal dimension of authoritarian regimes has been neglected. While it is easy to regard authoritarian legality with what E. P. Thompson called the "enormous condescension of posterity," ignoring these laws—and the people who struggled against them—will do little to enhance our understanding of how authoritarian regimes actually work.[5] Too often comparative political scientists become trapped by regime typologies that assume relationships and outcomes that should actually be researched and that upon closer inspection appear to be built on sand. In addition, we tend to study state organizations such as the military and the judiciary in isolation, neglecting relations between them and the way that they can change over time.[6] We need a fusion of formerly separate subfields if our understanding of authoritarian legality is to be enhanced.

This study has suggested that the classic distinction between de jure constitutional democracies and de facto authoritarian regimes based on force obscures an enormous gray area of legality perpetrated by legalistic authoritarian regimes. These regimes use law in a variety of bewildering, frightening, and sometimes absurd ways, and they have evolved over time toward more or less reliance on law. Furthermore, our assumptions about law under authoritarian regimes may blind us to the ability of defense lawyers to protect the individual rights of defendants even in these highly manipulated and repressive legal systems. In this regard, the courageous achievements of Brazilian defense lawyers in the military courts form one of the few bright spots in my narrative, filled as it is with torture, killing, and terror perpetrated by state agents acting with staggering cruelty and impunity.

Second, we need to focus more on how authoritarian regimes differ from one another due to variation in their approaches to the law. Equally, we need to examine the differences between authoritarian regimes and democracies that resort to emergency measures. This book suggests that an important way to measure regimes is to distinguish them along two axes: their degree of conservatism vis-à-vis preexisting law, and the degree to which they judicialize their repression.

Third, as Jennifer Schirmer writes, "we need to examine precisely how national security becomes, or remains, structured within democratic governing apparatuses" (1996, 94). Transitions to democracy very rarely wipe out—in one dramatic reform—the accretion of years and sometimes decades of authoritarian practices and mentalities in militaries and judiciaries. Democracies in Brazil and the southern cone have been rocked by continuing violence and repressive practices by state security forces; inefficient, politically manipulated and frequently corrupt judiciaries; and the failure to create genuinely democratic and durable institutions that link the public with political representatives. They share this condition with many other democracies created during the last thirty years in the so-called third wave of democratization in Latin America, Eastern Europe, Africa, and Asia (Huntington 1991). Third-wave democracies are all too often illiberal and unjust.

Responses to this reality have varied. Some scholars argue that too much democracy can be a bad thing, and that it may be better for third-wave polities to fortify the institutions of "liberty" before subjecting their leaders to majoritarian constraints (Zakaria 2003). But such a prescription stems from a faulty diagnosis—that new democracies are most threatened by unreasonable "masses" (rather than autocratic elites) and that narrow nineteenth-century conceptions of the rule of law are sufficient for twenty-first-century political systems.[7] A more promising line of work points to the creativity and energy of ordinary people in constructing new institutional solutions to problems of governance (Avritzer 2002). Thus legal institutions in new democracies can be vivified through reforms emanating from democratic participation, discussion, and debate. At present, they are too often the ossified remnants of previous processes of state formation, more reflective of their authoritarian foundational moments than of contemporary realities.

Finally, the historical-institutional approach to legality suggests that both authoritarian and democratic regimes are apt to modify legal structures in response to political emergencies. These modifications can parallel each other even if the overall political context under each type of regime is different. Leaders of democracies in the age of the "war on terrorism" may be tempted to create fortresslike protections of the state's national security interests, making extravagant claims of executive privilege and eroding the very civil liberties that they claim to defend (Arato 2002). At such a time, studying the history of prior attempts to codify the state's claims to national security in other times and places is not just an academic exercise. It is a sobering warning to citizens of democracies that their rights, too, may be dismantled one law, one executive order, one administrative procedure at a time. State violence, politically manipulated legality, and gross injustice are ever-present dangers in all political regimes.

Appendix 1

A NOTE ON SOURCES AND DATA

The sources for the evidence used in this book are many and varied. In Brazil, an archive of all the cases that reached the Superior Tribunal Militar (STM) from 1964 to 1979 exists and is open to the public. This is due not to the good graces of the military itself, which was always reluctant to make the record public, but to the Brasil: Nunca Mais project organized by the Archdiocese of São Paulo, which secretly photocopied the STM's cases over a period of five years. I consulted and made my own copies of some of these documents in the Edgar Leuenroth archive at the State University of Campinas (UNICAMP) in São Paulo, mostly in 1994 and 1995. The Brasil: Nunca Mais cases are now available in the United States. They can be ordered on microfilm from the Center for Research Libraries (see http://www.crl.edu).

The cases in the Nunca Mais archive were tried in the first instance in one of twenty-one courts in twelve military districts located throughout the country. The busiest venues by far were Rio de Janeiro and São Paulo. Cases were then appealed to the STM. Altogether, there are 707 cases involving 7,367 defendants in the archive. I compiled quantitative information on 257 of these cases (36 percent of the total) with 2,109 defendants (29 percent of the total). This information is presented in chapter 4. The samples of the tables in chapter 4 vary slightly, because information from some cases was missing. I consulted court documents from over fifty cases for the qualitative material presented in chapter 7. Law journals and books by defense lawyers and pro-regime legal experts were the sources for the discussion of the legal and ideological dimensions of the trials discussed throughout the book.

In Chile, no archive comparable to the Brazilian one exists. The military claimed that a terrorist attack—a terribly accurate and destructive one, at that—burned it down. Therefore, I was forced to rely on summaries of the cases written by defense lawyers working for the Vicaría de la Solidaridad (Vicariate of Solidarity), an umbrella organization of churches that provided legal defense to political prisoners. These summaries lack crucial documents that can be found in the Brasil: Nunca Mais archive, such as court opinions, but are quite detailed. The data on Chilean military trials presented in chapter 5 was culled from the Vicaría's four-volume compilation of cases, which I obtained in 1998. The data concern 406 cases with 2,689 defendants from 31 military courts throughout the country during the period 1973–1988. This constitutes about 45 percent of the roughly 6,000 defendants believed to have been tried in Chile's military courts from 1973 to 1978.

While there is a rich literature on Argentina's two most recent military regimes and their opponents, evidence from Argentina's political trials is sparser than it is for either Brazil or Chile. Neither an archive nor summaries of the few military court cases against civilians in the period 1976–1983 exist for consultation. The story of Argentine political justice presented in chapter 6 is thus based mainly on secondary sources, some primary documents including newspapers, and interviews. A list of the interviews conducted in Argentina, as well as Brazil and Chile, can be found in appendix 2.

Some mention should be made of the trial data on Brazil and Chile used in this book. The data come from trials in various parts of both countries, involving a variety of defendants over long periods of military rule. They allow an analyst to make important generalizations about patterns in the political trials that could not be made by reading through the archives on a case-by-case basis. However, they are not random samples and as such do not allow definitive statements about some topics. For example, the Brazilian archive only contains cases that were appealed to the higher military court, and thus omits all cases that ended at the first level of the system. Similarly, my sample has more cases from the early period of military rule (1964–1967) than it does from the period that contained the most trials (1967–1973). This book cannot therefore definitively settle certain quantitative issues such as the total number of people tried under military rule in Brazil and Chile and their sentences. I do, however, use the Brazilian and Chilean material to make inferences about the total universe of cases. In methodological terms this is not ideal, but in comparative politics, limitations of data should not prevent scholars from doing the best they can with the data they have. Comparative politics also struggles with the problem of too few cases and too many variables, but that does not necessarily constitute grounds for its abandonment.

In addition to the sources already mentioned, I conducted supplemental research in a variety of archives. The archive, its location, and the type of documents I consulted are listed below.

Government Documents, Bobst Library, New York University, NY: U.S. documents on Brazil from the 1960s and 1970s.

Government Documents, Widener Library, Harvard University, Cambridge, MA: transcripts of the national congresses of Argentine, Brazil, Chile, and Uruguay, various years.

Government Documents and Latin American Library, Howard-Tilton Library, Tulane University, New Orleans, LA: newspapers from Brazil, Chile, and the United States and U.S. government documents.

International Legal Studies Library, Harvard University Law School, Cambridge, MA: institutional acts and decrees issued by military governments in Argentina, Brazil, Chile, and Uruguay, various years.

Library of Congress, Buenos Aires, Argentina: newspapers during the years
1971–1973.

Military Club (*Circulo Militar*), Buenos Aires, Argentina: periodicals from the
years 1971–1983.

National Library, Buenos Aires, Argentina: magazines from the years 1971–1973. .

São Paulo State Archive, Sao Paulo, Brazil, Section on the Department of Political
and Social Order (DEOPS): political police files from the military regime.

Vicaría de la Solidaridad, Santiago, Chile: cases involving political prisoners from
the period 1973–1989.

Tortura Nunca Mais, Recife, Pernambuco, Brazil: press clippings from the period
of military rule.

The Latin American periodicals that I drew upon and their locations are listed below:

Brazil Focus Weekly Report, Brasília

Clarín, Buenos Aires

Folha de São Paulo, São Paulo

O Globo, Rio de Janeiro

Jornal da Bahia, Salvador

Jornal do Brasil, Rio de Janeiro

El Mercurio, Santiago

La Nación, Buenos Aires

El Observador, Santiago

Veja, São Paulo

Appendix 2

INTERVIEWS

Abregu, Martin, Executive Director, Center for Legal Studies (CELS), Buenos Aires, June 12, 1997.

Acuña, Carlos, former human rights activist with the Justice and Peace Service (human rights NGO) and academic, Buenos Aires, June 11, 1997.

Antunes, Rubmaier, Secretary for the Commission on the Disappeared, Brazilian Congress, Brasília, November 17, 1994.

Araújo, Amparo, President, local chapter of Torture Never Again, Recife, Pernambuco, Brazil, July 12, 2002.

Argibay, Carmen M., Judge, Oral Criminal Court Number 2, Buenos Aires, June 20, 1997.

Arns, Archbishop Dom Paulo Evaristo, São Paulo, November 1, 1994.

Barone Nucci, Fernando Sergio, prosecutor, state military justice system, São Paulo, October 17, 1996.

Bickford, Louis, consultant, Ford Foundation, Santiago, June 22 and June 26, 1998.

Bicudo, Deputado Hélio, Federal Deputy (Workers' Party), São Paulo, January 23, 1995.

Brett, Sebastian, researcher for Human Rights Watch, Santiago, July 6, 1998.

Caneva, Franco, Jr., prosecutor, state military justice system, São Paulo, October 17, 1996.

Caride, Susana, journalist and former political prisoner, Buenos Aires, June 26, 1997.

Carneiro, Maria Madalena, secretary for the Commission on the Disappeared, Brazilian Congress, telephone interview, Brasília, December 27, 1994.

Cattani, Judge Horacio R., member, Judges for Democracy (professional association), Buenos Aires, July 2, 1997.

Caucoto, Nelson, former lawyer for the Vicaría de la Solidaridad, Santiago, July 1, 1998.

Correa Sutil, Jorge, law professor at the Universidad Diego Portales and secretary of the Rettig Commission, Santiago, June 19, 1998.

Corrêa, Dr. Getúlio, President, Association of Judges in the State Military Justice System, Florianópolis, Santa Catarina, Brazil, September 25 and 30, 1996.

Dallari, Dalmo, law professor, former lawyer for political prisoners and former president, Justice and Peace Commission in São Paulo, 1970–80, São Paulo, October 30 1996.

Dalton, Army General (retired) Eugenio A., advisor to Senator Losada, Argentine Congress, Buenos Aires, July 1, 1997.

D'Angelis, Dr. Wagner Rocha, former defense lawyer for political prisoners and State Secretary of Human Rights in Paraná, Curitiba, Brazil, July 15, 2003.

de Bastos, Prof. Edmundo José, Júnior, former chief minister for military affairs in the state government of Santa Catarina, and former judge in the state military justice system, Florianópolis, Santa Catarina, Brazil, September 25, 1996.

de Oliveira, Dr. Edmundo Franca, judge in the Rio Centro bombing case and president, Association of Judges in the Federal Military Justice System, Rio de Janeiro, November 22, 1996.

de Sá Bierrenbach, Admiral Júlio, former judge, Superior Military Court, 1977–1987, Rio de Janeiro, November 27, 1996.

Duhalde, Judge Eduardo, 29th Oral Criminal Court, and former lawyer for political prisoners, Buenos Aires, June 12, 1997.

Espinoza Pino, Alberto, lawyer for political prisoners, Santiago, June 22 and 24, 1998.

Ferreira, Dr. Celio Lobão, former military court judge, Brasília, written response to questionnaire received December 10, 1996.

Fletes, Professor José Francisco, former political detainee, Florianópolis, Santa Catarina, Brazil, September 25, 1996.

Freire, Alipio, former political prisoner, São Paulo, January 31, 1995, October 21 and 30, 1996.

Frühling, Hugo, political scientist, Universidad de Chile, Santiago, June 30, 1998.

Funari, Antonio, former lawyer for political prisoners, former political prisoner, and president of the Justice and Peace Commission in São Paulo, São Paulo, November 6, 1996.

Gaggero, Manuel, former lawyer for political prisoners and political exile, Buenos Aires, July 2, 1997.

Garretón Merino, Carmen, Archivo de la Fundación de la Vicaría de la Solidaridad, Santiago, June 15, 1998.

Garretón Merino, Roberto, former chief of the Juridical Department of the Vicaría de la Solidaridad, Santiago, June 22 and 23, 1998.

Gaspari, Elio, journalist, São Paulo, November 11, 1996.

Genoíno Neto, José, Federal Deputy (Workers' Party), São Paulo, November 7, 1994.

Ghio, José Mario, historian, Di Tella University, Buenos Aires, June 12, 1997.

Godoy, João, director of documentary film about the disappeared, *Vala Comun (Mass Grave)*, São Paulo, January 28, 1995.

González Gartland, Dr. Carlos A., lawyer, former lawyer for political prisoners and human rights activist, Buenos Aires, June 17, 1997.

Gonzalez Poblete, Dr. Alejandro, organizer of 4-volume *Jurisprudencia* series on military court trials in 1975–1989, former member of the Vicaría, former president of the Corporación Nacional de Reparación y Reconciliación, Santiago, June 12, 1998.

Gonzalez, Felipe, professor of law, Universidad Diego Portales, Santiago, July 2, 1998.

Goyret, General (retired) Teofilo, Buenos Aires, June 23, 1997.

Groisman, Enrique, director, National High School of Buenos Aires, lawyer, and author on legal issues, Buenos Aires, June 30, 1997.

Guimarães, Cleber, public information officer, Superior Military Court, Brasília, November 19, 1996.

Hanashiro, Dr. Getúlio, former defendant in military court trial and state legislator, São Paulo, October 18, 1996.

Karam, Dra. Maria Lúcia, judge, federal military justice system, Rio de Janeiro, November 22, 1996.

Kushner, Beatriz, researcher into political police archives in São Paulo and Rio de Janeiro and university professor, Rio de Janeiro, November 27, 1996.

Limongi, Dr. Celso, secretary of the professional association Judges for Democracy and judge, São Paulo, November 14, 1996.

Lira, Elizabeth, psychologist and researcher, ILADES (Instituto Latinoamericano de Doctrina y Estudios Sociales), Santiago, June 8, 1998.

Lopez Dawson, Carlos, lawyer and author of *Justicia Militar: Una Nueva Mirada*, Santiago, June 30, 1998.

Maslaton, Carlos, lawyer, Buenos Aires, June 9, 1997.

Mera, Jorge, professor of law, Universidad Diego Portales, Santiago, July 2, 1998.

Mignone, Emilio, lawyer, human rights activist, and founder of CELS, Buenos Aires, June 19, 1997.

Miguel, Salim, former political prisoner, Franklin Cascães Foundation, Florianópolis, Santa Catarina, Brazil, September 26, 1996.

Millet, Paz, researcher on civil-military relations, FLACSO (Facultad Latinoamericana de Ciencias Sociales), Santiago, June 16, 1998.

Milutin, Lila, lawyer, Buenos Aires, June 10, 1997.

Miranda, Federal Deputy Nilmário (Workers' Party, Minas Gerais), member of the Commission on the Disappeared, Brazilian Congress, Brasília, November 20, 1996.

Motta, Roberto, former Brazilian Communist Party member and political prisoner, Florianópolis, Santa Catarina, Brazil, October 1, 1996.

Neto, Paulo de Mesquita, researcher, Núcleo de Estudos da Violência, University of São Paulo, São Paulo, November 8, 1996.

Ojea Quintana, Rodolfo, human rights lawyer and former political prisoner, Buenos Aires, June 19, 1997.

Oliveira, Alicia, lawyer and member of Centro de Estudios Legales y Sociales, Buenos Aires, June 17, 1997.

Oteiza, Eduardo, law professor and author of book on the Argentine Supreme Court, Buenos Aires, June 18, 1997.

Pauperio Serio, Darcio, lawyer, Justice and Peace Commission, Metropolitan Diocese, São Paulo, November 1, 1994.

Pereira dos Santos, Dona Helena, president of local branch of Torture Never Again [Tortura Nunca Mais], São Paulo, October 7, 1994.

Pereira Fernandez, Pamela, lawyer and author of report on military justice, Santiago, June 17, 1998.

Pereira, Francisco, former political prisoner and member of the Brazilian Communist Party, Florianópolis, Santa Catarina, Brazil, September 30, 1996.

Peruzzotti, Enrique, sociologist, Di Tella University, Buenos Aires, June 12, 1997.

Piveta, Idebal, former lawyer for political prisoners, political prisoner, playwright and theatre director, São Paulo, November 15, 1996.

Raimondi, Navy Captain (retired) Carlos, Buenos Aires, June 10, 1997.

Rehren, Alfredo, political scientist, Universidad Católica de Chile, Santiago, June 25, 1998.

Rodríguez Espada, Army General (retired) Héctor, Buenos Aires, June 25, 1997.

Sabsay, Daniel, law professor, Buenos Aires, July 1, 1997.

Salazar, Hector, lawyer for political prisoners, Santiago, July 6, 1998.

Schiffrin, Judge Leopoldo, La Plata, Buenos Aires, June 23, 1997.

Schilling, Paulo, former advisor to Governor Leonel Brizola, Rio Grande do Sul, and political exile, São Paulo, January 5, 1995.

Simas, Mario former lawyer for political prisoners and member, Justice and Peace Commission in São Paulo, São Paulo, November 4 and November 14, 1996.

Smulovitz, Catalina, political scientist, Di Tella University, Buenos Aires, June 18, 1997.

Soares, Severino Manuel, former president of the Timbauba rural workers' union (prosecuted for national security crimes under the military regime) Taguatinga, near Brasília, November 17, 1994.

Sobiejarsky, Professor José Luis, former victim of political persecution, Federal University of Santa Catarina, Florianópolis, Santa Catarina, Brazil, September 25, 1996.

Storni, Judge Ernestina, former union official for judicial employees, Buenos Aires, July 1, 1997.

Szmukler, Dr. Benusz, lawyer and law professor, former lawyer for political prisoners, Buenos Aires, June 16, 1997.

Tibiletti, Army Captain (retired) Luis Eduardo, Seguridad Estratégica Regional (NGO in the area of security and military studies), Buenos Aires, June 18, 1997.

Ulloa Gonzalez, Mirtha, juridical consultant, Ministry of Justice, Santiago, June 26, 1998.

Valenzuela, Lucia, former functionary at the Vicaría de la Solidaridad and the Corporación Nacional de Reparación y Reconciliación, Santiago, June 19, 1998.

Vannucchi, Paulo, former member of the armed left group Ação Libertadora Nacional (ALN) and political prisoner, São Paulo, October 14, 1996.

Vannucchi Leme, Dona Egle, mother of slain political prisoner Alexandre Vannucchi Leme, telephone interview, Sorocaba, São Paulo, January 6, 1995.

Varella, Admiral Alberto, director, National Intelligence School, Buenos Aires, June 13, 1997.

Vieira, Emanuel, former political prisoner and fiction writer, Brasília, November 21, 1996.

Wedekin, Nelson, ex-lawyer for political prisoners, former member of the Justice and Peace Commission, and former federal senator, Florianópolis, Santa Catarina, Brazil, September 28 1996.

Wilde, Alexander, representative, Ford Foundation, Santiago, June 22, 1998.

Notes

Chapter 1: *Repression, Legality, and Authoritarian Regimes*

1. The names of defendants in the cases discussed in this book have been changed, except where indicated, in cases of well-known defendants whose stories are already part of the public record. Real names are used for the defense lawyers cited. All translations from Spanish and Portuguese texts, both primary documents and secondary sources, are the author's unless otherwise indicated.

2. Seven other defendants in the case received sentences ranging from five to twenty-five years. All defendants were stripped of their political rights, including the right to vote and run for elected office, for ten years.

3. This and all other quotes are from the Brasil: Nunca Mais archive, case 98 (these cases are hereafter referred to as BNM cases). The BNM or archive number of a case is not the same number as that used by the lower military court and the appeal courts. In the case of Oliveira Brandt, the case was number 43/71 from the Second Courtroom of the Second District of Military Justice in São Paulo, case number 39,085 in the STM (Superior Tribunal Militar, or Superior Military Court, the appeals court of military justice located in the federal capital in Brasília), and case number 1,190 in the STF (Supremo Tribunal Federal, the civilian Federal Supreme Court, where military court cases could be appealed for a final decision, also located in Brasília).

4. Western Union telegram from Paris, France dated June 7, 1971, protesting the treatment of Oliveira Brandt, signed by professors at the Ecole Pratique des Hautes Etudes and addressed to Doctor Nelson da Silva Machado Guimaraes, Avenida Brigadeiro Luís Antonio, 1249, São Paulo. Found in the trial transcript of BNM 98.

5. Two other defendants were sentenced to seven years and three years, respectively, for their alleged role in aiding and abetting Bolaños and Perez.

6. This is her real name. This case is part of the public record and is mentioned in Andersen (1993, 252).

7. Author's interview with Monica's father, Emilio Mignone (lawyer and founder of Centro de Estudios Legales y Sociales), Buenos Aires, June 19, 1997. Monica's story is also recounted in Mignone (1986, 1), and Nino (1996, 55).

8. By using the term "dirty war," I refer to the extrajudicial, at least partly clandestine, and extremely violent character of the repression. I am not endorsing the view of some military officers and their supporters that these operations approximated a conventional

war, nor would I accept that the actions of the armed left justified such an extraordinary abandonment of legal constraints on the use of force.

9. Writs of habeas corpus are legal orders from courts to prison officials ordering that prisoners be brought to the courts so that judges can decide whether prisoners have been lawfully imprisoned and whether or not they must be released. The Latin term means "you have the body" (Black 1979, 638). The inoperability of writs of habeas corpus was one of the features of the military regimes in Brazil and the southern cone that made them so repressive.

10. These distinctions between the modes of political repression under the three regimes are not absolute. Disappearances, summary executions, and trials took place under all three regimes. The regimes also frequently ignored their own laws. Nevertheless, the proportion of one form of repression to the others varied considerably across regimes, and I have used the available data as the basis for my classification.

11. A rare exception is Lopez (1984, 70).

12. Brooker (2000). Despite this gap, the book is an otherwise useful attempt to classify twentieth-century authoritarian regimes.

13. It should be noted that in this passage, Kirchheimer is referring to political trials under a constitutional regime. His generalization seems to hold for some, although probably not all authoritarian regimes.

14. The originator of this term is Guillermo O'Donnell, whose seminal work is *Modernization and Bureaucratic Authoritarianism* (1973).

15. The politics of different regimes are sometimes conventionally analyzed purely in terms of the interaction of key members of the political elite. In this perspective, courts and political trials reveal nothing essential about regimes. However, in this work I have been influenced by theorists who argue that relationships between rulers and ruled are constantly being negotiated and renegotiated in everyday settings such as courts. Some important works that inspire researchers in this vein are Gramsci (1971), Thompson (1966), and Scott (1985).

16. See, for example Giorgio Agamben, "L'état d'exception," *Le Monde*, December 12, 2002.

17. In this regard, the present book complements the perspective offered by Loveman (1993). Loveman's book gives valuable insights into the way that Spanish American constitutions granted extraordinary powers to presidents, while I point to the continued existence of an undercurrent of liberal traditions in the judiciary, at least in Brazil.

18. Charles Ragin argues that a legitimate purpose of social science, in addition to the essential task of explaining social phenomena, is that of "giving voice" to people and groups who otherwise might not be understood (1994, 43–45).

19. For an interesting analysis of the role of antislavery judges in upholding slavery laws in the antebellum United States, see Cover (1975). Cover's judgment on these judges could apply equally well to prosecutors and judges in Brazil's and Chile's political trials: whatever their personal views, they ultimately served an oppressive legal system.

20. I take the notion of structured, focused comparison from George (1979, esp. 61–63). David Laitin argues that theoretically informed narrative is one of the three

major methods of contemporary political science, along with statistics and formal modeling (2002, 630–33, 637–41).

21. I owe this distinction between preemptive and rollback coups to Drake (1996, 32–33). A preemptive coup is one that occurs before extensive mass mobilization by the incumbent government and is intended to forestall feared or incipient mobilization. A rollback coup is less conservative in that it seeks to reverse the reforms of the deposed regime and to crush high levels of prior mass mobilization.

22. Some authors contest this, arguing that the armed left had been largely annihilated by the time of the 1976 coup in Argentina. See, for example, Andersen (1993).

23. Another example of the point being made here is that the Tupamaros in Uruguay were one of the strongest armed movements in Latin America in the 1970s, but the Uruguayan military regime did not resort to a large-scale dirty war, as did its Argentine counterpart.

24. A status group is a collection of people who share an effective claim to social esteem—and perhaps also status monopolies—based on lifestyle, formal education or training, or traditions. See Weber (1978, 305–7).

25. While I agree with Gerardo Munck that overall elite consensus was probably higher in Chile's military regime than it was in Brazil's, I argue that in the specific area of authoritarian legality and judicial-military cooperation, Brazilian consensus was higher (see Munck 1998, 166–84, esp. 172).

26. The Chilean Vicaría de la Solidaridad has published a detailed four-volume study of political trials under Chilean military rule. See Arzobispado de Santiago (1989–1991). The great bulk of the material is on trials in the 1973–1978 period, although Tomo 1 contains material on eighty-seven cases that were tried in peacetime courts after 1978 (see pp. 311–13). However, these are lawyers' summaries of cases and are not comparable in richness and detail to the cases I examined in the Brasil: Nunca Mais archive.

27. For the Brazilian trials, an exception is Skidmore (1988, 131–33), in which he argues that the traditionalism of the military justice system imposed some institutional restraints on the repressive forces, gave the military regime a "symbolic rallying point" that its treatment of the opposition had been decent, and gave the opposition detailed evidence that torture of detainees had been widespread. However, this is only a passing reference. Four works treat the Brazilian trials in more detail: Arquidiocese de São Paulo (1991), Reis Filho (1989), Ridenti (1993), and Fernandes (2004). However, none of these works use the military court records to analyze the regime's authoritarian legality in comparative perspective. I am not aware of comparable works on the Chilean military trials under the Pinochet regime.

Chapter 2: *National Security Legality in Brazil and the Southern Cone in Comparative Perspective*

This chapter uses some material from my 2003 article "Political Justice under Authoritarian Regimes in Argentina, Brazil, and Chile," *Human Rights Review* 2 (2): 27–47. Permission to use this material was granted by the Transaction Periodicals Consortium.

1. Enrique Groisman (lawyer and author on legal issues), interview with author, Buenos Aires, June 30, 1997.

2. Brazil is famous for the *jeito*, the informal, improvised, quasi-legal or outright illegal maneuver designed to solve a particular problem. See Rosenn (1971) as well as Da Matta (1991, esp. 138).

3. An official commission found that, during the same period, 8,960 persons had been "disappeared." See Argentine National Commission on the Disappeared (1986, 447). However, a commonly accepted range for the total number of killed and disappeared is 20,000–30,000. In the Chilean military courts more than 6,000 political prisoners were tried between the coup in 1973 and 1978 (Barros 2002, 139). An official commission found that 2,279 people had been killed or disappeared during the entire regime, and this figure was later revised to more than 3,000 (Chilean National Commission on Truth and Reconciliation 1993, 2:900). Human rights groups frequently refer to 4,000 to 5,000 as the likely total death toll. In Brazil, 7,367 people were prosecuted in military courts in cases that were appealed to the second level of military justice between 1964 and 1979; from Projeto "Brasil: Nunca Mais" (1988, 9). While the government officially recognized 284 people as killed or disappeared, a human-rights organization estimated that the correct number was 364 (Miranda and Tibúrcio 1999, 12, 15–16, 633, 635). See also Pinheiro (2000, 119–43, esp. 140, note 2).

4. In Brazil four defendants were sentenced to death under military rule, but their sentences were all commuted to prison terms.

5. From *El Mercurio* (Santiago), "Piden procesamentos por 'caravana,'" June 8, 1999, "Proceso contra Arellano Stark y 4 ex altos oficiales," June 9, 1999, "Proceso a militares," June 12, 1999, "Una caravana de procesos," June 13, 1999. For an in-depth analysis of these events, see Verdugo (2001).

6. Dr. Benusz Szmukler (lawyer, law professor, and former defense lawyer for political prisoners), interview by author, Buenos Aires, June 16, 1997.

7. Carlos Acuña (political scientist), interview by author, Buenos Aires, June 11, 1997.

8. Nino (1996, 80). Reportedly, almost all of these people had been apprehended before the 1976 coup.

9. To resort to the jargon of political science, this comparison of cases builds in variation on the dependent variable. For the injunction to adopt such a strategy, designed to avoid the problem of "selection bias," see King, Keohane, and Verba (1994, 129–32).

10. For example, while a labor-repressive political economy probably contributed to the army massacres of villagers in the highlands of Guatemala in the early 1980s—the bloodiest instance of state violence in the Americas in the last three decades—the ethnic cleavage between Mayans and ladinos (and whites) also seems crucial to explaining this repression.

11. For an example of such an approach to the explanation of politics, see Ames (1987); Bates et al. (1998); Cohen (1994); Geddes (1994); Hunter (1997); Przeworski (1991); Tsbelis (1990).

12. See Geddes (1995). For persuasive critiques of rational choice theory, see Green and Shapiro (1994); Elster (2000); Weyland (2002).

13. For a discussion of the pitfalls of this kind of evolutionary paradigm, see Roe (1996).

14. From a lecture by Douglass North at Tulane University, November 8, 2002. "Ergodic" is a term from math and statistics that means of or pertaining to the condition that, in a time period of sufficient length, a system will return to a state that is roughly similar to previous ones.

15. For cultural approaches to politics, see Graziano (1992); Sosnowski and Popkin (1993).

16. The political scientist Karl Loewenstein wrote in the early 1940s that "It is not in the Brazilian character to kill people for political reasons"(Loewenstein 1942, 226). For recent scholarship that casts doubt on such a judgment, see Rose (1998); Smallman (2002).

17. In doing so it implicitly rejects the rational choice theorists' admonition that *all* explanations of political outcomes must be reducible to individual behavior. For this methodologically individualist position, see Elster (1989, 13–21). Instead, I agree with Steven Lukes (1977, 177–86) that explanations at the level of institutions can be valid in particular instances.

18. The literature on institutionalism is vast. For example, see Hall and Taylor (1996); Steinmo, Thelen, and Longstreth (1989).

19. For useful discussions of the historical turn in political science see Rogers Smith (1996, 1997). See also Orren and Skowronek (1995); Pierson and Skocpol (2002).

20. From Pierson (2000, 264). While I accept this and other insights from scholars of path dependency, I do not make a fully path-dependent argument in this book. Like Miguel Centeno (2002, 19 n. 57), I avoid the term so as not to get distracted by the particular methodological debates associated with its use.

21. Pierson (2000). For a less elaborate statement of a similar approach see Roe (1996).

22. Pierson (2000, 251) uses the concept of increasing returns to add rigor to the insight that the initial advantages accruing from the choice of a certain path widen over time, while the costs of exit rise.

23. Quoted in ibid., p. 255.

24. Granted, in some sense all trials are political, in that ordinary crimes are considered a threat to the established order, and prosecuted by the state for that reason. Scholarship challenging the distinction between public and private, and attempting to link the workings of power on the macro and micro levels, reinforces the suspicion that labeling certain trials as political and others as nonpolitical can be somewhat artificial. See, for example, Foucault (1979), as well as MacKinnon (1989). On the other hand, some specialists might claim that no trials are political whenever they involve alleged crimes clearly specified in the criminal code. However, these debates shall not be entered into here. The trials examined in this book were ones in which the political views of defendants, and alleged threats to the political regime, were seen by protagonists on both sides as relevant to the proceedings. Hence they qualify for our purposes as political trials.

25. Kirchheimer (1961, 49). For other analyses of political trials, see Christenson (1986, 1–6); Becker (1971, xi–xvi); and Barkan (1985, 1–9).

26. This distinction comes from the German theorist Carl Schmitt via Andrew Arato (2000a). Arato uses the term "commissarial" rather than "conservative."

27. For a discussion of historical memory see Aguilar (1996, 32–42).

28. Stanley (1996, 12, quote p. 13). Stanley's "protection racket" differs from that of Charles Tilly (1985), who first used the term. In Tilly's formulation, the state as a whole operates a protection racket vis-à-vis its citizens, extracting revenue from them in return for protecting them from other states and nonstate actors.

Chapter 3: *The Evolution of National Security Legality in Brazil and the Southern Cone*

This chapter draws on some of the material in my 1998 article "'Persecution and Farce': The Origins and Transformation of Brazil's Political Trials," *Latin American Research Review* 33 (1): 43–66. Copyright permission for this material was granted by *Latin American Research Review*.

1. Constitutions such as that of Belgium's 1831 document, which expressly forbade the suspension of constitutional rights in part or in their entirety, were rare in Latin America (Loveman 1993, 373).

2. A major accomplishment of the recent wave of constitutional reform in Latin America has been to remove these provisions and to make congressional approval more important in the declaration of a state of siege or state of emergency. See Mainwaring and Shugart (1997).

3. The terminology comes from Damaška (1986, 181). Damaška divides justice systems into four basic types, evaluating them on the basis of two dichotomies: policy-implementing versus conflict-solving systems, and hierarchical versus coordinate forms of authority.

4. In Germany, for example, people who made allegations "apt to disrupt the operations of the armed forces" could be punished with a prison term under a 1957 law, as they could in France for trying to "bring discredit to any legal decision," according to a 1958 law. See Kirchheimer (1961, 41).

5. A previous generation of scholars did believe that Latin America's civil law system contained a philosophical bias against the protection of individual rights and in favor of the reflexive legitimation of state power. However, the emergence of strong, relatively independent judiciaries capable of protecting individual rights in such civil law countries as France and Germany should warn us against too easy generalizations in this regard. See Verner (1984).

6. Mid-twentieth-century Latin American populism, while consisting of multiclass coalitions of urban workers (and more rarely peasants and rural workers), members of the middle class, and industrialists, was usually not based on the autonomous organized power of labor. Instead, labor's power tended to be dependent on middle- and upper-middle-class leaders who often ruled in a personalistic, clientelistic, or charismatic manner. Populism usually combined some measure of commitment to redistribution, anti-imperialist nationalism, and socialism and was often hostile to bourgeois or liberal conceptions of the rule of law. Unlike populism in most other parts of the world, Latin

American populism sought inspiration primarily among urban rather than rural masses. See Hennessy (1969).

7. For an exploration of Brazilian conservatism, see Mercadante (2003).

8. Avritzer (2002, 177 n. 6). In the quoted passage, Avritzer summarizes the argument of Wanderley Guilherme dos Santos.

9. Beattie (2001, 281–82). Impressment was a common method of recruitment before conscription. In both Chile and Brazil conscription in practice reached only the working class and below; members of the middle and upper classes rarely failed to obtain exemptions from service. In Argentina, conscription seems to have been closer to universal than in other Latin American cases.

10. The *intentona* continued to be evoked by the military for many years afterwards. For example, Giordani wrote a defense of the military regime and an attack on the Brasil: Nunca Mais project that begins with a chapter entitled "Remember '35!" See Giordani (1986).

11. Quoted in Pompeu de Campos (1982, 39). In a remarkable parallel, a legal scholar in Argentina used similar language in the early 1980s to justify the dirty war, arguing, as had Ráo, that while traditional law protects the individual from society, this is exploited by terrorists (Communists in Ráo's case), and that new law must protect society from these dangerous individuals (Domínguez 1983, 11).

12. See Pompeu de Campos (1982); Pinheiro (1991, 325); and Loewenstein (1942, 212–34). Loewenstein indicates that the TSN was compared at the time to the People's Court in Nazi Germany, discussed in chapter 9.

13. The Força Expedicionária Brasileira (Brazilian Expeditonary Force; FEB) was an army infantry division that served in the Italian campaign with the U.S. Fifth Army in 1944–1945 (de Abreu et al. 2001, 2284–87). For a critical appraisal of the way that the FEB was commanded, see Udihara (2002). U.S.-Brazilian military cooperation probably reached its high-water mark in 1965, when the Brazilians furnished troops to the U.S. invasion of the Dominican Republic.

14. For more on Oliveira Vianna, see Bastos and Quartim de Morães (1993).

15. Quoted in Johnson (1964, 231). The article appeared on October 9, 1955; the translation is Johnson's.

16. Unlike in the United States, at this time in Brazil the heads of the armed services served directly in the president's cabinet, without the intermediation of a civilian minister of defense. The ministers were Marshall Odílio Denis of the army, Vice Admiral Sílvio Heck of the navy, and Brigadier Gabriel Grün Moss of the air force (Barbosa 2002, 41–42).

17. From de Abreu et al. (2001, 1825) and Barbosa (2002, 99). The order is paralleled by the tragedy of 1973 in Chile, when the air force did actually bomb the palace of President Allende.

18. All three men were leading figures in the 1964 coup, conspiring as of early 1963 with generals Eduardo Gomes, Osvaldo Cordeiro de Farias, Nélson de Melo, and Olympio Mourão Filho, as well as jurists Francisco Campos and Antônio Neder (de Abreu et al. 2001, 3924).

19. This can be found in article 63 of Brazil's 1934 constitution (Costa Filho 1994, 38).

20. Dos Santos, Monteiro, and Lustosa Caillaux report that ninety-six people were forcibly retired or fired from the federal judiciary between 1964 and 1973 (1990, 251). This includes twenty-six officials from the Public Ministry, twenty-six members of official registries (*cartórios* and *varas*), and only forty-four members of the civilian, labor, and military courts.

21. One of the most famous cases of interference in the courts was the removal of General Peri Bevilaqua from the STM in 1969. For an account of his decisions as an STM judge from 1965 to 1969, see Lemos (2004).

22. I thank Professor Maria da Glória Bonelli of the Department of Social Sciences at the Federal University of São Carlos for pointing this out to me (comments during the international symposium "Forty Years after the 1964 Coup: New Dialogues, New Perspectives," Federal University of São Carlos, São Paulo, June 14, 2004).

23. In January of 1925 a revolutionary committee headed by Lieutenant Colonel Ibáñez and Lieutenant Colonel Marmaduke Grove Vallejo overthrew the interim government (Nunn 1989, 120).

24. Gil (1966, 61). The ensuing socialist republic lasted from December 1931 to September 1932. According to Gil, some important and long-lasting reform legislation was passed during that time.

25. From Quiroga and Maldonado (1988, 40–41). Frederick Nunn (1989) also writes of the Chilean army's Prussianization. Sater and Herwig (1999, 25–27) dispute as myth the image of Chile as the Prussia of South America, alleging that the transformation was superficial. Nevertheless, the authors report that the German general staff in the early twentieth century believed that the Chilean army was qualitatively superior to the Argentine's, and far superior to the Peruvian and Bolivian armies.

26. Collier and Collier (1991, 181). Loveman (1988, 220) reports that twelve hundred workers were killed.

27. Pinochet Ugarte (1979, 27); the entire incident is recounted in pp. 23–28. Thanks to Krystin Krause for finding and translating this passage. The story is retold in Manns (1999, 160–64).

28. This is Nunn's term (1976, 186, 187–94).

29. See also "Presidente Eduardo Frei señala responsibilidades," *El Mercurio*, March 12, 1966; and the transcripts of the March 12 debate in the Senate in "Incidentes en El Mineral de El Salvador," *El Mercurio*, March 17, 1966.

30. The first German training mission to Argentina helped to establish the Superior War College along Prussian lines (Goldwert 1989, 44).

31. Commentary by Salvador M. Lozada on Law 17,401, in Gobierno de Argentina (1967, 27B:1633–35).

32. The military regime of 1966 inserted its numerous decree-laws into the consecutive numbering of previous congressional legislation. These laws were not automatically abrogated after the 1973 transition. Instead, the courts were pragmatic and decided that laws had to be specifically struck down; if they were not, they endured (McSherry 1997, 315, n. 19 to chap. 3). McSherry seems concerned about this legal continuity, but at least

with regard to the treatment of political prisoners, it is irrelevant, since the leaders of the 1976–1983 regime largely ignored this previous legislation.

33. Lewis (2002, 107, 138–141) cites French counterinsurgency theorists Colonel Roger Trinquier and General André Beaufre, both participants in the Algerian conflict, as major influences on the leaders of the Argentine dirty war.

Chapter 4: *Political Trials in Brazil: The Continuation of a Conservative Tradition*

1. From U.S. Foreign Broadcast Information Service, transcript of broadcast on Radio Tupi, May 13, 1964, Rio de Janeiro 03:00 GMT, accessed at the Widener Library, Government Documents Section, Harvard University.

2. See Skidmore (1967); Morel (1965); Parker (1979, 58); Black (1977). I also base this statement on declassified documents: CIA Information Reports (sanitized copies) number TDCS-3/543, 633, April 10 1963; number TDCS-3/544, 130, April 16 1963; number TDCS-3/545, 753, April 24–28 1963; number TDCS-3/548, 655, May 24 1963; and number TDCS-3/555, 725, August 4 1963 (Government Documents, Bobst Library, New York University). Former Ambassador Gordon unconvincingly claims that U.S. government officials did not pledge any support to Brazil's coup plotters; see Gordon (2003, esp. 63–73).

3. In his *New York Times* column of April 7, 1964, conservative columnist Arthur Krock, for example, criticized Washington for recognizing the Brazilian government too quickly. Observers in other countries were more critical (Skidmore 1967, 327).

4. Afonso Arinos reported this in an interview to TV Globo in 1981 (de Abreu et al. 2001, 1:1007).

5. Ibid., entries on Francisco Campos (1:997–1008), Carlos Medeiros (3:3666–67), and Antônio Neder (4:4045–46).

6. Dos Santos, Monteiro, and Lustosa Caillaux (1990, 256). Elected officials denied their political rights were also stripped of their mandates.

7. "Debate ocioso," *Jornal do Brasil*, February 6, 1971.

8. Martins Filho (1996, 59) gives more evidence of President Castelo Branco's legalism, citing a letter written in September 1964 in which the president declares that he would free political prisoners whose habeas corpus writs were granted by the Supreme Court.

9. The quote comes from AI-1 as reprinted in Heller (1988, 627). The point about the initially limited duration of AI-1 is made in Fragoso (1975, 108).

10. The quote and the observation are from Couto (1999, 194).

11. The case against the alleged bomber is BNM 160 in the Brasil: Nunca Mais archive.

12. "Limites da repressão," *Jornal do Brasil*, January 14, 1971.

13. Quoted in Fragoso (1975, 117). Interestingly, Pessoa dedicated his book on national security law to the writer Gilberto Freyre. Freyre shared Pessoa's views and characterized Brazil under AI-5 as a variant of democracy. See Freyre (1970, xxiii).

14. For an analysis of the Brazilian military regime's search for legitimacy, see Rezende (2001).

15. Fragoso (1975, 104). Fragoso's bewildering diagram on page 107 does little to simplify this complicated system.

16. An example of this can be seen in the early 1970s in the Inter-American Commission on Human Rights (IACHR). In 1970, after receiving credible complaints of human-rights abuses in Brazil, the IACHR requested additional information from the Brazilian government. In its official response, dated January 11, 1971, the Brazilian government pointed to the fact that the alleged victims of human-rights abuses had been tried in public trials in military courts that were part of the judicial branch, had enjoyed the right to counsel, and had appealed their cases to the STM, where sentences were often reduced. At the beginning of 1974, the IAHCR in effect slapped the Brazilian government on the wrist and then moved on to consider other issues. From Inter-American Commission on Human Rights (1982, 112–22).

17. Elio Gaspari (journalist), interview by author, São Paulo, November 11, 1996.

18. For example, in a study of the ALN (Ação Libertadora Nacional, or National Liberationist Action), Vannucchi Leme found that the period 1969–1971 accounts for 75 percent of the ALN members charged with crimes in military justice and almost 40 percent of the deaths of ALN militants in the state of São Paulo. The period 1972–1974, on the other hand, accounts for just 25 percent of the ALN members charged but 60 percent of the deaths of militants. In the state's response to the ALN, judicial action was apparently largely replaced by extrajudicial action in the later period. From Vannucchi Leme de Matos (2002, 57).

19. This is a sample of the 707 cases in the Brasil: Nunca Mais archive, which contains all national security cases appealed to the Supreme Court in the period 1964–1979. They thus represent 36 percent of the total universe of cases without constituting a random sample of that universe. The samples in the tables that follow vary slightly because relevant information is missing for some cases.

20. "STM absolveu mais em 70 do que condenou," *Jornal do Brasil*, January 25, 1971. The article mentions that two-thirds of the twelve hundred cases it discusses dealt with subversion. It is likely that the STM rounded the number of cases in each category up or down.

21. I am grateful to Kurt Weyland for persuasively making this argument to me.

22. Simas divides the history of his defense of political defendants into two phases. The first is 1963 to 1969, when judicial institutions were weakened, but the prior legal structure was basically in place; the second is 1969 to 1979, when there was an "absolute contempt for the most elementary rights of man" because torture was institutionalized. Again, the lawyer's periodization is different from the conventional tripartite division (1986, 11).

23. These figures are based on a nonrandom sample of 224 cases from the Nunca Mais archive compiled by the author.

24. Carlos Lamarca was a prized marksman who defected from the army with some subordinates to join the armed left. He was eventually tracked down and killed in Bahia.

25. O'Donnell (1973) pointed out that the Brazilian "bureaucratic-authoritarian" regime "demobilized" labor, and the point has been reemphasized by many other authors in the literature on authoritarian regimes.

26. Gaspari interview. "The punishment was not imprisonment," said Gaspari. "The punishment was torture . . . [and] torture generated a kind of paternalism. When someone confessed and told everything to the military, he could be acquitted." See also Gaspari (2002a, 2002b).

27. I am using the concept of a frame as explained by Sidney Tarrow (1998, 21–22). Tarrow is interested in how social movements frame issues, but regimes also engage in such framing.

28. Lesser (2002, 5). Lesser's estimate might be high. Joan Dassin refers to six thousand individuals involved in the armed struggle at its height (1992, 161).

29. "Hora inaugural," editorial, *Jornal do Brasil*, March 19, 1971. Despite the fierce tone of this editorial, it goes on to demand legal and institutional normality.

30. BNM 635, Aud: 6a RM, Salvador de Bahia, processo 61/70. "Auditoria baiana inaugura pena de morte no Brasil republicana," *Jornal do Brasil*, March 19, 1971.

31. From the following articles in the *Jornal do Brasil*, March 20, 1971: "Clóvis Stenzel julga Teodomiro recuperável," "Cardeal Dom Eugenio Sales se diz supreso," "Fragoso ve em causa a dignidade," "Auditor carioca justifica pena," and "Ninguem na Bahia quer autorizar as visitas ao condenado a morte." See also "CNBB condena a aplicação da pena do morte no Brasil," *Jornal do Brasil*, March 23, 1971; "Deputado mineiro pede intervenção de Medici," *Jornal do Brasil*, March 23, 1971; "Confiança na Justica," editorial, *Jornal do Brasil*, March 23, 1971.

32. Case number 38,590, appealed to STM, in BNM 635.

33. Recurso 1232, appealed to STF, in BNM 635.

34. From case number 38,590, appealed to STM, in BNM 635.

35. From another newspaper article, with no reference given, in BNM 635.

36. "Exército convocará a imprensa, diz acusador," *Jornal do Brasil*, March 23, 1971.

37. "Auditoria baiana inaugura pena de morte no Brasil republicano," *Jornal do Brasil*, March 19, 1971.

38. "Conselho Especial ouve em Minas acusado de subversão sujeito a pena de morte," *Jornal do Brasil*, March 16, 1971.

39. "Ceará sujeita 9 a pena capital," *Jornal do Brasil*, March 24, 1971.

40. "Procurador quer pena máxima para 4," *Jornal do Brasil*, March 26, 1971.

41. "Contra o esquadrão," *Jornal do Brasil*, February 21–22, 1971.

42. From "Alem dos tribunais," *Veja*, May 19, 1971, pp. 33–34.

43. "Juiz marca depoimento de Fleury," *Jornal do Brasil*, March 7 and 8, 1971.

Chapter 5: *"Wartime" Legality and Radical Adaptation in Chile*

1. Robert Barros (2002, 139) reports that the wartime military courts operated from the time of the coup until October 1978, when the state of siege was lifted.

2. Marlise Simons, "The Brazilian Connection," *Washington Post*, January 6, 1974.

3. São Paulo State Archive, Section on the Department of Political and Social Order (DEOPS), São Paulo, Brazil, 1994–95. Arquivo do Estado, Seção de DEOPS, Ordem Social—Pasta 14—Diversos.

4. Created in 1975, Operation Condor was apparently spurred by the Chilean military authorities, who were anxious about stifling the efforts of Chilean exiles abroad to undermine their regime (Mariano 1998).

5. Carlos Lopez Dawson (lawyer and author of *Justicia militar: Una nueva mirada*), interview by author, Santiago, June 30, 1998.

6. Transcripts of the Chilean Congress, Legislatura Extraordinaria, Sessiones 13–21, January–February 1971, pp. 629–630.

7. "Allende anuncia criação de côrtes populares no Chile," *Jornal do Brasil*, January 8, 1971, and "Governo chileno elogia os tribunais populares," *Jornal do Brasil*, January 9, 1971.

8. "PDC vota contra projeto de Allende," *Jornal do Brasil*, January 27, 1971.

9. "PDC do Chile se opõe a tribunais populares," *Jornal do Brasil*, January 27, 1971.

10. "En el estado de derecho se cumplen normalmente las decisiones judiciales," *El Mercurio*, March 2, 1973.

11. "Derecho y justicia de clases," *El Mercurio*, March 3, 1973.

12. "Advogado acusa conspiração contra Allende," *Jornal do Brasil*, January 11, 1971.

13. Transcripts of the Chilean Congress, Legislatura Extraordinaria, Sessiones 23–33, March–April 1971, March 9, 1971, p. 1630.

14. "Allende ameaça quem faz oposição armada," *Jornal do Brasil*, January 11, 1971.

15. For an example of the first view, see Panish (1987). Hilbink (1999, esp. pp. 217–19) shows how the judiciary contributed to the antagonism and polarization of Chilean politics under Allende.

16. Cavallo, Salazar, and Sepúlveda (1997, 15–16). The junta accepted the Supreme Court president's recommendation, but they could not reach him, and ended up choosing someone else instead.

17. Garretón Merino et al. (1998, 59). For a discussion of the *bandos*, see the above-mentioned text and Barros (2002, 44–45, n. 16).

18. Barros (2002, 34). One would have to add that after 1894 and prior to 1964 the Brazilian military's interventions were to moderate political conflicts rather than to directly rule, so in many ways the Brazilian military faced the same dilemmas in 1964 that Barros ascribes to the Chilean military in 1973.

19. Constable and Valenzuela (1991, 129). Although the Civil Code required all laws to be published, the military regime got around this restriction by publishing the laws in limited editions of the official daily record (Diário Oficial), which circulated only among high-level officials within the regime.

20. For more on the caravan of death, see "Proceso contra Arellano Stark y 4 ex altos oficiales," *El Mercurio*, June 9, 1999; "El método de la comitiva de Arellano," *El Mercurio*, June 9, 1999; and "Procesan a militares de la era Pinochet," *El Observador*, June 9, 1999.

21. Article 12 of Bando Number 5 of September 11, 1973, reproduced in Garretón Merino et al. (1998, 61).

22. Quotation from Arriagada Herrera (1986, 119–20). The translation is by Arriagada Herrera.

23. Quotation from Arriagada Herrera (1986, 120–21). Once again the translation is by Arriagada Herrera.

24. Arzobispado de Santiago (1989–1991, 1989, Tomo 1). Some prisoners were tried for violations of the Law of State Security in civilian courts, with the right of appeal to a higher court, but these were a minority of all such cases.

25. Arzobispado de Santiago (1989–1991, 1990, Tomo 2, Vol. 1, 7).

26. These percentages are based on the total cases compiled by the Vicaría in its four-volume *Jurisprudencia* series that catalogues political trials under the military regime. The Vicaría acknowledges that there are gaps in this compilation, so we cannot take the percentages as definitive. Nevertheless, since the military regime's own archives of the court cases were allegedly destroyed, they are probably the best data that we will ever have.

27. Arzobispado de Santiago (1989–1991, 1990, Tomo 2, Vol. 1, 6).

28. Contra Oyarce Oyarce Juan Gustavo, Rol 5–73, Consejo de Guerra de Tejas Verdes, January 12, 1973, in ibid., pp. 415–416.

29. Contra Plaza Vera Renato del Carmen, Rol 10–73, Consejo de Guerra de Tejas Verdes, November 24, 1973, in ibid., pp. 417–418. This case is extraordinary because another justification for the guilty verdict against the taxi driver was that he had violated a strike declared by the taxi driver's union by continuing to work. Thus a military court in Pinochet's Chile punished a man for breaking his union's strike!

30. Contra Betancourt Barrera Justo Pastor, Rol 13–73, Consejo de Guerra de Tejas Verdes, November 24, 1973, in ibid., p. 419.

31. Contra Vidal Pérez Germán Cayetano y otros, Rol 34–73, Consejo de Guerra de Tejas Verdes, May 24, 1974, in ibid., pp. 428–429.

32. Contra Rojas González Patricio y otros, Rol 18–73, Consejo de Guerra de Tejas Verdes, November 17, 1973, in ibid., pp. 421–422. In this case the brigadier general in charge of the military zone, Julio Polloni, lowered the sentences of three of the convicted defendants almost two years after the original verdicts were issued.

33. Contra Arriagada Ungo Eduardo y otro, Rol 20–73, Consejo de Guerra de Tejas Verdes, December 10, 1973, in ibid., pp. 423–424. The revision of the sentence was dated November 21, 1974.

34. A comparison of table 4.1 and table 5.1 shows that in Chile, the lowest local acquittal rate is 0, while the highest is 46.34 percent, giving a range of the latter number. This is only slightly lower than the Brazilian range between localities of 54.07.

35. This fact must be tempered by the reality that the greatest number of extrajudicial killings also took place in middle Chile. The acquittal rate in the military courts should by no means be taken as a gauge of the overall severity of the repression.

36. Table 5.2 slightly understates the severity of Chilean military court sentences, because it excludes 67 people who were exiled from the country, most for a period of one to five years. Furthermore, 269 were sentenced to *relegación*, a type of internal exile; 240 for sentences of one to five years; and the rest for six years or more.

37. This figure is not strictly comparable to the Chilean one because the categories are different—ten years or more compared to more than ten years. However, even if we assume the implausible, that all Brazilian defendants in the 83–120 months category received maximum sentences of ten years, the Brazilian figure would still be around 16 percent of all defendants, lower than the Chilean figure of more than 20 percent.

38. Roberto Garretón Merino, interview by the author, Santiago, June 23, 1998.

39. Rigby (2001, 92n34). Another source claims that only 10 of 5,400 habeas corpus petitions filed between 1973 and 1983 were accepted. Constable and Valenzuela (1991, 122).

40. Constable and Valenzuela (1991, 132).

Chapter 6: *Antilegalism in Argentina*

1. While the original *Nunca más* report stated that there were 340 secret detention centers, in later editions of this report, the number has been increased to 365. See Argentine National Commission on the Disappeared (1986); I thank Krystin Krause for this information.

2. Feitlowitz takes a linguistic approach and argues that a virulent strain of conservative thought permeated the Argentine right, so that the enemy was discursively "killed" even before the repression began (see 1998, 20). Pion-Berlin, like Feitlowitz, explains the dirty war with reference to discourse, but in his case the relevant language is monetarist or what are now called "neoliberal" economic doctrines (1989, 10). Buchanan basically concurs with this analysis (see 1989). Anderson shares this perspective when he writes that the dirty war was not really waged against the armed left, because the latter had already been defeated, but was primarily an attempt to terrorize the population into submitting to the regime's radical policies of economic and political reorganization (1993). Marchak considers no fewer than four explanations for the dirty war: that it was a "holy war" (expressed in terms of national security doctrine) on the part of the military to wipe out revolutionary groups; that it was primarily to impose economic restructuring, as Pion-Berlin, Buchanan, and Anderson argue; that it was a proxy struggle in the Cold War; and that it was a struggle for power between factions of the middle class. She finds some explanatory power in the first, third, and fourth of these explanations. She also suggests that another important conditioning factor in the dirty war was the purge of the "Third World priest" movement within the Catholic Church, making the Argentine church far more conservative and supportive of repression than the Chilean church and certainly the Brazilian (Marchak 1999, 235–65, 322–39).

3. This is true even of economic doctrine and the role of the Catholic Church. While Brazilian economic policy under military rule was never "neoliberal," it did rely on the repression of labor and the containment of wage increases. And while Brazil's church was not as conservative as its Argentine counterpart, many of its leaders did take quite conservative positions with regard to the repression.

4. The creation of the special court was the culmination of a series of laws promulgated by the military regime to stiffen penalties against political crimes and to deal with the growing armed opposition.

5. From "Fue creada la Cámara Federal en lo Penal," *Clarín,* May 29, 1971, and "Créose la nueva Cámara Federal," *La Nación,* May 29, 1971. The law creating the Cámara was Number 19,053 of May 28, 1971.

6. Lewis (2002, 72) reports that the court dealt with over 2,000 political prisoners,

of whom roughly 600 were found guilty, 800 were released, and the rest were being processed when the court was dissolved. For his part Judge Eduardo Luís Duhalde (not the same Duhalde who later became president), who defended some 200 defendants in the National Penal Court, stated that to his knowledge between 1,000 and 1,200 people were tried in the court. This fits roughly with the numbers reported by Lewis. Judge Duhalde, interview by author, Buenos Aires, June 12, 1997.

7. For this reason I consider the National Penal Court to be an example of the authoritarian legality that characterizes the other military courts that are the focus of this book.

8. The Onganía government reestablished the death penalty for the crime of kidnapping resulting in murder by decreeing Law Number 18,701 of June 2, 1970, after the kidnapping and killing of General Aramburu. The penalty was abolished in 1972 under President Lanusse. As is mentioned later, it was restored again—but never formally applied—after the 1976 coup in Law 21,338. It was abolished again in 1984. From Silvina Quintans (2000) "En contra de la pena de muerte," www.legalmania.com.ar (accessed August 2004).

9. Dr. Carlos A. González Gartland, a former lawyer for political prisoners and human rights activist, told me that there were cases in which political prisoners were tortured in front of a court judge or functionary (interview, June 17, 1997). This matches a similar anecdote told to me about a São Paulo military court judge who had a defendant tortured in his court. The anecdote was told to me by Paulo Vannucchi, former member of the National Liberationist Action and political prisoner (interview by the author, October 14, 1996).

10. Benusz Szmukler (former defense lawyer for political prisoners), interview by author, Buenos Aires, June 16, 1997.

11. Rodolfo Ojea Quintana, a former political prisoner and defense lawyer, reports that his wife was sentenced to fifteen years in prison by the National Penal Court for "illicit association" with Peronists while he was underground (interview by the author, Buenos Aires, June 19, 1997).

12. The bar association (Asociacion Gremial de los Abogados) often provided lawyers for political prisoners free of charge. Another source of defense lawyers was the Argentine League for the Rights of Man (Liga Argentina para los Derechos de lo Hombre), an organization founded in the 1930s with ties to the Communist Party.

13. González Gartland interview.

14. Former defense lawyer for political prisoners Benusz Szmukler said that the archives of the Cámara may still be in the possession of the Supreme Court (Szmukler interview). However, my efforts to gain access to them were unsuccessful.

15. Judge Eduardo Luís Duhalde, interview by author, Buenos Aires, June 12, 1997. Judge Duhalde had been a partner of Ortega Peña.

16. González Gartland interview.

17. This interpretation was given to me by human rights activist Emilio Mignone (interview, Buenos Aires, June 19, 1997) and by Judge Carmen Argibay (interview, Buenos Aires, June 20, 1997).

18. Schiffrin (1974); Judge Leopoldo Schiffrin, interview by author, La Plata, June 23, 1997; Enrique Groisman, interview by author, Buenos Aires, June 30, 1997.

19. The dramatic scenes are recounted by Bonasso (1997, 476–85).

20. Law 20,509 of May 27, 1973. At the same time the Congress passed Law 20,508, abolishing many of the political crimes under which the defendants in the National Penal Court had been convicted.

21. The law abolishing the Cámara en lo Penal de la Nación was 20,510 of May 27, 1973.

22. Carlos Raimondi (retired naval captain), interview by author, Buenos Aires, June 10, 1997.

23. Lewis (2002, 72). Cameron Judge Carlos Malbran was also shot and wounded in the legs in 1972.

24. Quiroga played a prominent role in judicially whitewashing the navy massacre of political prisoners in Trelew in August 1972. See "No interviene un juez en el caso de Trelew," *La Nación*, August 31, 1972; Urondo (1973). A plaque commemorating Quiroga's life and career and condemning the "terrorist delinquents" who killed him can be seen on the building that used to house the National Penal Court in Buenos Aires.

25. Szmukler interview.

26. Cámara de Senadores de la Nación, Septiembre 11/12 de 1975, Reunion 31, Tomo 3, 7 de Agosto al 11/12 de Septiembre, p. 2133.

27. Cámara de Senadores de la Nación, Septiembre 30 de 1975, Reunion 38, Tomo 4, 17 de Septiembre al 30 de Septiembre de 1975, pp. 2999–3011.

28. Cámara de Senadores de la Nación, 22 de Octubre de 1975 al 12/13 de Febrero de 1976, Reunion 47, Tomo 5, 12/13 de Febrero de 1976, pp. 3757–3758.

29. Cámara de Senadores de la Nación, 10 de Marzo de 1975, Reunion 48, Tomo 6, pp. 3872–3873.

30. Cámara de Diputados de la Nación, 25/26 de Febrero de 1976, Reunion 57, Tomo 9, 25/26 de Febrero al 17/18 de Marzo de 1976, p. 6259.

31. Cámara de Diputados de la Nación 17/18 de Marzo de 1976, Reunion 62, Tomo 9, 25/26 de Febrero al 17/18 de Marzo de 1976, p. 6483.

32. The quote was originally reported in the Rosario newspaper *La Capital* on June 14, 1980. From Argentine National Commission on the Disappeared (1986, 413).

33. González Gartland interview. A large plaque at the Tribunal de Justicia building at the Plaza Lavalle in Buenos Aires memorializes the lawyers and judicial functionaries killed in the dirty war and lists a total of 113 names.

34. Judge Ernestina Storni (former union official for judicial employees), interview by author, Buenos Aires, July 1, 1997. Judge Storni believes that he may have been killed for his role in shutting down the National Penal Court.

35. Dr. Manuel Gaggero (lawyer and former political prisoner), interview by the author, Buenos Aires, July 2, 1997.

36. Guest (1990, 433). The cable is reproduced on pp. 430–35. For newly declassified documents on U.S. relations with Argentina during the "dirty war," see the Web sites of the National Security Archive (www.nsarchive.org) and the U.S. Department of State (www.foia.state.gov).

37. Raimondi interview.

38. Pinochet remained head of the army until 1998.

39. In *1984*, the protagonist Winston Smith reflects several times on the fate of people arbitrarily executed in this manner. As Orwell writes, in Oceania "nothing was illegal, since there were no longer any laws." Furthermore, records of the state's violence were destroyed by state functionaries such as Winston Smith, so that "the lie passed into history and became truth" (Orwell 1977, 9, 32).

40. In an important essay on the Brazilian military regime, Juan Linz noted that national security doctrine was essentially negative and could not serve as a foundation for stable authoritarian institutions such as those that existed in Franco's Spain. This conclusion can also be applied to the regimes in Chile and Argentina (Linz 1973, 235). Despite the usefulness of Linz's insight, I feel that it is misleading to describe a twenty-one-year regime as a mere "situation."

41. Feitlowitz (1998, 33). The translation is by Feitlowitz.

42. Argentine National Commission on the Disappeared (1986, 404). After the end of military rule, the Argentine government compensated former PEN prisoners for their illegal detentions. I thank former New School student Marta Panero for furnishing me with the documentation of her compensation under this program.

43. Some of these points come from the author's interviews with Professor Carlos Acuña, Buenos Aires, June 11, 1997, and Professor Catalina Smulovitz, Buenos Aires, June 18, 1997.

44. Cheresky (1998, 84–85, n. 17). The comment by General Videla was first reported in *Revista gente*, December 22, 1977, and also cited in Argentine National Commission on the Disappeared (1986, 53).

45. Feitlowitz (1998, 28, 262, n. 30). Videla appeared on U.S. television on September 14, 1977.

46. Arceneaux (2001, 113–14). This picture of the autonomy of zone commanders was confirmed in my interview of former navy captain Carlos Raimondi, Buenos Aires, June 10, 1997. See also Argentine National Commission on the Disappeared (1986, xxiii).

47. The source for the names of political prisoners in 1973 is "Fueron 371 los presos politicos indultados," *La Nación*, May 27, 1973; the source for the names of the disappeared is Comisión Nacional sobre la Desaparición de Personas (1984a).

48. This figure was obtained by dividing the high estimate of the disappeared (thirty thousand) by the population of thirty-two million, and rounding up.

49. Alison Brysk (1994, 45–56).

Chapter 7: *Defense Lawyers in Brazil's Military Courts*

1. This generalization is corroborated by my own research as well as Arquidiocese de São Paulo (1991); and Vannucchi Leme de Matos (2002).

2. These distinctions come from Idebal Piveta, a lawyer who defended hundreds of political prisoners from 1964 to 1979 and was imprisoned himself on six occasions under the military regime (interview by the author, São Paulo, November 15, 1996).

3. Piveta interview.

4. Some of the most important defense lawyers in São Paulo were Airton Soares, Idebal Piveta, Mario Simas, José Carlos Dias, Luís Eduardo Greenalgh, and Antonio Mercado; in Rio de Janeiro, Heleno Fragoso, Heráclito Sobral Pinto, and Marcelo Alencar; in Brasília, Sepulveda Pertence; and in Pernambuco, Paulo Cavalcanti. For more on the activities of some of the lawyers above, see Fernandes (2004, esp. 201–82); Fragoso (1984); Fragoso (1980); and Simas (1986).

5. Piveta interview.

6. Vannucchi Leme de Matos finds this to have been the case even with defendants linked to the ALN, one of the most violent of the armed left groups (2002, 84–85).

7. Martin Schapiro (1975) emphasizes the triadic nature of courts.

8. From a defense brief dated November 7, 1973, and sent from Rio de Janeiro to a military court in São Paulo. Found in BNM 68.

9. STM judgment in case number 35,145 on June 17, 1966, in BNM 142.

10. Prosecution brief dated April 23, 1973, from BNM 180, a case in the 1st Court of the 2nd District of Military Justice in São Paulo, decided upon on June 20, 1973, and appealed to the STM as case number 40,233, decided upon on August 10, 1977.

11. BNM 242, case number 52/70 in the 4th District of Military Justice in Juiz de Fora, appealed to the STM as case number 38,919.

12. Defense brief by Heleno Fragoso dated December 22, 1969, in BNM 235, case number 11/69 in the 2nd Court of the 1st District of Military Justice in Rio de Janeiro, in which the regional military court acquitted Pellegrino on February 27, 1970, by a unanimous vote. The acquittal was upheld by the STM in case number 37,894 on November 3, 1972.

13. Regional military court sentence dated February 27, 1970, in BNM 235.

14. Quoted in Fragoso (1980, 29). For more on the case, see Gaspari (2002b, 214–15). *Correio da Manhã* eventually stopped circulating in 1974 (de Abreu et al. 2001, 1632).

15. Case number 1069/75 in the 1st Court of the 2nd Military Justice District, São Paulo, leading to acquittal on September 30, 1975. The case was appealed to the STM as case number 41,059. From BNM 422.

16. From STM judgment in case number 41,059, upholding the acquittal of the defendant, dated April 12, 1976. From BNM 422.

17. This was during the period when the prosecutor in military justice was obligated to appeal acquittals to the STM. From STM ruling in case number 39,188 on July 12, 1972. The original case was 99/71, in the Court of the 7th Military Justice District in Recife, in which the defendant was acquitted on January 19, 1972. From BNM 463.

18. From regional military court decision of February 12, 1974, in case number 141/69 in the 2nd Court of the 2nd Military Justice District in São Paulo and case number 9/73 in the 3rd Court of the 2nd Military Justice District in São Paulo. This seems to be another example of double jeopardy, common in Brazil's political trials.

19. The letter was from Henrique Afonso de Araújo, Subprocurador Geral da República (Assistant Attorney General) dated May 20, 1970. From BNM 538.

20. The opposition candidate for mayor was a member of the MDB (Movimento Democrático Brasileiro, or Brazilian Democratic Movement) while the other candidate

was from the pro-military ARENA (Aliança Renovadora Nacional, or National Alliance for Renewal).

21. STM ruling dated November 27, 1974, in case number 40,271. From BNM 538.

22. Defense brief submitted April 7, 1971, to the regional military court in Belém. From case number 224/70 tried in Belém in Pará state, with an acquittal of all defendants on June 14, 1971. The case was appealed to the STM as case number 38,791 and the acquittal was upheld on June 12, 1972. From BNM 405.

23. For an examination of the politics of music, and in particular the Tropicália movement of the 1960s, see Dunn (2001).

24. For more on press censorship, see Ann-Marie Smith (1997).

25. STM judgment in case number 35,145 on June 17, 1966, in BNM 142.

26. STM case number 35,590, upholding the conviction of a student on October 21, 1966, in BNM 398. The composition of the STM in June, at the time of the previous case, and in October, at the time of this one, differed by only two people.

27. BNM 37. The ruling at the first level came on June 4, 1970, and the STM upheld the sentence on October 12, 1970. One defendant managed to avoid serving her six-month sentence. On August 23, 1972, her lawyer obtained a pardon (*extinção de punibilidade*) for his client.

28. BNM 427, involving the acquittal of Marcio Pereira. The case was number 1138/75, heard in the 3rd Court of the 2nd Military Justice District, which acquitted on February 17, 1976. The STM upheld the acquittal on June 2, 1976, in STM case number 41,241.

29. Alberto João Rocha was prosecuted under article 39, sections 1 and 2, and article 45, section 5 of Decree-Law 898 of September 29, 1969. All details and quotes from this case recounted here are from BNM 107, 8th Regional Military District Court case number 162/70, decided on August 4, 1970. The case was appealed to the STM, where it became case number 39,366, decided on September 22, 1972.

30. The faculty in Brazil's public colleges and universities, unlike their counterparts in the United States, are members of the state or federal civil service, i.e., regular government employees.

31. The judges found Alberto guilty of violating article 45, section 5, but not guilty of violating article 39, sections 1 and 2 of Decree-Law 898 of 1969.

32. This was the minimum sentence, the maximum being three years.

33. From the transcript of the interrogation of Nascimento by DEOPS agents dated October 10, 1969, found in the file of BNM 148.

34. BNM 148, involving the acquittal of Nascimento in the 3rd Court of the 1st Military Justice District in Rio de Janeiro, in case number 44/70, on September 21, 1970. The STM verdict came in case number 38,938 on January 10, 1972.

35. Brief of the military justice prosecutor dated June 8, 1970, found in BNM 110, in case number 19/70 in the Air Force Court of the 1st Military Justice District, Rio de Janeiro, in which the verdict—an acquittal of all defendants—was reached on July 22, 1970. The case was appealed to the STM as case number 39,220. The STM upheld the acquittals on July 12, 1972.

36. DEOPS report dated September 19, 1969, found in BNM 110.

37. Defense brief from Heleno Fragoso dated June 8, 1970, submitted to the judges in the Air Force Court of the First Military Justice District, Rio de Janeiro, found in BNM 110.

38. From STM sentence dated July 12, 1972, found in BNM 110.

39. In a significant 1979 ruling, the STM actually acquitted a defendant on the grounds that his confession had been extracted by torture. However, this was an exceptional ruling rather than the norm, and the police agents responsible were never investigated. From author's interview with Júlio de Sá Bierrenbach (judge, Superior Tribunal Militar, 1977–1987), Rio de Janeiro, November 17, 1996; and written comments made by Admiral de Sá Bierrenbach to his fellow judges in appeal case number 41,264. See also Godinho (1982, 49–51).

40. Lawyers in Chile could file writs of habeas corpus—possibly a factor in moving the Pinochet regime toward a more selective and secretive application of violence, and the constitutionalization of its rule. This point is made by Frühling (1984). See also Policzer (2001 and forthcoming).

41. The phrase "communities of memory" comes from Jules Lobel, "Winning Lost Causes," *Chronicle of Higher Education*, February 6, 2004.

42. I take this notion of "judicial space" from Bourdieu (1987).

43. This is not to deny the cases of disappearance and killing in Brazil. The work of Marco Aurélio Vannucchi Leme de Matos, for example, shows how many ALN members were systematically tracked down and executed in the early 1970s (2002, 88–89).

44. The campaign is described by Gaspari (2002b, 399–464).

45. Admittedly these ratios are produced from rough and contested estimates. However, the differences between them are so large that widely differing numbers would produce similar results.

Chapter 8: *Transitional Justice and the Legacies of Authoritarian Legality*

1. For a somewhat narrower definition of transitional justice, see Elster (1998, 14).

2. For more on transitional justice, see Minow (1998), Nino (1996), and Kritz (1995). For works on transitional justice in the southern cone, see Roniger and Sznajder (1999) and Barahona de Brito (1997).

3. The commission to indemnify relatives of the killed and disappeared was not a truth commission along the lines of those established in Argentina and Chile because it only investigated the killings of certain individuals whose cases were brought to it, and it issued no official report.

4. For a broader definition of authoritarian legacies that goes beyond formal institutions, see Hite and Cesarini (2004, 4).

5. This is an overall assessment. The Chilean military's prerogatives are higher than those of their Brazilian counterparts. But because Chile has undergone extensive judicial reform, while Brazil has not, I rank it below Brazil.

6. Nino suggests that the longer the time span between human rights abuses and the democratic transition, the lower the probability of transitional justice (1996, 126–27).

7. The homicide rate in Brazil in 1995 was 23.3 killings per 100,000 people, while the rate in Argentina was 4.8 in 1996, and in Chile 2.9 in 1994 (Yunes and Zubarew 1999).

8. For the argument that high levels of everyday violence diminish the salience of punishment for past human rights abuses in a post-authoritarian situation, see Barahona de Brito, González-Enríquez, and Aguilar (2001, 311).

9. The PDS was an outgrowth of the ARENA (Aliança Renovadora Nacional, or National Alliance for Renewal) party, the pro-regime party that existed from 1965 until 1982. The Brazilian transition reflects the "*trasformismo*" of both Italian and Brazilian politics, in which even the political movements that seem most oppositional get sucked into the political establishment, where they are unable to achieve more than incremental reform. See Perry Anderson, "FHC Deixou Saldo negatívo, diz historiador," *Folha de São Paulo*, November 10, 2002. See also "Transformismo" in Bobbio, Matteucci, and Pasquino (1983, 1259–60).

10. For evidence that leading figures in the founding of the military regime were calling for a return to constitutional and legal normality by the end of the 1970s, see de Abreu et al. (2001, vol. 3, 3667; vol. 4, 3924 and 4046).

11. Brazil's military police are not to be confused with military police in the U.S. armed forces.

12. *Brasil: Nunca mais*, unlike the publications of the truth commissions of Argentina and Chile, was not an official document commissioned by the government.

13. Some observers disagree with this assessment. In the author's interview with Dom Paulo Evaristo Arns (then archbishop of São Paulo) on November 1, 1994, Dom Paulo declared that Brazil's repression "wiped out the credibility of the judiciary."

14. Four Brazilian states (São Paulo, Santa Catarina, Paraná, and Pernambuco) have reportedly initiated processes of indemnifying political prisoners who had been tortured (Dr. Wagner Rocha D'Angelis, former defense lawyer for political prisoners and state secretary of human rights in Paraná, interview by author, Curitiba, July 15, 2003).

15. See the statement of government officials in response to demands to investigate the disappeared in Larry Rohter, "Long after Guerrilla War, Survivors Demand Justice from Brazil's Government," *New York Times*, March 28, 2004.

16. When authoritarian regimes judicialize their repression, post-authoritarian demands for transitional justice will usually center around the opening of official archives. This applies to post–martial law Poland as well as Brazil. See Barahona de Brito, González-Enríquez, and Aguilar (2001, 310).

17. It was a local branch of Torture Never Again (Tortura Nunca Mais) that raised the funds for a statue of a political prisoner being tortured on the parrot's perch in Recife, one of the few monuments to the victims of the military regime's repression to be found in Brazil. For information on other commemorative acts, see also Carvalho and da Silva Catela (2002). For human rights work in one Brazilian state, see D'Angelis (1990). An interesting example of the voluminous testimonial literature by victims of the repression is Freire, Almada, and de Granville Ponce (1997).

18. On November 22, 1996, I visited the bookstore in the army's Duque de Caxias Palace on President Vargas Avenue in Rio de Janeiro and saw the copies of the book on sale.

19. The photographs that sparked this incident were originally thought to be of the journalist Vladimir Herzog, killed while in the custody of the Second Army in São Paulo

in 1975. From "A força dos generais," *Veja*, November 17, 2004, 54–55. For information on the November 2004 apology of the commander of the Chilean Army, General Emilio Cheyre, see "O Chile abre os porões," *Veja*, November 17, 2004, 140. In April of 1995, the then commander of the Argentine Army, General Martín Balza, recognized the military's responsibility for human rights violations during the 1976–1983 dictatorship. From "Participantes en procesos de paz de 4 paises expusieron sus inquietudes," Agencia Latinoamericana y Caribeña de Comunicación, June 9, 2003, at http://www.alcnoticias.org (accessed March 13, 2005).

20. From a 2004 Ministry of Justice report summarized in David Fleischer, *Brazil Focus Weekly Report*, August 14–20, 2004, 6–7.

21. See, for example, Figueroa (1998) and López Dawson (1995). These are both excellent critical analyses of military justice's past, present, and possible future. I have encountered no equivalent of them in Brazil.

22. The *Revista do Superior Tribunal Militar* and other STM publications are the chief sources of this kind of analysis. See, for example, Ferreira (1984/85), Fernandes (1983), and Costa Filho (1994).

23. From Costa Filho (1994, 39–40). The essay, written on the occasion of the sixtieth anniversary of military justice's integration with the civilian judiciary, is by a retired assistant prosecutor (*subprocurador*) in military justice. The quote is interesting in that it recognizes that the judicial power under military rule did not follow the rule of law, but was somehow responsible for the latter's reestablishment.

24. Law 23,040, passed in 1983, was the reopened Congress' first decision. According to Nino, the bill passed unanimously, with members of the Madres de Plaza de Mayo in attendance (1996, 74).

25. Law 23,049, passed on February 9, 1984. Article 3 definitively removed civilians from the jurisdiction of military justice. See also Sancinetti (1988, 76, 185–93).

26. One author writes, "the new judges appointed by the Alfonsín administration were young and inexperienced; those originally appointed by the military regime and reappointed in 1983 were suspected of not having democratic convictions" (Malamud-Goti 1996, 185).

27. The so-called Full Stop Law (*punto final*) was passed in December 1986. It set a deadline of February 23, 1987, for the initiation of further prosecutions of the military for dirty war violations (Lewis 2002, 224). The Due Obedience Law (*obediencia debida*), enacted in June of 1987, stated that military personnel who had committed human rights abuses while following orders would not be liable for prosecution (Nino 1996, 100–101).

28. Nino (1996) argues that trials in Argentina were effective in repudiating military rule and promoting democracy, despite President Menem's pardons. For a different assessment, see Malamud-Goti (1996).

29. From "The Empty-Handed Social Democrat," *Economist*, May 31, 2003, 35.

30. Janaína Figueiredo, "Argentina: 97 militares presos na era Kirchner," *O Globo*, June 12, 2004.

31. For the argument that legal continuity creates formidable obstacles to transitional justice, see Nino (1996, 120).

32. From the presentation by Nibaldo Galleguillos on the panel LAW01: "Authoritarian Legacies and Institutions of Coercion: Legal Reform and the Rule of Law in Latin America" at the 23rd International Congress of the Latin American Studies Association, Washington, D.C., September 6, 2001.

33. The Concertación de Partidos por la Democracia (Coalition of Parties for Democracy) includes the Socialist Party, the Radical Party, the Party for Democracy, and the Christian Democratic Party. Created as an electoral alliance in the 1989 presidential election, it won the first three presidential elections after the end of military rule.

34. Aylwin was a member of the "Group of 24," a group of prominent members of the opposition who originally met to analyze and critique the 1980 constitution and who later became leading figures in the first Concertación government.

35. Personal communication from Carlos Maldonado, an official in the Public Security and Information section of the Ministry of the Interior, Chile, June 26, 2003.

36. From Claudia Heiss and Patricio Navia (2003, 17, 30–38).

37. Alexander Wilde characterizes truth and justice issues as having a peculiarly "muffled" tone in Chile. See Wilde (1999).

38. The reforms are all discussed in Prillaman (2000, 143–44, 150). For a much less positive view of them, see Galleguillos (2001).

39. "Chile's Top Court Strips Pinochet of Immunity," *New York Times*, August 27, 2004; and "Pinochet Entangled in Web of Inquiries," *New York Times*, February 7, 2005.

Chapter 9: *The Sword and the Robe*

1. For example, Kirk Bowman argues that Latin American militaries are unique in the developing world because of their long, almost two-hundred-year histories as relatively autonomous organizations within independent states, and for their primarily internal focus (2002, 37).

2. I define military regimes here broadly as regimes in which the executive is controlled by a military junta or cabinet, as well as regimes with military presidents who to some degree control or represent the armed forces. Regimes with civilian presidents in which real power and control lie with the armed forces should also be included in this category, although such regimes can be difficult to evaluate. (An example is the Uruguayan regime headed by civilian president Juan María Bordaberry from 1972 to 1976.) See the discussion by Brooker (2000, 44–52).

3. See Brooker (2000, 4) for twentieth-century authoritarian regimes.

4. One source lists only four contemporary military regimes (Burma, Libya, Syria, and Sudan) with Pakistan classified as a military-led "transitional government." The latter may have more to do with U.S. foreign policy than analytical concerns. From Central Intelligence Agency (2004) World Fact Book, http://www.cia.gov/cia/publications/factbook (accessed August 2004).

5. For purposes of this discussion, I do not place Nazi Germany in a distinctive category of totalitarian regimes. For some types of analysis in comparative politics, the totalitarian label is no longer seen as useful; see Brooker (2000, 8–21).

6. I am not the first to make a connection between the authoritarian regimes founded in inter-war Europe and the Brazilian and southern cone military regimes. The "bureau-cratic-authoritarian" label that O'Donnell applied to the latter was borrowed from Janos's analysis of Eastern European regimes in the 1920s and 1930s. See Janos (1970).

7. Miller (1995, 52). The Brazilian military regime also used this tactic in cases involving national security.

8. Scholars of Nazi legality seem to agree that rigid adherence to legal positivism was not a characteristic of Nazi justice and not responsible for the horrors of the regime. Köch (1989), Miller (1995), and Müller (1991) all agree that the problem was the opposite—that judges engaged in politically motivated searches for the "fundamental idea" of the laws and often disregarded statutory language.

9. Miller (1995, 44). Miller reports the acquittal rate in Germany's criminal trials in 1932 as 15 percent, similar to that in the People's Court.

10. From the Harvard Law School Library Nuremberg Trials Project: A Digital Document Collection, "Introduction to NMT Case 4, U.S.A. v. Pohl et al." at http://nuremberg .law.harvard.edu.

11. The People's Court was not the only venue for judicialized repression under the Nazis. From 1933 to 1945, German military courts sentenced about fifty thousand people to death, most of them after 1942 (Stölleis 1998, 151–52). Another author estimates the number to have been thirty-three thousand (see Müller 1991, 194).

12. Quoted in H. L. Mathews (2003) "Half of Spain Died," http://www.rigeib.com/ heroes/unamuno/franco.html (accessed October 2003).

13. This is not to imply that there were equal numbers of killings on each side. Payne concludes that more people belonged to leftist organizations than to identifiably right groups, so the Nationalists had more perceived enemies to eliminate, and their executions probably exceeded those on the other side. See Payne (1967, 415).

14. The Falangists were members of a fascist political party called the Falange Española founded in 1933 by José António Primo de Rivera, son of a former Spanish dictator.

15. Payne (1967, 411–12). Franco also personally approved the execution of his first cousin, Major Lapuente Bahamonde, in Morocco in 1936 (ibid., 413).

16. All figures and the anecdote in this paragraph are from Gallo (1974, 67–70). The total population figure is from Gallo (21).

17. From 1968 to 1974 Portugal was ruled by Salazar's successor Marcelo Caetano, but I refer to the whole period of authoritarian rule as the Salazar regime.

18. This distinction comes from Cruz (1988, 84).

19. After the 1926 coup d'etat that ended the Portuguese Republic, Salazar, formerly an economics professor at the University of Coimbra, became minister of finance in 1928 and prime minister in 1932 (Bermeo 1986,13–14). In many ways, the Salazar regime is a better approximation of Juan Linz's ideal-type of a nonmobilizing authoritarian regime than is Franco's Spain; see Linz (1975).

20. Under Salazar's successor, Caetano, the PIDE was again renamed, this time to DGS (Direção Geral de Segurança, or General Directorate of Security). After the revolution of April 25, 1974, the DGS was abolished.

21. Cruz (1988, 83–85). The trials were aimed primarily at the lower strata of society; between 1932 and 1945, 48 percent of political prisoners were workers while only 14 percent were middle-class professionals (95).

22. As a precedent, the Bush administration cited the military tribunal that tried and sentenced to death German spies captured on U.S. soil during World War II. But this case occurred before the United States signed several major treaties, including the Geneva Conventions.

23. At the time of writing—March 2005—the best-known detainee in this category was the alleged "dirty bomber" José Padilla, arrested in Chicago after a trip to Pakistan in the spring of 2002. "Detention Cases Before Supreme Court Will Test Limits of Presidential Power," *New York Times*, April 18, 2004.

24. The detainees in Guantánamo, alleged Taliban and al Qaeda combatants from more than forty countries, numbered about 540 in March of 2005. Douglas Jehl, "Detainee Numbers in Cuba to Be Cut," *Times-Picayune*, March 11, 2005. In response to the Supreme Court decision of June 2004 discussed below, some pretrial screenings of detainees have taken place to determine their status. From Ian James, "Detainees Plead for Release in Guantánamo Tribunals," *Sacramento Bee*, August 6, 2004. Meanwhile, the first trial in the military tribunals has been initiated; see Neil A. Lewis, "Military Tribunal Begins in Cuba," *Times-Picayune*, August 25, 2004.

25. For different views of these and other post-9/11 measures, see Etzioni and Marsh (2003) and Schulz (2003).

26. Seymour Hersh, "Annals of National Security: Torture at Abu Ghraib," *New Yorker*, May 10, 2004, 42–53.

27. See Eyal Press, "Tortured Logic," *Amnesty Now*, Summer 2003, 20–28; and "Ends, Means and Barbarity," *Economist*, January 11, 2003, 18–20.

28. From Barry Gewen, "Thinking the Unthinkable," review of Alan M. Dershowitz, *Why Terrorism Works: Understanding the Threat, Responding to the Challenge*, *New York Times Book Review*, September 15, 2002, 12. See also Jeremy Waldron, "The Great Defender," review of Alan M. Dershowitz, *Shouting Fire: Civil Liberties in a Turbulent Age*, *New York Times Book Review*, February 3, 2002, 13; and "Ends, Means and Barbarity," *Economist*, January 11, 2003, 18–20.

29. From Seymour Hersh, "Torture at Abu Ghraib," *New Yorker*, May 10, 2004, 42–47.

30. As of January 2005, more than 130 U.S. military personnel have been disciplined or convicted in connection with the abuse or killing of prisoners in Afghanistan, Iraq, and Guantánamo Bay. It is notable that these punishments do not extend high up the chain of command. See "Just a Few Bad Apples?" *Economist*, January 22, 2005, 29.

31. The complete name of the USA PATRIOT act is H.R. 3162, Uniting and Strengthening America by Providing Appropriate Tools Required to Intercept and Obstruct Terrorism. The full name of the earlier law is the Antiterrorism and Effective Death Penalty Act of 1996. For an analysis of the latter act, see Cole and Dempsey (2002, 107–75). For more on changes to law enforcement and intelligence gathering after 9/11, see Schulhofer (2002).

32. For example, the Justice Department investigated the Holy Land Foundation for

234 Notes to Pages 186–88

Relief and Development for alleged ties to Hamas, a Palestinian organization placed on the U.S. government's list of terrorist organizations in 1997. Furthermore, the Treasury Department froze $5 million of the foundation's assets, and the foundation has sued the government in an attempt to recover the funds. From "Islamic Charity Says Feds' Case Flawed," *Times-Picayune*, September 21, 2003.

33. See "Army Detains One of its Own in War on Terror," *Times-Picayune*, September 21, 2003; and "Airman Accused of Spying for Syria," *Times-Picayune*, September 24, 2003.

34. For an argument against this provision of the regulations, see Edward J. Klaris, "Justice Can't Be Done in Secret," *Nation*, June 10, 2002, 16–20.

35. John Mintz, "Rumsfeld Details Tribunal for War Captives," *Manchester Guardian Weekly*, March 28–April 3, 2002, 32.

36. Paisely Dodds, "Arraignments on Tap for Cuba Detainees," *Times-Picayune*, August 23, 2004. This article claims that several former prisoners at Guantánamo have said that they made false confessions after interrogations.

37. For these and other insights into the military commissions I am indebted to the participants in the symposium "The Judiciary and the War on Terror" held at the Tulane University Law School on February 21, 2003, especially Robin Shulberg, a federal public defender; Eugene Fidell, the president of the National Institute of Military Justice; Edward Sherman, a professor of Tulane Law School; Jordan Paust, of the University of Houston Law Center; and Derek Jinks, of the St. Louis University School of Law.

38. Wolfe (2001, 284, 293, and esp. 287–88).

39. Mike van Winkle, a spokesperson for the California Anti-Terrorism Information Center, quoted in Jim Hightower, "Bush Zones Go National," *Nation*, August 16/23, 2004, 27–29; the quote is on p. 29.

40. Arato (2000b, 328). Arato suggests that there is a general tendency for U.S. presidents to seek a way out of the gridlock inherent in the U.S. presidential and federal system by invoking emergency powers. However, the open-ended nature of the "war on terrorism" and the unconventional nature of the presumed war make this particular push for emergency powers particularly dangerous from a constitutional point of view.

41. Quoted in Miles Benson and David Wood, "Terrorism Suspect's Detention by Military Faces Tide of Criticism," *Miami Herald*, June 16, 2002.

42. The outpouring of commentary on the military commissions is too great to list here. For significant criticisms of the tribunals, see Arato (2002, 457–76); William Safire, "Kangaroo Courts Betray Our Values," *Times-Picayune*, November 16, 2001; Anthony Lewis, "Wake Up America," *New York Times*, November 30, 2001; Judith Butler, "Guantánamo Limbo," *Nation*, April 1, 2002, 20–24; and Aryeh Neier, "The Military Tribunals on Trial," *New York Review of Books*, February 14, 2002, 1–9. For a defense of the commissions, see Albert R. Gonzales, "Martial Justice, Full and Fair," in *New York Times*, November 30, 2001; and Wedgwood (2002).

43. For some examples of this work, see Gathii (2003, 335), Lugosi (2003, 225), and Amann (2004, 263).

44. Stuart Taylor Jr., "Lawless in the Dungeon," *Legal Times*, January 12, 2004, 46.

45. Jess Bravin, "Capital Charges Thrown Out in Moussaoui Terrorism Trial," *Wall*

Street Journal, October 3, 2003. Government lawyers responded to the ruling by saying that they would appeal it and if they lost the appeal would designate Moussaoui as an "enemy combatant" so that he could be held without charges indefinitely or tried in a military commission. This shows how the creation of a special court can change the impact of legal decisions in the civilian judiciary, in effect giving the prosecution an entirely new and highly favorable jurisdiction.

46. Cass R. Sunstein, "The Smallest Court in the Land," *New York Times*, July 4, 2004, Week in Review section.

47. Esther Schrader, "Tribunals Unconstitutional, Judge Rules," *Times-Picayune*, February 1, 2005; and "Free Him, or Charge Him," *Economist*, March 5, 2005, 31.

48. Andrew Arato takes the optimistic view that resistance to "the illegitimate and dangerous expansion of emergency government" after 9/11 will succeed (2002, 472).

49. Interestingly, Supreme Court Chief Justice William Rehnquist has written a book on civil liberties in wartime. (I thank Miguel Schor for alerting me to this fact.) Rehnquist's measured conclusion might give hope to both supporters and critics of the executive's assertion of broad war powers in the "war on terrorism": "It is neither desirable nor it is remotely likely that civil liberty will occupy as favored a position in wartime as it does in peacetime. But it is both desirable and likely that more careful attention will be paid by the courts to the basis for the government's claims of necessity as a basis for curtailing civil liberty. The laws will thus not be silent in time of war, but they will speak with a somewhat different voice" (Rehnquist 1998, 224–25).

Chapter 10: *The Puzzle of Authoritarian Legality*

1. Friedrich's argument is paraphrased in Finn (1991, 16–17). For more on emergency powers in contemporary politics, see Giorgio Agamben, "L'État d'exception," *Le Monde*, December 12, 2002; Arato (2002); Franz Schurmann, "The Rise of Emergency Powers and the Fall of the Law," *Sacramento Bee*, December 29, 2002; and Rehnquist (1998).

2. Friedrich's guidelines are useful in assessing the ongoing debate in Brazil about whether or not the military regime was a dictatorship, leading to the conclusion that it was. For this debate, see Rezende (2001, 17–18 nn. 3, 5).

3. Michel Foucault (1979) seems to come close to endorsing such a view. He writes, "the prison is not the daughter of laws, codes, or the judicial apparatus; . . . it is not subordinate to the court and the docile or clumsy instrument of the sentences that it hands out and of the results that it would like to achieve; . . . it is the court that is external and subordinate to the prison" (307–8).

4. As we have seen, the independence of military courts in both Brazil and Chile was very limited, because most judges were active-duty officers in the military chain of command, and none of them had security of tenure. Furthermore, judges were highly biased rather than neutral arbiters of defendants' behavior. Court autonomy therefore refers to the limited ability of judges, under certain circumstances, to interpret national security laws in ways that upheld individual rights and to acquit defendants who might otherwise have faced continued imprisonment.

5. Thompson (1966, 12). Thompson was writing about eighteenth- and nineteenth-century English workers, but his phrase is also wonderfully appropriate in this context.

6. In their brief for historical-institutional scholarship, Pierson and Skocpol argue that such work has three essential features: it is oriented to large, important questions; it makes temporal sequence a part of its explanatory arguments; and it examines "the combined effects of institutions and processes, their contexts and configurations, not just one institution or process at a time" (2002, 695–96). I agree that there is a need for more work with these characteristics. For a survey of the literature on judicial politics in the United States that reveals how courts have often been studied in isolation from other organizations and processes, see Maveety (2004).

7. In my view, Zakaria's conception of law is too narrow in that it emphasizes the rights of property and contract but gives insufficient attention to more modern civil and human rights. See Zakaria (2003, 86).

Works Cited

Abreu, Alzira Alves de, Israel Beloch, Fernando Lattman-Weltman, and Sérgio Tadeu de Niemeyer Lamarão, eds. 2001. *Dicionário histórico-biográfico brasileiro pós-1930.* 5 vols. Rio de Janeiro: Fundação Getúlio Vargas, Centro de Pesquisa e Documentação de História Contemporanea.

Acuña, Carlos, and Catalina Smulovitz. 1997. "Guarding the Guardians in Argentina: Some Lessons about the Risks and Benefits of Empowering the Courts." In *Transitional Justice and the Rule of Law in New Democracies,* ed. A. James McAdams, 93–122. Notre Dame, IN: University of Notre Dame Press.

Aguilar, Paloma. 1996. *Memoria y olvido de la guerra civil española.* Madrid: Alianza Editorial.

Almeida, General Heitor Luiz Gomes de. 1986/87. "A justiça militar e as propostas pré-constitucionais." *Revista do Superior Tribunal Militar* 9 (11/12): 17–27.

Alves, Maria Helena Moreira. 1987. *Estado e oposição no Brasil. 1964–1984.* 4th ed. Petrópolis: Editora Vozes.

Amann, Diane Marie. 2004. "Guantánamo." *Columbia Journal of Transnational Law* 42:263–348.

Ames, Barry. 1987. *Political Survival: Politicians and Public Policy in Latin America.* Berkeley: University of California Press.

Andersen, Martin Edward. 1993. *Dossier Secreto: Argentina's Desaparecidos and the Myth of the 'Dirty War'.* Boulder, CO: Westview Press.

Arato, Andrew. 2000a. "Good-bye to Dictatorships?" *Social Research* 67 (4): 927–28.

———. 2000b. "Constitutional Lessons." *Constellations* 7 (3): 316–40.

———. 2002. "The Bush Tribunals and the Specter of Dictatorship." in *Constellations* 9 (4): 457–76.

Arceneaux, Craig. 2001. *Bounded Missions: Military Regimes and Democratization in the Southern Cone and Brazil.* University Park, PA: Pennsylvania State University Press.

Arendt, Hannah. 1958. *The Origins of Totalitarianism.* 2nd ed. New York: World Publishing Company.

Argentine National Commission on the Disappeared. 1986. *Nunca más.* New York: Farrar, Strauss, Giroux.

Arquidiocese de São Paulo. 1991. *Brasil: Nunca mais.* 26th ed. Petrópolis: Editora Vozes.

Arriagada Herrera, Genero. 1986. "The Legal and Institutional Framework of the Armed Forces." In *Military Rule in Chile: Dictatorship and Oppositions,* ed. J. Samuel Valenzuela and Arturo Valenzuela, 117–43. Baltimore: Johns Hopkins University Press.

Arzobispado de Santiago. 1989–1991. *Jurisprudencia: Delitos contra la seguridad del estado.* 4 vols. Santiago: Vicaría de la Solidaridad.

Avritzer, Leonardo. 2002. *Democracy and the Public Space in Latin America.* Princeton, NJ: Princeton University Press.

Barahona de Brito, Alexandra. 1997. *Human Rights and Democratization in Latin America: Uruguay and Chile.* New York: Oxford University Press.

Barahona de Brito, Alexandra, Carmen González-Enríquez, and Paloma Aguilar, eds. 2001. *The Politics of Memory: Transitional Justice in Democratizing Societies.* Oxford: Oxford University Press.

Barbosa, Vivaldo. 2002. *A Rebelião da Legalidade.* Rio de Janeiro: Editora Fundação Getúlio Vargas.

Barkan, Steven E. 1985. *Protestors on Trial: Criminal Justice in the Southern Civil Rights and Vietnam Antiwar Movements.* New Brunswick, NJ: Rutgers University Press.

Barros, Robert. 1996. "By Reason and Force: Military Constitutionalism in Chile, 1973–1989." PhD diss., University of Chicago.

———. 2001. "Chile: Personalization and Institutional Constraints." *Latin American Politics and Society* 43 (1): 5–28.

———. 2002. *Constitutionalism and Dictatorship: Pinochet, the Junta, and the 1980 Constitution.* New York: Cambridge University Press.

Bastos, Elide Rugai, and João Quartim de Morães, eds. 1993. *O pensamento de Oliveira Vianna.* Campinas: Editora da UNICAMP.

Bates, Robert, Avner Greif, Margaret Levi, Jean-Laurent Rosenthal, and Barry Weingast. 1998. *Analytic Narratives.* Princeton, NJ: Princeton University Press.

Beattie, Peter M. 2001. *The Tribute of Blood: Army, Honor, Race, and Nation in Brazil, 1864–1945.* Durham, NC: Duke University Press.

Becker, Theodore, ed. 1971. *Political Trials.* Indianapolis, IN: Bobbs-Merrill Company.

Bermeo, Nancy. 1986. *The Revolution within the Revolution: Workers' Control in Rural Portugal.* Princeton, NJ: Princeton University Press.

Black, Henry Campbell. 1979. *Black's Law Dictionary.* 5th ed. St. Paul, MN: West Publishing Co.

Black, Jan Knippers. 1977. *United States Penetration of Brazil.* Manchester: Manchester University Press.

Bobbio, Norberto, Nicola Matteucci, and Gianfranco Pasquino, eds. 1983. *Dicionário de política.* Vol. 2. Brasília: Editora Universidade de Brasília.

Boeninger, Edgardo. 1998. *Democracia en Chile: Lecciones para la gobernabilidad.* Santiago: Editorial Andrés Bello.

Bonasso, Miguel. 1997. *El presidente que no fue: Los archivos ocultos del peronismo.* Buenos Aires: Planeta.

Bourdieu, Pierre. 1987. "The Force of Law: Toward a Sociology of the Juridical Field." *Hastings Law Journal* 38:805–53.

Bowman, Kirk S. 2002. *Militarization, Democracy, and Development: The Perils of Praetorianism in Latin America.* Philadelphia: Pennsylvania State University Press.

Brennan, James. 1994. *The Labor Wars in Cordoba, 1955–1976.* Cambridge, MA: Harvard University Press.

Brooker, Paul. 2000. *Non-Democratic Regimes: Theory, Government, and Politics.* New York: St. Martin's Press.

Bryce, James. 1916. *South America: Observations and Impressions.* New York: Macmillan. Company.

Brysk, Alison. 1994. *The Politics of Human Rights in Argentina: Protest, Change, and Democratization.* Stanford, CA: Stanford University Press.

Buchanan, Paul. 1989. "State Terror as a Complement of Economic Policy: The Argentine Proceso, 1976–1981." In *Dependence, Development, and State Repression,* ed. George A. Lopez and Michael Stohl, 33–66. New York: Greenwood Press.

Cardoso, Fernando Henrique, and Enzo Faletto. 1979. *Dependency and Development in Latin America.* Berkeley: University of California Press.

Carey, John. 2000. "Parchment, Equilibria, and Institutions." *Comparative Political Studies* 33 (6/7): 735–61.

Carleton, David. 1989. "The New International Division of Labor, Export-Oriented Growth, and State Repression in Latin America." In *Dependence, Development, and State Repression,* ed. George A. Lopez and Michael Stohl, 211–36. New York: Greenwood Press.

Carvalho, Alessandra, and Ludmila da Silva Catela. 2002. "31 de marzo de 1964 en Brasil: Memorias deshilachadas." In *Las conmemoraciones: Las disputas en las fechas 'infelices',* ed. Elizabeth Jelin, 195–242 Buenos Aires: Siglo Veintiuno de Argentina Editores/New York: Social Science Research Council.

Cavallo, Ascanio, Manuel Salazar, and Oscar Sepúlveda. 1997. *La historia oculta del régimen militar: Chile 1973–1988.* Santiago: Grijalbo.

Centeno, Miguel. 2002. *Blood and Debt: War and the Nation-State in Latin America.* University Park: Pennsylvania State University Press.

Cheresky, Isidoro. 1998. "Régimen estatal de desaparición." *Sociedad* 12/13 (November): 81–102.

Chiavenato, Júlio José. 2000. *O golpe de '64 e a ditadura militar.* São Paulo: Editora Moderna.

Chilean National Commission on Truth and Reconciliation. 1993. *Report of the National Commission on Truth and Reconciliation,* vols. 1–2. Notre Dame, IN: University of Notre Dame Press.

Christenson, Ron. 1986. *Political Trials: Gordian Knots in the Law.* New Brunswick, NJ: Transaction Books.

Cohen, Youssef. 1994. *Radicals, Refomers, and Reactionaries: The Prisoner's Dilemma and the Collapse of Democracy in Latin America.* Chicago: University of Chicago Press.

Cole, David, and James X. Dempsey. 2002. *Terrorism and the Constitution.* New York: New Press.

Collier, David, and Ruth Collier. 1991. *Shaping the Political Arena.* Princeton, NJ: Princeton University Press.

Comisión Nacional sobre la Desaparición de Personas. 1984a. *Anexos del informe de la Comisión Nacional sobre la Desaparición de Personas.* 2nd ed. Buenos Aires: Eudeba.

———. 1984b. *Nunca más.* Buenos Aires: Martes.

Constable, Pamela, and Arturo Valenzuela. 1991. *A Nation of Enemies: Chile under Pinochet*. New York: W. W. Norton.

Corradi, Juan. 1985. *The Fitful Republic: Economy, Society, and Politics in Argentina*. Boulder, CO: Westview Press.

Costa Couto, Ronaldo. 1999. *História indiscreta da ditadura e da abertura*. São Paulo: Editora Record.

Costa Filho, Milton Menezes da. 1994. *A justiça militar no poder judiciário*. Brasília: Superior Tribunal Militar, DIDOC, Seção da Divulgação.

Couto, Adolpho João de Paula. 1999. *Revolução de 1964: A versão e o fato*. Porto Alegre: Gente do Livro.

Cover, Robert. 1975. *Justice Accused: Antislavery and the Judicial Process*. New Haven, CT: Yale University Press.

Craig, Gordon. 1955. *The Politics of the Prussian Army, 1640–1945*. New York: Oxford University Press.

Cruz, Manuel Braga da. 1988. *O partido e o estado no salazarismo*. Lisbon: Editorial Presença.

Da Matta, Roberto. 1991. "'Do You Know Who You're Talking To?!' The Distinction between Individual and Person in Brazil." In *Carnivals, Rogues, and Heroes: An Interpretation of the Brazilian Dilemma*, 137–97. Notre Dame, IN: University of Notre Dame Press.

Damaška, Mirjan R. 1986. *The Faces of Justice and State Authority*. New Haven, CT: Yale University Press.

D'Angelis, Wagner Rocha. 1990. *Centro Heleno Fragoso pelos Direitos Humanos*. 3rd. ed. Curitiba: Centro Heleno Fragoso Pelos Direitos Humanos.

D'Araújo, Maria Celina, Glaucio Ary Dillon Soares, and Celso Castro, eds. 1994. *Os anos de chumbo: A memória militar sobre a repressão*. Rio de Janeiro: Relume Dumará.

Dassin, Joan. 1992. "Testimonial Literature and the Armed Struggle in Brazil." In *Fear at the Edge: State Terror and Resistance in Latin America*, ed. Juan Corradi, Patricia Weiss Fagen, and Manuel Antonio Garretón, 161–83. Berkeley: University of California Press.

Davis, Nathaniel. 1985. *The Last Two Years of Salvador Allende*. Ithaca, NY: Cornell University Press.

Dellasoppa, Emilio. 1998. *Ao inimigo, nem justiça: Violência política na Argentina 1943–1983*. São Paulo: Editora Hucitec.

Domínguez, Carlos Horacio. 1983. *El terrorismo en el estado de derecho*. Buenos Aires: Editorial Abaco de Rodolfo Depalma.

Domínguez, Virginia. 1986. *White by Definition: Social Classification in Creole Louisiana*. New Brunswick, NJ: Rutgers University Press.

dos Santos, Wanderley Guilherme, Violeta Maria Monteiro, and Ana Maria Lustosa Caillaux. 1990. *Que Brasil é este?: Manual de indicadores políticos e sociais*. Rio de Janeiro: IUPERJ and Vertice.

Drake, Paul. 1991. "Chile, 1930–58." In *The Cambridge History of Latin America*, vol. 8, *1930 to the Present*, ed. Leslie Bethell, 269–310. New York: Cambridge University Press.

———. 1996. *Labor Movements and Dictatorships: The Southern Cone in Comparative Perspective.* Baltimore, MD: Johns Hopkins University Press.

Dunn, Christopher. 2001. *Brutality Garden: Tropicália and the Emergence of a Brazilian Counterculture.* Durham: University of North Carolina Press.

Elster, Jon. 1989. *Nuts and Bolts for the Social Sciences.* New York: Cambridge University Press.

———. 1998. "Coming to Terms with the Past: A Framework for the Study of Justice in the Transition to Democracy." *Archives européenes de sociologie* 39(1): 7–48.

———. 2000. "Rational Choice History: A Case of Excessive Ambition." *American Political Science Review* 94 (3): 685–95.

Etzioni, Amitai, and Jason Marsh, eds. 2003. *Rights vs. Public Safety after 9/11: America in the Age of Terrorism.* Boulder, CO: Rowman and Littlefield.

Feitlowitz, Marguerite. 1998. *A Lexicon of Terror: Argentina and the Legacies of Torture.* New York: Oxford University Press.

Fernandes, Fernando Augusto. 2004. *Voz humana: A defesa perante os tribunais da república.* Rio de Janeiro: Editora Revan.

Fernandes, Octávio J. S. 1983. "O Superior Tribunal Militar e a legislação de segurança nacional." *Revista do Superior Tribunal Militar* 7 (8): 7–50.

Ferreira, Célio Lobão. 1984/85. "Crimes contra a segurança do estado." *Revista do Superior Tribunal Militar* 8 (9/10): 23–88.

Figueroa, Jorge Mera. 1998. "Justicia militar y estado de derecho." *Cuadernos de análisis jurídico* 40.

Finn, John E. 1991. *Constitution in Crisis: Political Violence and the Rule of Law.* New York: Oxford University Press.

Foucault, Michel. 1979. *Discipline and Punish: The Birth of the Prison.* New York: Vintage Books.

Fragoso, General Augusto. 1975. "Legislação de segurança nacional." *Revista do Superior Tribunal Militar* 1 (1): 103–93.

Fragoso, Heleno. 1980. *Lei de segurança nacional: Uma experiencia antidemocrática.* Porto Alegre: Sergio Antonio Fabris Editor.

———. 1984. *Advocacia da liberdade: A defesa nos processos políticos.* Rio de Janeiro: Foresnse.

Freire, Alipio, Izaías Almada, and J. A. de Granville Ponce, eds. 1997. *Tiradentes, um presídio da ditadura.* São Paulo: Scipione Cultural.

Freyre, Gilberto. 1970. *Order and Progress: Brazil from Monarchy to Republic.* Trans. Rod W. Horton. New York: Alfred A. Knopf.

Frühling, Hugo. 1984. "Repressive Policies and Legal Dissent in Authoritarian Regimes: Chile 1973–1981." *International Journal of the Sociology of Law* 12: 351–74.

Galleguillos, Nibaldo H. 2001. "Judicial and Legal Reforms in the Democratic Transition: An Assessment of the Changing Roles of the Judiciary in Chile." Paper prepared for the 23rd International Congress of the Latin American Studies Association, September 6–9, Washington, DC.

Gallo, Max. 1974. *Spain under Franco: A History.* New York: E. P. Dutton and Company.

Gardner, James. 1980. *Legal Imperialism: American Lawyers and Foreign Aid in Latin America.* Madison: University of Wisconsin.

Garretón Merino, Manuel Antonio, Roberto Garretón Merino, and Carmen Garretón Merino. 1998. *Por la fuerza sin la razon: Analisis y textos de los bandos de la dictadura militar.* Santiago: LOM Ediciones.

Gaspari, Elio. 2002a. *A ditadura envergonhada.* As ilusões armadas. São Paulo: Companhia das Letras.

———. 2002b. *A ditadura escancarada.* As ilusões armadas. São Paulo: Companhia das Letras.

Gathii, James Thuo. 2003. "Torture, Extraterritoriality, Terrorism, and International Law." *Albany Law Review* 67:335–70.

Geddes, Barbara. 1994. *Politician's Dilemma: Building State Capacity in Latin America.* Berkeley: University of California Press.

———. 1995. "Uses and Limits of Rational Choice." In *Latin America in Comparative Perspective: New Approaches to Methods and Analysis,* ed. Peter Smith, 81–108. Boulder, CO: Westview Press.

George, Alexander. 1979. "Case Studies and Theory Development: The Method of Structured, Focused Comparison." In *Diplomacy: New Approaches in History, Theory, and Policy,* ed. Paul Gordon Lauren, 43–67. New York: Free Press.

Gil, Frederico. 1966. *The Political System of Chile.* Boston: Houghton Mifflin.

Giordani, Marco Polo. 1986. *Brasil: Sempre.* Porto Alegre: Tche Editora.

Gobierno de Argentina. 1967. Laws 17,292–17,453. *Anales de legislación argentina,* 27B.

———. 1971. Laws 18,969–19,162. *Anales de legislación argentina,* 31B.

Godinho, Gualter. 1982. *Legislação de segurança nacional e direito penal militar.* São Paulo: Revista dos Tribunais.

Goldwert, Marvin. 1989. "The Rise of Modern Militarism in Argentina." In *The Politics of Anti-Politics,* 2nd ed., ed. Brian Loveman and Thomas Davies, 43–45. Lincoln: University of Nebraska Press.

Gordon, Lincoln. 1964. "Novas perspectivas das relações brasileiro-norte-americanas (New Perspectives in Brazilian–North American Relations)." Speech of U.S. Ambassador to Brazil to the Superior War College, May 5.

———. 2001. *Brazil's Second Chance: En Route toward the First World.* Washington, DC: Brookings Institution Press.

———. 2003. *Brazil, 1961–64: The United States and the Goulart Regime.* Washington, DC: Brookings Institute.

Gramsci, Antonio. 1971. *Selections from the Prison Notebooks.* Ed. and trans. Quintin Hoare and Geoffrey Nowell-Smith. New York: International Publishers.

Graziano, Frank. 1992. *Divine Violence: Spectacle, Psychosexuality, and Radical Christianity in the 'Dirty War'.* Boulder, CO: Westview Press.

Green, Donald, and Ian Shapiro. 1994. *Pathologies of Rational Choice Theory.* New Haven, CT: Yale University Press.

Groisman, Enrique. 1983. *Poder y derecho en el "proceso de reorganización nacional."* Buenos Aires: Centro de Investigaciones sobre el Estado y la Administración.

Grothe, Mardy. 2004. *Oxymoronica.* New York: Harper Collins.

Guest, Ian. 1990. *Behind the Disappearances: Argentina's Dirty War against Human Rights and the United Nations.* Philadelphia: University of Pennsylvania Press.

Hall, Peter, and Rosemary Taylor. 1996. "Political Science and the Three New Insitutionalisms." *Political Studies* 44:936–57.

Halperín Donghi, Tulio. 1993. *The Contemporary History of Latin America.* Durham, NC: Duke University Press.

Hayner, Priscilla. 2001. *Unspeakable Truths: Confronting State Terror and Atrocity.* New York: Routledge.

Heinz, Wolfgang. 1992. "Determinants of Gross Human Rights Violations by State and State-Sponsored Actors in Brazil, 1960–1990." 2 vols. Manuscript, Leiden University.

Heller, Milton Ivan. 1988. *Resistência democrática: A repressão no Paraná.* São Paulo: Editora Paz e Terra/Secretario de Estado da Cultura do Paraná.

Hennessy, Alistair. 1969. "Latin America." In *Populism: Its Meaning and National Characteristics*, ed. Ghita Ionescu and Ernest Gellner, 28–61. London: Macmillan.

Hess, Claudia, and Patricia Navia. 2003. "You Win Some and You Lose Some: Vote Bargaining and Constitutional Reform in Chile's Transition to Democracy." Paper presented at the Ninety-ninth Annual Meeting of the American Political Science Association, August 23–31, Philadelphia, PA.

Hilbink, Elizabeth. 1999. "Legalism against Democracy: The Political Role of the Judiciary in Chile, 1964–94." PhD diss., University of California at San Diego.

Hite, Katherine, and Paula Cesarini. 2004. "Introducing the Concept of Authoritarian Legacies." In *Authoritarian Legacies and Democracy in Latin America and Southern Europe*, ed. Katherine Hite and Paula Cesarini, 1–24. Notre Dame, IN: University of Notre Dame Press.

Holston, James, and Teresa Caldeira. 1998. "Democracy, Law, and Violence: Disjunctions of Brazilian Citizenship." In *Fault Lines of Democracy in Post-Transition Latin America*, ed. Felipe Agüero and Jeffrey Stark, 263–96. Coral Gables, FL: North-South Center Press.

Horowitz, Irving Louis. 1970. "The Politics of Reform and the Brazilian Counterrevolution." In *Political Power in Latin America: Seven Confrontations*, ed. Richard A. Fagen and Wayne Cornelius, 206–11. Englewood Cliffs, NJ: Prentice Hall.

Hunter, Wendy. 1997. *Eroding Military Influence: Politicians against Soldiers.* Chapel Hill: University of North Carolina Press.

Huntington, Samuel P. 1968. *Political Order in Changing Societies.* New Haven: Yale University Press.

———. 1991. *The Third Wave: Democratization in the Late Twentieth Century.* Norman: University of Oklahoma Press.

Hutchful, Eboe. 1986. "The Modern State and Violence: The Peripheral Situation." *International Journal of the Sociology of Law* 14:153–78.

Ingraham, Barton. 1979. *Political Crime in Europe: A Comparative Study of France, Germany, and England.* Berkeley: University of California Press.

Inter-American Commission on Human Rights. 1982. *Ten Years of Activities 1971–1981.* Washington, DC: General Secretariat of the Organization of American States.

James, Daniel. 1988. *Resistance and Integration: Peronism and the Argentine Working Class, 1946–1976*. New York: Cambridge University Press.

Janos, Andrew. 1970. "The One-Party State and Social Mobilization: East Europe between the Wars." In *Authoritarian Politics in Modern Societies: The Dynamics of Established One-Party Systems*, ed. Samuel Huntington and C. Moore. New York: Basic Books.

Jelin, Elizabeth. 2003. *State Repression and the Labors of Memory*. Trans. Judy Rein and Marcial Godoy-Anativia. Minneapolis: University of Minnesota Press.

Johnson, John J. 1964. *The Military and Society in Latin America*. Stanford, CA: Stanford University Press.

Kant de Lima, Roberto. 1995. "Bureaucratic Rationality in Brazil and the United States: Criminal Justice Systems in Comparative Perspective." In *The Brazilian Puzzle: Culture on the Borderlands of the Western World*, ed. David J. Hess and Roberto Da Matta, 241–69. New York: Columbia University Press.

Keck, Margaret E., and Kathryn Sikkink. 1998. *Activists beyond Borders: Advocacy Networks in International Politics*. Ithaca: Cornell University Press.

King, Gary, Robert O. Keohane, and Sidney Verba. 1994. *Designing Social Inquiry*. Princeton, NJ: Princeton University Press.

Kirchheimer, Otto. 1961. *Political Justice*. Princeton, NJ: Princeton University Press.

Kittrie, Nicholas. 2000. *Rebels with a Cause: The Minds and Morality of Political Offenders*. Boulder, CO: Westview Press.

Koch, H. W. 1989. *In the Name of the Volk: Political Justice in Hitler's Germany*. London: I. B. Tauris and Co.

Kritz, Neil, ed. 1995. *Transitional Justice*, vols. 1–3. Washington, DC: United States Institute of Peace.

Laitin, David. 2002. "Comparative Politics: The State of the Subdiscipline." In *Political Science: The State of the Discipline*, ed. Ira Katznelson and Helen Milner, 630–59. New York: W. W. Norton and Company.

Lamounier, Bolivar. 1996. "Brazil: The Hyperactive Paralysis Syndrome." In *Constructing Democratic Governance: South America in the 1990s*, ed. Jorge Domínguez and Abraham Lowenthal, 166–87. Baltimore, MD: Johns Hopkins University Press.

Lane, David. 1985. *State and Politics in the USSR*. New York: NYU Press.

Langer, Maximo. 2001. *Reforms to the Criminal Justice Systems in the Nineties in Latin America: A Real Break with Authoritarian Legal Practices?* Paper presented at the 23rd International Congress of the Latin American Studies Association, September 6–9, Washington, DC.

Lemos, Renato, ed. 2004. *Justiça fardada: O General Peri Bevilaqua no Superior Tribunal Militar. 1965–1969*. Rio de Janeiro: Bom Texto.

Lesser, Jeffrey. 2002. "Rethinking Armed Struggle in Brazil—An Ethnic Perspective." Paper prepared for presentation at Tulane University, September 27, New Orleans.

Lewis, Paul H. 2002. *Guerrillas and Generals: The 'Dirty War' in Argentina*. Westport, CT: Praeger.

Lichbach, Mark Irving, and Alan S. Zuckerman. 1997. "Research Traditions and Theory in Comparative Politics: An Introduction." In *Comparative Politics: Rationality, Culture, and Structure*, ed. Mark Irving Lichbach and Alan S. Zuckerman, 3–16. New York: Cambridge University Press.

Linz, Juan. 1973. "The Future of an Authoritarian Situation or the Institutionalization of an Authoritarian Regime: The Case of Brazil." In *Authoritarian Brazil: Origins, Policies and Future*, ed. Alfred Stepan, 233–54. New Haven, CT: Yale University Press.

———. 1975. "Totalitarian and Authoritarian Regimes." In *Handbook of Political Science: Macropolitical Theory*, vol. 3, ed. Fred I. Greenstein and Nelson W. Polsby, 175–411. Reading: Addison-Wesley Publishing Company.

Linz, Juan, and Alfred Stepan. 1996. *Problems of Democratic Transition and Consolidation: Southern Europe, South America, and Post-Communist Europe*. Baltimore, MD: Johns Hopkins University Press.

Loewenstein, Karl. 1942. *Brazil under Vargas*. New York: Macmillan.

Lopez, George A. 1984. "A Scheme for the Analysis of Government as Terrorist." In *The State as Terrorist*, ed. Michael Stohl and George A. Lopez, 59–81. Westport, CT: Greenwood Press.

López Dawson, Carlos. 1995. *Justicia Militar: Una Nueva Mirada*. Santiago: Comisión Chilena de Derechos Humanos; Editora Nacional de Derechos Humanos.

Loveman, Brian. 1988. *Chile: The Legacy of Hispanic Capitalism*. 2nd ed. New York: Oxford University Press.

———. 1993. *The Constitution of Tyranny: Regimes of Exception in Spanish America*. Pittsburgh, PA: University of Pittsburgh Press.

Loveman, Brian, and Thomas M. Davies Jr., eds. 1989. *The Politics of Antipolitics: The Military in Latin America*, 2nd ed. Lincoln: University of Nebraska Press.

Lugosi, Charles. 2003. "Rule of Law or Rule by Law: The Detention of Yaser Hamdi." *American Journal of Criminal Law* 30 (Spring): 225–78.

Lukes, Steven. 1977. *Essays in Social Theory*. New York: Columbia University Press.

MacKinnon, Catharine. 1989. *Toward a Feminist Theory of the State*. Cambridge, MA: Harvard University Press.

Mainwaring, Scott, and Matthew Shugart, eds. 1997. *Presidentialism and Democracy in Latin America*. New York: Cambridge University Press.

Malamud-Goti, Jaime. 1996. *Game without End: State Terror and the Politics of Justice*. South Bend, IN: University of Notre Dame Press.

Mann, Michael. 1993. *The Sources of Social Power*. Vol. 2, *The Rise of Classes and Nation-States, 1760–1914*. New York: Cambridge University Press.

Manns, Patricio. 1999. *Chile: Una dictadura militar permanente. 1811–1999*. Santiago: Editorial Sudamericana.

Maravall, José María, and Adam Przeworski, eds. 2003. *Democracy and the Rule of Law*. New York: Cambridge University Press.

Marchak, Patricia. 1999. *God's Assassins: State Terrorism in Argentina in the 1970s*. Montreal: McGill-Queen's University Press.

Mariano, Nilson. 1998. *Operacion Condor: Terrorismo de estado en el cono sur*. Buenos Aires: Ediciones Lohle Lumen.

Martins Filho, João Roberto. 1996. *O palácio e a caserna: A dinâmica militar das crises políticas na ditadura (1964–1969)*. São Carlos: Editora da UFSCar.

Maveety, Nancy. 2004. *The Vagaries of the Founding Field of the Discipline of Political Science*. Paper presented at the conference The Science of Politics, Tulane University, January 9–11.

McCubbins, Matthew D., and Barry R. Weingast. 1984. "Congressional Oversight Overlooked: Police Patrols Versus Fire Alarms." *American Journal of Political Science* 28 (1): 165–79.

McGuire, James W. 1997. *Peronism without Perón: Unions, Parties, and Democracy in Argentina*. Stanford, CA: Stanford University Press.

McSherry, J. Patrice. 1997. *Incomplete Transition: Military Power and Democracy in Argentina*. New York: St. Martin's Press.

———. 1999. "Cross-Border Terrorism: Operation Condor." *NACLA Report on the Americas* 32 (6): 34–35.

Melanson, Richard A. 1991. *Reconstructing Consensus: American Foreign Policy since the Vietnam War*. New York: St. Martin's Press.

Méndez, Juan E., Guillermo O'Donnell, and Paulo Sérgio Pinheiro, eds. 1999. *The (Un)rule of Law and the Underprivileged in Latin America*. Notre Dame, IN: Notre Dame University Press.

Mercadante, Paulo. 2003. *A consciência conservadora no Brasil*. 4th ed. Rio de Janeiro: Topbooks. First published in 1965.

Mesquita Neto, Paulo de. 1997. "Armed Forces, Police, and Democracy in Brazil." Paper presented to the Sawyer Seminar on the Military, Politics, and Society, New School for Social Research, November 4, New York.

Mignone, Emilio. 1986. *Witness to the Truth: The Complicity of the Church and Dictatorship in Argentina, 1976–1983*. Maryknoll, NY: Orbis Books.

Miller, Richard Lawrence. 1995. *Nazi Justiz: Law of the Holocaust*. Westport, CT: Praeger.

Minow, Martha. 1998. *Between Vengeance and Forgiveness: Facing History after Genocide and Mass Violence*. Boston: Beacon Press.

Miranda, Nilmário, and Carlos Tibúrcio. 1999. *Dos filhos deste solo. Mortos e desaparecidos políticos durante a ditadura militar: A responsibilidade do estado*. São Paulo: Editora Fundação Perseu Abramo/Boitempo Editorial.

Miranda, Nilmário, and Roberto Valadão. 1994. *Relatório final da comissão externa destinada a atuar junto aos familiares dos mortos e desaparecidos políticos após 1964, na localização dos seus restos mortais*. Brasília: Câmara dos Deputados, Congresso Nacional, September.

Moore, Barrington. 1966. *The Social Origins of Dictatorship and Democracy: Lord and Peasant in the Making of the Modern World*. Boston: Beacon Press

Morel, Edmar. 1965. *O golpe começou em Washington*. Rio de Janeiro: Editora Civilização Brasileira.

Morse, Richard. 1964. "The Heritage of Latin America." In *The Founding of New Societies*, ed. Louis Hartz, 123–77. New York: Harcourt.

Müller, Ingo. 1991. *Hitler's Justice: The Courts of the Third Reich*. Cambridge: Harvard University Press.

Munck, Gerardo. 1998. *Authoritarianism and Democratization: Soldiers and Workers in Argentina, 1976–1983.* University Park: Pennsylvania State University Press.

Neumann, Franz. 1957. *The Democratic and the Authoritarian State.* London: Collier-Macmillan.

Nino, Carlos. 1996. *Radical Evil on Trial.* New Haven, CT: Yale University Press.

North, Douglass C. 1990. *Institutions, Institutional Change and Economic Performance.* New York: Cambridge University Press.

Nunn, Frederick. 1976. *The Military in Chilean History: Essays on Civil-Military Relations, 1810–1973.* Albuquerque: University of New Mexico Press.

———. 1989. "The Military in Chilean Politics, 1924–32." In *The Politics of Anti-Politics,* 2nd ed., ed. Brian Loveman and Thomas Davies, 118–25. Lincoln: University of Nebraska Press.

O'Donnell, Guillermo. 1973. *Modernization and Bureaucratic Authoritarianism: Studies in South American Politics.* Berkeley: Institute of International Studies, University of California.

———. 1980. "Comparative Historical Formations of the State Apparatus and Socio-Economic Change in the Third World." *International Social Science Journal* 32 (4): 717–29.

———. 1988. *Bureaucratic Authoritarianism: Argentina, 1966–1973, in Comparative Perspective.* Berkeley: University of California Press.

———. 1999. *Counterpoints: Selected Essays on Authoritarianism and Democratization.* Notre Dame, IN: University of Notre Dame Press

Olavarria, Margot. 2002. "Andean Hope: Autonomy and Alliances in Chile's Poblador Movement." PhD diss., New School University.

Orren, Karen, and Stephen Skowronek. 1995. "Order and Time in Institutional Study: A Brief for the Historical Approach." In *Political Science in History,* ed. James Farr, John Dryzek, and Stephen Leonard, 296–317. New York: Cambridge University Press.

Orwell, George. 1977. *1984.* New York: Signet Classic. First published in 1948.

Oteiza, Eduardo. 1994. *La Corte Supreme: Entre la justicia sin política y la política sin justicia.* La Plata: Libreria Editora Platense.

Ottaway, Marina. 2003. *Democracy Challenged: The Rise of Semi-Authoritarianism.* Washington, DC: Carnegie Endowment for International Peace.

Ozlak, Oscar. 1981. "The Historical Formation of the State in Latin America: Some Theoretical and Methodological Guidelines for its Study." *Latin American Research Review* 16 (2): 3–33.

Panish, Neal P. 1987. "Chile under Allende: The Decline of the Judiciary and the Rise of a State of Necessity." *Loyola of Los Angeles International and Comparative Law Journal* 9 (3): 693–709.

Parker, Phyllis R. 1979. *Brazil and the Quiet Intervention.* Austin: University of Texas Press.

Payne, Stanley. 1967. *Politics and the Military in Modern Spain.* Stanford, CA: Stanford University Press.

Pereira, Anthony W. 1998. "'Persecution and Farce': The Origins and Transformation of Brazil's Political Trials." *Latin American Research Review* 33 (1): 43–66.

————. 2001. "'Virtual Legality': Authoritarian Legacies and the Reform of Military Justice in Brazil, the Southern Cone, and Mexico." *Comparative Political Studies* 34 (5): 555–74.

————. 2003a. "Explaining Judicial Reform Outcomes in New Democracies: The Importance of Authoritarian Legalism in Argentina, Brazil, and Chile." *Human Rights Review* 4 (3): 3–16.

————. 2003b. "Political Justice under Authoritarian Regimes in Argentina, Brazil and Chile." *Human Rights Review* 4 (2): 27–47.

Pessoa, Mário. 1971. *O direito da segurança nacional.* São Paulo: Editora Revista dos Tribunais.

Petras, James. 1997. "Political Economy of State Terror: Chile, El Salvador, and Brazil." *Crime and Social Justice* 27–28:88–109.

Pierson, Paul. 2000. "Increasing Returns, Path Dependence, and the Study of Politics." *American Political Science Review* 94 (2): 251–67.

Pierson, Paul, and Theda Skocpol. 2002. "Historical Institutionalism in Contemporary Political Science." In *Political Science: The State of the Discipline*, ed. Ira Katznelson and Helen Milner, 693–721. New York: W. W. Norton and Company.

Pinheiro, Paulo Sergio. 1991. *Estrategias da ilusão.* São Paulo: Companhia das Letras.

————. 2000. "Democratic Governance, Violence, and the Rule of Law." *Daedalus* 129 (2): 119–43.

Pinochet Ugarte, Augusto. 1979. *El día decisivo.* Santiago: Editorial Andrés Bello.

Pion-Berlin, David. 1989. *The Ideology of State Terror: Economic Doctrine and Political Repression in Peru.* Boulder, CO: Lynne Rienner.

Policzer, Pablo. 2001. "Organizing Coercion in Authoritarian Chile." PhD diss., Massachusetts Institute of Technology.

————. Forthcoming. *The Rise and Fall of Repression in Chile under Pinochet: Organization and Information in Authoritarian Regimes.* Notre Dame, IN: University of Notre Dame Press.

Pompeu de Campos, Reynaldo. 1982. *Repressão judicial no Estado Novo.* Rio de Janeiro: Achiame.

Potash, Robert A. 1969. *The Army and Politics in Argentina 1928–1945: Yrigoyen to Perón.* Stanford, CA: Stanford University Press.

————. 1980. *The Army and Politics in Argentina 1945–1962: Perón to Frondizi.* Stanford, CA: Stanford University Press.

————. 1989. "The Military and Argentine Politics." In *The Politics of Anti-Politics*, 2nd ed., ed. Brian Loveman and Thomas Davies, 93–105. Lincoln: University of Nebraska Press.

————. 1996. *The Army and Politics in Argentina 1962–1973: From Frondizi's Fall to the Peronist Restoration.* Stanford, CA: Stanford University Press.

Prillaman, William. 2000. *The Judiciary and Democratic Decay in Latin America: Declining Confidence in the Rule of Law.* Westport, CT: Praeger.

Projeto "Brasil: Nunca Mais." 1988. *Perfil dos atingidos*, vol. 3. Petrópolis: Editora Vozes.

Przeworski, Adam. 1991. *Democracy and the Market: Political and Economic Reforms in Eastern Europe and Latin America.* New York: Cambridge University Press.

Quiroga, Patricio, and Carlos Maldonado. 1988. *El prusianismo en las fuerzas armadas chilenas: Un estado histórico, 1885–1945.* Santiago: Ediciones Documentas.

Rabêlo, Jose Maria, and Thereza Rabêlo. 2001. *Diaspora: Os longos caminhos do exilio.* São Paulo: Geração Editorial.

Ragin, Charles. 1994. *Constructing Social Research.* Thousand Oaks, CA: Pine Forge Press.

Rawls, John. 1971. *A Theory of Justice.* Cambridge: Harvard University Press.

Rehnquist, William H. 1998. *All the Laws but One: Civil Liberties in Wartime.* New York: Alfred A. Knopf.

Reis Filho, Daniel Aarão. 1989. *A revolução faltou ao encontro.* São Paulo: Brasiliense.

Remmer, Karen. 1989. *Military Rule in Latin America.* Boston: Unwin Hyman.

Rezende, Maria José de. 2001. *A ditadura militar no Brasil: Repressão e pretensão de legitimidade, 1964–1984.* Londrina: Editora UEL.

Ridenti, Marcelo. 1993. *O fantasma da revolução brasileira.* São Paulo: UNESP.

Rigby, Andrew. 2001. *Justice and Reconciliation: After the Violence.* Boulder: Lynne Rienner.

Rodríguez Espada, Héctor. 1997. "Nuestra guerra contra la subversión terrorista." *Revista militar* (Buenos Aires) 739 (April/June): 19–25.

Roe, Mark J. 1996. "Chaos and Evolution in Law and Economics." *Harvard Law Review* 109 (3): 641–68.

Roldan, Alberto Polloni. 1972. *Las fuerzas armadas de Chile.* Santiago: Editorial Andrés Bello.

Romero, Hugo Monsante. 1985. *Manual y codigo de justicia militar,* vol. 2. Santiago: Ediar Conosur Ltda.

Roniger, Luís, and Mario Sznajder. 1999. *The Legacy of Human-Rights Violations in the Southern Cone: Argentina, Chile, and Uruguay.* New York: Oxford University Press.

Rose, R. S. 1998. *Beyond the Pale of Pity: Key Episodes of Elite Violence in Brazil to 1930.* San Francisco: Austin and Winfield.

Rosenn, Keith. 1971. "The Jeito: Brazil's Institutional Bypass of the Formal Legal System and its Developmental Implications." *American Journal of Comparative Law* 29 (3): 514–49.

Rueschemeyer, Dietrich A., Evelyne Huber Stephens, and John D. Stephens. 1992. *Capitalist Development and Democracy.* Chicago: University of Chicago Press.

Sancinetti, Marcelo. 1988. *Derecho humanos en la Argentina pos-dictatorial.* Buenos Aires: Lerner Editores Associados.

Sater, William F., and Holger H. Herwig. 1999. *The Grand Illusion: The Prussianization of the Chilean Army.* Lincoln: University of Nebraska Press.

Schamis, Hector. 1991. "Reconceptualizing Latin American Authoritarianism in the 1970s: From Bureaucratic Authoritarianism to Neoconservatism." *Comparative Politics* 23 (January): 201–20.

Schapiro, Martin. 1975. "Courts." In *Handbook of Political Science: Macropolitical Theory.* Vol. 5, *Governmental Institutions and Processes,* ed. Fred I. Greenstein and Nelson W. Polsby, 321–71. Reading: Addison-Wesley Publishing Company.

Schiffrin, Leopoldo. 1974. "El 'forum delicti commissi' como exigencia del art. 102 de la constitucion nacional." *El derecho* 52:531–50.

Schirmer, Jennifer. 1996. "The Looting of Democratic Discourse by the Guatemalan Military: Implications for Human Rights." In *Reconstructing Democracy: Human Rights, Citizenship, and Society*, ed. Elizabeth Jelin and Eric Hershberg, 84–96. Boulder, CO: Westview Press.

———. 1998. *The Guatemalan Military Project: A Violence Called Democracy*. Philadelphia: University of Pennsylvania Press.

Schulhofer, Stephen. 2002. *The Enemy Within: Intelligence Gathering, Law Enforcement, and Civil Liberties in the Wake of 9/11*. New York: The Century Foundation Press.

Schulz, William. 2003. *Tainted Legacy: 9/11 and the Ruin of Human Rights*. New York: Thunder's Mouth Press/Nation Books.

Scott, James. 1985. *Weapons of the Weak: Everyday Forms of Peasant Resistance*. New Haven, CT: Yale University Press.

Serbin, Kenneth P. 2000. *Secret Dialogues: Church-State Relations, Torture, and Social Justice in Authoritarian Brazil*. Pittsburgh, PA: University of Pittsburgh Press.

Shklar, Judith. 1964. *Legalism*. Cambridge, MA: Harvard University Press.

Silva, Eduardo. 1996. *The State and Capital in Chile: Business Elites, Technocrats, and Market Economics*. Boulder, CO: Westview Press.

Simas, Mario. 1986. *Gritos de justiça: Brasil 1963–1979*. São Paulo: Editora FTD.

Skidmore, Thomas. 1967. *Politics in Brazil 1930–1964: An Experiment in Democracy*. New York: Oxford University Press.

———. 1988. *The Politics of Military Rule in Brazil 1964–85*. Oxford: Oxford University Press.

Smallman, Shawn C. 2002. *Fear and Memory in the Brazilian Army and Society, 1889–1954*. Chapel Hill: University of North Carolina Press.

Smith, Ann-Marie. 1997. *A Forced Agreement: Press Acquiescence to Censorship in Brazil*. Pittsburgh, PA: University of Pittsburgh Press.

Smith, Rogers. 1996. "Science, Non-Science, and Politics." In *The Historic Turn in the Human Sciences*, ed. Terrence J. McDonald, 119–59. Ann Arbor: University of Michigan Press.

———. 1997. "Still Blowing in the Wind: The American Quest for a Democratic, Scientific Political Science." In *American Academic Culture in Transformation*, ed. Thomas Bender and Carl Schorske, 271–305. Princeton, NJ: Princeton University Press.

Snyder, Edward C. 1995. "The Dirty Legal War: Human Rights and the Rule of Law in Chile 1973–1995." *Tulsa Journal of Comparative and International Law* 2:253–87.

Sosnowski, Saúl, and Louise Popkin, eds. 1993. *Repression, Exile, and Democracy: Uruguayan Culture*. Durham, NC: Duke University Press.

Stanley, William. 1996. *The Protection Racket State: Elite Politics, Military Extortion, and Civil War in El Salvador*. Philadelphia: Temple University Press.

Steinmo, Sven, Kathleen Thelen, and Frank Longstreth, eds. 1989. *Structuring Politics: Historical Institutionalism in Comparative Analysis*. New York: Cambridge University Press.

Stepan, Alfred. 1971. *The Military in Politics: Changing Patterns in Brazil*. Princeton, NJ: Princeton University Press.

Stölleis, Michael. 1998. *The Law under the Swastika: Studies on Legal History in Nazi Germany*. Chicago: University of Chicago Press.

Tarrow, Sidney. 1998. *Power in Movement*. New York: Cambridge University Press.

Thompson, E. P. 1966. *The Making of the English Working Class*. New York: Vintage Books.

Tilly, Charles. 1985. "The State as Organized Crime." In *Bringing the State Back In*, ed. Peter Evans, Dieter Rueschemeyer, and Theda Skocpol, 169–91. New York: Cambridge University Press.

———. 1998. *Durable Inequality*. Berkeley: University of California Press.

Tsbelis, George. 1990. *Nested Games: Rational Choice in Comparative Politics*. Berkeley: University of California Press.

Udihara, Massaki. 2002. *Um medico brasileiro no front*. São Paulo: Hacker Editores, Imprensa Oficial do Estado, Editora Narrative Um.

Ungar, Mark. 2002. *Elusive Reform: Democracy and the Rule of Law in Latin America*. Boulder, CO: Lynne Rienner.

Uricoechea, Fernando. 1980. *The Patrimonial Foundations of the Brazilian Bureaucratic State*. Berkeley: University of California Press.

Urondo, Francisco. 1973. *La patria fusilada*. Buenos Aires: Ediciones de Crisis.

U.S. Department of State. 1964. *Bulletin*, vol. 50, no. 1295, April 20.

Vannucchi Leme de Matos, Marco Aurélio. 2002. "Em nome da segurança nacional: Os processos da justiça militar contra a Ação Libertadora Nacional, ALN, 1969–1979." PhD diss., University of São Paulo.

Verdugo, Patricia. 2001. *Chile, Pinochet, and the Caravan of Death*. Boulder, CO: Lynne Rienner.

Verner, Joel. 1984. "The Independence of Supreme Courts in Latin America: A Review of the Literature." *Journal of Latin American Studies* 16 (2): 463–506.

Vidal, Hernán. 1989. *Mitología militar chilena: Surrealismo desde el superego*. Literature and Human Rights Series, no. 6. Minneapolis: Institute for the Study of Ideologies and Literature.

Waisman, Carlos. 1999. "Argentina." In *Democracy in Developing Countries: Latin America*, ed. Larry Diamond, Jonathan Hartlyn, Juan J. Linz, and Seymour Martin Lipset, 71–129. Boulder, CO: Lynne Rienner.

Weber, Max. 1978. *Economy and Society*. Vol. 1, edited by Guenther Roth and Claus Wittich. Berkeley: University of California Press.

Wedgwood, Ruth. 2002. "Al Qaeda, Military Commissions, and American Self-Defense." *Political Science Quarterly* 117 (3): 357–72.

Weyland, Kurt. 2002. "Strengths and Limitations of Rational Choice Institutionalism in the Study of Latin American Politics." *Studies in Comparative International Development* 37 (1): 57–85.

Wilde, Alexander. 1999. "Irruptions of Memory: Expressive Politics in Chile's Transition to Democracy." *Journal of Latin American Studies* 31 (2): 473–500.

Wolfe, Alan. 2001. "The Home Front: American Society Responds to the New War." In *How Did This Happen? Terrorism and the New War*, ed. James F. Hoge Jr. and Gideon Rose, 283–94. New York: Public Affairs.

Wolpin, Miles. 1986. "State Terrorism and Repression in the Third World: Parameters and Prospects." In *Government Violence and Repression: An Agenda for Research*, ed. Michael Stohl and George Lopez, 97–164. New York: Greenwood Press.

Yunes, João, and Tamara Zubarew. 1999. "Mortalidad por causas violentas en adolescentes y jóvenes: Un desafío para la región de las Américas." *Revista brasileira de epidemiologia* 2 (3): 102–71.

Zakaria, Fareed. 1997. "The Rise of Illiberal Democracy." *Foreign Affairs* 76 (6): 22–43.

———. 2003. *The Future of Freedom: Illiberal Democracy at Home and Abroad.* New York: W. W. Norton and Company.

Zaverucha, George. 2000. *Frágil Democracia: Collor, Itamar, FHC e os Militares, 1990–1998.* Rio de Janeiro: Civilização Brasileira.

Index

Note: Page numbers in *italic* type refer to figures or tables.

Abu Ghraib prison, 185
Acuña, Carlos, 129
Addison, Joseph, 63
Afanasiev, V., 154
AI-1. *See* First Institutional Act (Brazil, 1964)
AI-2. *See* Second Institutional Act (Brazil, 1965)
AI-5. *See* Fifth Institutional Act (Brazil, 1968)
Al Odah v. United States (2004), 189
al Qaeda, 188, 233
Albuquerque, Francisco Roberto de, 164–65
Alencar, Marcelo, 226n4
Alessandri, Arturo, 49, 50
Alfonsín, Raul, 124, 162, 165–67
Alianza Anticomunista Argentina (Triple A), 25, 124, 126, 127, 131
Allende, Salvador, 2–3, 16, 40, 50–52, 92–98, 114, 124–25
Altamirano, Luís, 48
Alvarez Guerrero, Osvaldo, 127
amnesty: Argentina, 126, 130, 136, 166; Brazil, 21, 68, 158, 161; Chile, 168, 170–71; self-amnesty, 158, 166, 170. *See also* pardons, in Argentina
amnesty committees (Comites Brasileiros pela Anistia, CBAs), 75
Amnesty International, 137, 142
Andersen, Martin Edward, 222n2
Andrade Abreu, Hugo de, 72
Angeloz, Eduardo César, 127
Angola, 182
antilegalism: Argentina, 117–39; Nazi Germany, 175–78
Aramburu, Pedro Eugenio, 128, 223n8
Arato, Andrew, 74, 187
Araucanians (Mapuches), 49
Arceneaux, Craig, 6–7, 58, 135
Arellano Stark, Sergio, 25, 102–3, 108, 110, 171
ARENA. *See* National Alliance for Renewal (Aliança Renovadora Nacional, ARENA)

Arendt, Hannah, 135
Argentina: amnesty in, 126, 130, 136, 166; anti-legalism in, 117–39; armed left in, 121–22; authoritarian legality in, 26, 124–25, 138–39; comparative study of, 9–14, 120–21; conservative versus revolutionary legality in, 119; coups in, 16, 18, 25–26, 54, 55, 56, 120–21, 128–32; disappearances in, 3, 4, 26, 119, 126, 129–30, 166; judicial-military relations in, 12–13, 55, 119, 124–25, 129–31, 138–39, 172; judiciary in, 54, 58, 119, 121–28, 166–67; map of, *118*; military courts in, 124, 133; military in, 40, 52–59, 120, 166–67; National Penal Court, 121–27; Nazi Germany compared to, 175, 177; 1966–1973 military regime, 57–59; Operation Condor and, 24; opposition in, 137; political prisoners in, 135–37; political repression in, 4, 25–26; political repression in, history of, 52–59; political trials in, 133–34; populism in, 40, 55–56; security forces in, 88; transitional justice outcomes, 165–68; truth commission in, 166. *See also* dirty war
Argentine League for the Rights of Man (Liga Argentina por los Derechos del Hombre), 137
Argibay, Carmen, 223n17
Armed Forces High Command (Oberkommando der Wehrmacht, OKW), 178
Arms Control Law (Chile, 1972), 92, 97–98, 101, 106, 108, 115
Arns, Dom Paulo Evaristo, 229n13
Arriagada, Genaro, 94
Asociación Gremial de los Abogados (Argentine bar association), 126
assassinations. *See* killings, state-sponsored
association, crimes of, 76
authoritarian legality: Argentina, 26, 124–25, 138–39; Brazil, 1–2, 22–23, 47, 61–62, 63–89;

authoritarian legality *(cont.):*
  Chile, 2–3, 24–25, 90–116; comparisons of,
    23, 173–90; degree of repression indicated
    by, 6; democracy and, 7–8; evolution of,
    71–73; as framing device, 7; Franco's Spain,
    178–81; gray areas of, 18–19; individuals
    prosecuted versus killed, 23; judicial-mili-
    tary relations as key to, 191–92; legacies of,
    159–72, 177, 196–97, 199–200; Nazi Ger-
    many, 175–78; patterns in, 18–27, 59–60;
    perpetuation of, 36; Portugal, 181–83; rea-
    sons for, 192; study of, 5–8, 198–200; targets
    of, 8; varieties of, 2, 6–7, 27–32, 194–95. *See
    also* judicialization of repression; national
    security legality; political trials
authoritarianism: conservative versus revolu-
    tionary, 32, 68–70, 100–101; extralegal, 74;
    under political party direction, 174; politi-
    cal trial role under, 32–36, 192, 196. *See also*
    authoritarian legality; bureaucratic au-
    thoritarian regimes; political repression
Avritzer, Leonardo, 41–42, 164
Aylwin, Patricio, 162, 168–70

Balza, Martín, 230n9
bandos, 99, 100
Barkan, Steven, 183
Barros, Robert, 96, 100, 101, 103, 104, 105
Barthes, Roland, 2
Bastide, Roger, 2
Beattie, Peter M., 42
belief, crimes of, 145–47
Bevilaqua, Peri, 216n21
Bicudo, Hélio, 88, 113
Bierrenbach, Júlio de Sá, 228n39
"big trial" (1985), 124, 131
Bolaños, Jorge, 2–3
Bordaberry, Juan María, 16
Bourdieu, Pierre, 2
Braga da Cruz, Manuel, 182
Brasil: Nunca mais (Archdiocese of São Paulo),
    21, 163, 201, 209n3, 229n12
Brazil: amnesty in, 21, 68, 158, 161; armed left
    in, 72, 79, 81, 86–87, 89, 151, 164; authoritar-
    ian legality in, 1–2, 22–23, 47, 61–62, 63–89;
    centralized versus local power in, 41, 78–80;
    civil society in, 86–88, 143; comparative
    study of, 9–14, 92–94, 120–21; Congress in,
    22; conservative versus revolutionary legal-
    ity in, 68–70, 89; coup in, 16, 20, 45, 60, 63,
    65–67, 92–94; disappearances in, 21, 22, 157;
    Estado Novo, 43, 66; hard-liners in, 70–71,
    103–4; judicial-military relations in, 12,
    45–47, 66–67, 88–89, 156–58, 165, 172; judici-

ary in, 163, 165; map of, *64;* military courts
    in, 22, 47, *64,* 75–86, 87, 89, 140–58, 162–63,
    165; military in, 40, 42, 45, 47, 55, 67, 161–65;
    1961 crisis, 45–46; Operation Condor and,
    24; opposition in, 88, 143; political repres-
    sion in, 3–4, 20–23, 67–68, 70–71; political
    repression in, history of, 41–47; political
    trials in, 75–88; political trials in military
    courts, *64;* populism in, 40; Salazarist Por-
    tugal compared to, 181–83; state above law
    in, 74–75; transitional justice outcomes,
    161–65; truth commission in, 163; U.S. mili-
    tary and, 43–44
Brazilian Bar Association (Ordem dos Advoga-
    dos do Brasil, OAB), 75, 162–63
Brazilian Communist Party (Partido Comu-
    nista Brasileiro, PCB), 20, 44, 145, 155
Brazilian Democratic Movement (Movimento
    Democrático Brasileiro, MDB), 226–27n20
Brazilian Labor Party (Partido Trabalhista
    Brasileiro, PTB), 47
Brazilian Revolutionary Communist Party
    (Partido Comunista Brasileiro Revolu-
    cionário, PCBR), 42, 44, 86
Brizola, Leonel, 45–46
Bryce, James, 140–58
Brysk, Alison, 137
Buchanan, Paul, 222n2
bureaucratic authoritarian regimes, 6–7, 232n6
Bush, George W., 184, 186, 189

Caetano, Marcelo, 232n17
Camara Couto, Antônio da, 92
cámara del terror (court of terror), 121, 123–24
cameron (big court), 121
Cámpora, Hector, 125–26
Campos, Francisco, 66
carabineros, 49, 113
caravan of death, 101–4, 171
Cardoso, Fernando Henrique, 27, 163
Carey, John, 35
Carmona, Juan de Dios, 51
Carrasco, Washington, 94
Castelo Branco, Humberto de Alencar, 65, 66,
    68–71
Castillo, Ramón S., 55
Catholic Church: Argentina, 222n2; Brazil, 83,
    115, 143, 163; Chile, 106
Cavalcanti, Paulo, 226n4
Cavallo, Gabriel, 167
Center for Law and Social Policy, 137
Center for Legal and Social Studies (Centro de
    Estudios Legales y Sociales, CELS), 137
Central Intelligence Agency (CIA), 185–86

centralization of power: Argentina, 135; Brazil, 41, 78–80; Chile, 111
Cerda, Carlos, 113
Cerro, Francisco, 127
Cheyre, Emilio, 230n19
Chile: amnesty in, 168, 170–71; armed resistance in, 97; authoritarian legality in, 2–3, 24–25, 90–116; caravan of death, 101–4, 171; centralized versus local power in, 111; comparative study of, 9–14, 92–94, 120–21; conservative versus revolutionary legality in, 100–101, 104; coup in, 16, 51, 60, 92–94, 98–101; disappearances in, 113; Franco's Spain compared to, 178–81; hard-liners in, 103–4; judicial-military relations in, 12, 49–50, 99–100, 113–16, 172; judiciary in, 95, 168, 170; land invasions in, 95–96; map of, 91; military courts in, 2–3, 4, 10–12, 25, 51–52, 91, 101, 102–3, 105–7, 169, 171; military in, 40, 48–52, 55, 97–100, 102–5, 169; nationalization in, 98; Operation Condor and, 24; political repression in, 4, 23–25, 103–4; political repression in, history of, 48–52; political trials in, 104–14; populism in, 40, 95; Prussianization of military in, 12, 48–49; rule of law in, 94–98; transitional justice outcomes, 168–71; truth commission in, 169–70
Chilean National Commission on Truth and Reconciliation, 90
Chilean-Soviet Cultural Institute of San Antonio, 110
China, 45, 152–53
Christian Democratic Party, 95, 98
civil society, in Brazil, 86–88, 143
CJMs. *See* military court districts (Circunscrições Judiciárias Militares, CJMs)
class: Argentina, 53, 120; Chile, 95, 96, 110; political repression and, 27–28. *See also* elites
CODI. *See* Operational Command for Internal Defense (Comando Operacional de Defesa Interna, CODI)
Collier, David, 53–54
Collier, Ruth, 53–54
commissions, post-authoritarian investigative. *See* truth commissions
Communism, 61; Argentina, 56–57; Brazil, 20, 42–45, 65, 67, 145–46, 155; Chile, 23, 41, 49–50, 93, 113; Portugal, 182
compensation, in Argentina, 166
CONADEP. *See* National Commission on the Disappearance of Persons
Concertación, 168–69, 231n33
Conference of Brazilian Bishops (Conferência Nacional dos Bispos do Brasil), 86

conscription, 42
Consejos de Guerra Especialies Estables, 133
consensus: in Brazil, 141; in Chile, 94–95; judicial-military relations and, 10–11
Constable, Pamela, 48
constitutions: Argentina, 53, 56; authoritarian approaches to, 32; Brazil, 22, 65–71; Chile, 50–51, 100; presidential powers in, 38; United States, 189
Contreras Sepúlveda, Manuel, 108, 113
Cordobazo, 58
Corradi, Juan, 132
Correio da Manhã (newspaper), 146, 148
Costa e Silva, Artur da, 71, 148
coups: Argentina, 16, 18, 25–26, 54, 55, 56, 120–21, 128–32; Brazil, 16, 20, 45, 60, 63, 65–67, 92–94; Chile, 16, 51, 60, 92–94, 98–101; preemptive versus rollback, 9, 92, 99, 211n21
courts: Argentina, 54; Brazil versus Chile, 24; faceless, 186; hybrid military-civilian (Brazil), 1–4, 10, 22, 47, 158, 165; implementation and enforcement as role of Latin American, 38, 40; inquisitorial procedures in Latin American, 38–39; trustworthy, 190, 192, 198. *See also* judicial-military relations; military courts; political trials
Cover, Robert, 173
Craig, Gordon, 177
criminal justice system. *See* authoritarian legality; courts; legality; national security legality
criticism of government, crimes of, 147–49
Cruz Ponce, Lisandro, 95
Cuba, 155
cultural explanations of political repression, 29–30

Damaška, Mirjan R., 37
Dávila Espinoza, Carlos Gregorio, 40–41
Davis, Nathaniel, 93, 94
de facto government, 56, 100, 199
de jure government, 199
dead, accounting of: Argentina, 127, 135; Chile, 112
death penalty: Argentina, 133, 134; Brazil, 86–88; Chile, 92, 101, 106, 112, 114; U.S. military commissions, 186, 188
death squads: Argentina, 126; Brazil, 87–88. *See also* disappearances; killings, state-sponsored
"Declaration of Principles of the Government of Chile," 104
Decree-Law 5 (Chile, 1973), 101

Decree-Law 314 (Brazil, 1967), 151
Decree-Law 898 (Brazil, 1969), 151, 152–53, 154
Decree-Law 4,214 (Argentina, 1963), 56
Decree-Law 17,245 (Argentina, 1967), 56
Decree-Law 17,401 (Argentina, 1967), 57
Decree-Law 18,787 (Argentina, 1956), 56
defendants: access to lawyers, 143; charges against, 76–77, *84*, 84–85, 106, 145–55; defenses presented by, 141–42; professional background of, 82–84, *83*; rights of, 106, 133; time served by, 85; in U.S. military commissions, 186
defense lawyers: access to clients, 143; Argentina, 123, 126, 128, 156; Brazil, 140–58; Chile, 156; and crimes of belief, 145–47; and criticisms of government, 147–49; and dissemination of subversive propaganda, 149–51; roles and resources of, 140–45; significant achievements of, 156–58; in U.S. terrorism cases, 188
Dellasoppa, Emilio, 129
democracy: authoritarian legality and, 7–8, 73, 183–89; judiciary-military relations and, 15; political offender treatment under, 33; third-wave, 200; threats to, from within, 187, 189; transition to, 159, 199–200
Democratic Social Party (Partido Democrático Social, PDS), 162
Denis, Odílio, 46
DEOPS. *See* Departamento Estadual de Ordem Político e Social
Departamento de Ordem Político e Social (DOPS), 146, 155
Departamento Estadual de Ordem Político e Social (DEOPS), 20, 164
Department of Homeland Security, 186
Department of Internal Operations (Departamento de Operações Internas, DOI), 1, 20
detention centers, 85, 119. *See also* Navy Mechanics' School (ESMA)
Devoto Prison, 125
Dias, José Carlos, 226n4
Diaz Lestrem, Guillermo Raul, 128
dictatorship. *See* authoritarianism
Diez, Sérgio, 100
DINA. *See* National Intelligence Directorate (Dirección Nacional de Inteligencia, DINA)
Dios Carmona, Juan de, 51
diretas-já (direct elections now) campaign, 162
dirty war, 18, 128–32, 166, 209–10n8; as corrective to failed policy, 59, 121, 126, 129, 136–37, 138, 192; explanations of, 119, 222n2; French role in, 60; institutional matrix of, 4; origination and expansion of, 25–26; victims of

from judiciary, 128, 224n33; U.S. relations with Argentina during, 129–30, 224n36
disappearances: Argentina, 3, 4, 26, 119, 126, 129–30, 166, 195, 212n3; Brazil, 21, 22, 157, 212n3; Chile, 113, 171, 212n3; conduct of, 136; effects of, 135; locations of, 136; number of, 134, 212n3; policy of, 129–30, 134–35, 138; truth commission on, 166; United States, 187; victims of, 136. *See also* death squads
dissemination of subversive propaganda, crimes of, 149–51
dissent, intolerance of, 39
Division of Political Order of the Federal Police, 123
documents, Brazilian release of, 164
DOI. *See* Department of Internal Operations (Departamento de Operações Internas, DOI)
DOI-CODI (Departamento de Operações Internas and Comando Operacional de Defesa Interna), 20
Domínguez, Virginia, 29
DOPS. *See* Departamento de Ordem Político e Social
Drummond de Andrade, Carlos, 147
Due Obedience Law (Argentina, 1987), 167, 230n27
Duhalde, Eduardo Luís, 223n6

Ecumenical Movement for Human Rights (Movimiento Ecuménico por los Derechos Humanos), 137
Egypt, 185
Elbrick, Charles, 150
elites: Argentine military's support of, 54; as audience for subversive ideas, 152–55; in Brazil and southern cone countries, 193; in Brazilian democratic transition, 162, 165; judicial and military (*see* judicial-military relations); in post-9/11 United States, 184, 188–89
emergency powers: Argentina, 126, 136, 193–94; Brazil, 66, 193–94; Chile, 51, 101, 105, 193–94; Latin America, 38, 39; Roman limitations on, 193; United States, 184, 187, 189
enemy combatants, 184, 187, 188
ERP. *See* Revolutionary People's Army (Ejército Revolucionário del Pueblo, ERP)
ESG. *See* Superior War College (Escola Superior de Guerra, ESG)
O Estado de São Paulo (newspaper), 44
eugenics, 42
executions. *See* disappearances; killings, state-sponsored

expression of ideas, crimes of, 152–55

faceless courts, 186
Faletto, Enzo, 27
Falklands/Malvinas War (1982), 165
Family Members of those Detained and Disappeared for Political Reasons (Familiares de Detenidos y Desaparecidos por Razones Políticas), 137
Fatherland and Liberty (Patria y Libertad), 93
Federal Bureau of Investigation (FBI), 185
federal prosecutor (Procuradoria Geral da República), 76
Federal Resources Court (Tribunal Federal de Recursos, TFR), 66
Feitlowitz, Marguerite, 7, 222n2
Fifth Institutional Act (Brazil, 1968), 21, 72–73, 162
Figueiredo, João Baptista de Oliveira, 150
Final Solution, 175, 178
First Institutional Act (Brazil, 1964), 66, 67, 69
Fiúza de Castro, Adyr, 81–82
Fleury, Sérgio, 88, 113, 148
Foucault, Michel, 2, 235n3
Fragoso, Augusto, 73
Fragoso, Heleno, 86, 144–45, 147, 149, 155
France, 60
Franco y Bahamonde, Francisco, 174, 179–81
freedom of speech, 149–55
Frei Montalva, Eduardo, 51
Friedrich, Carl, 193
Full Stop Law (Argentina, 1986), 167, 230n27
Fundamentals of Philosophy (Afanasiev), 154–55

Gaggero, Manuel, 128–29
Gallo, Max, 180
Garré, Nilda Celia, 127
Garretón Merino, Roberto, 112
Garzón, Baltazar, 171
Geddes, Barbara, 28
Geisel, Ernesto, 150, 162
Geisel, Orlando, 46
Geneva Conventions, 184–85
Germany, 48, 53. *See also* Nazi Germany
Gestapo, 175
González Gartland, Carlos A., 123
Gordon, Lincoln, 65, 70
Goulart, João, 16, 20, 44–46, 63, 65, 67, 93, 94, 98
Grandmothers of the Plaza de Mayo (Abuelas de Plaza de Mayo), 137
Gray Dawn (*Manhã Cinza*) (film), 154
Greenalgh, Eduardo, 226n4
Groisman, Enrique, 56

Grove Vallejo, Marmaduke, 40, 48
Guantánamo naval base, Cuba, 185, 186, 189
Guarda, Florentino de la, 49
Gueiros, Nehemias, 71
Guevara, Ché, 146
Guzmán, Jaime, 100, 170
Guzzetti, César, 132

habeas corpus, 21, 72, 112–13, 210n9
habeas data, 164
Halperín Donghi, Tulio, 54
Hamdi v. Rumsfeld (2004), 188
hard-liners: Argentina, 124; Brazil, 70–71, 103–4; Chile, 103–4; judiciary distrusted by, 8, 70
Hersh, Seymour, 185
Herzog, Vladimir, 229–30n19
Hilbink, Elizabeth, 96–97, 98
historical institutionalism, 30–32, 194, 200, 236n6
Hitler, Adolf, 175, 177–78
human rights: Argentina, 88, 137, 165, 167; Brazil, 161, 218n16; Chile, 105, 112, 165, 170; democratic transition and, 160; United States, 185
Human Rights Commission, Organization of American States, 137
Huntington, Samuel, 98

IACHR. *See* Inter-American Commission on Human Rights
Ibáñez del Campo, Carlos, 40, 48–50
ideology, political trials and, 34
Illia, Arturo, 16
information access, in Brazil, 164
infrastructural power, 193
Ingraham, Barton, 39
Inqueritos Policial-Militares (IPMs), 67, 155
Institute of Research and Social Studies (Instituto de Pesquisa e Estudos Sociais, IPES), 93
institutional matrix, 30, 59, 119
intelligence agencies: Brazil, 94; Chile, 24, 94; Operation Condor and, 24
intentona, 42
Inter-American Commission on Human Rights (IACHR), 218n16
Inter-American Legal Commission, 66
International Commission of Jurists, 137
international groups, and Argentine opposition, 137
International Police for the Defense of the State (Polícia Internacional de Defesa do Estado, PIDE), 182
interpretation of laws, in Brazil, 140–43
intimidation, political trials used for, 19, 32, 33, 77

intraregime conflict: executions and, 103; political trials and, 34–35
investigative commissions. *See* truth commissions
IPMs. *See* Inqueritos Policial-Militares (IPMs)

jeito, 212n2
Jewish Movement for Human Rights (Movimiento Judío por los Derechos Humanos), 137
Jews, 175–76
Johnson, Lyndon, 66
Jordán, Servando, 113
Jornal do Brasil (newspaper), 68, 72, 77, 86
judges, role in political trials of, 144
judicial space, 156, 189
judicial system. *See* authoritarian legality; courts; law; legality; national security legality
judicialization of repression: Argentina, 57; effects of, 6, 13, 195–98; judicial-military relations and, 174, 191–92; reasons for, 192; Spain, 179–81; variation in, 5. *See also* authoritarian legality
judicial-military relations, 10–13, 173–90; Argentina, 12–13, 55, 119, 124–25, 129–31, 138–39, 172, 194–95; authoritarian versus democratic regimes, 15, 190, 198; Brazil, 12, 45–47, 66–67, 88–89, 156–58, 165, 172, 194–95; Chile, 12, 49–50, 99–100, 113–16, 172, 194–95; Franco's Spain, 178–81; military constrained by, 197–98; Nazi Germany, 175–78; Portugal, 181–83; United States, 189
justice. *See* transitional justice
Justice and Peace Commission (Comissão de Justiça e Paz, CJP), 75, 115

killings, state-sponsored: Argentina, 54, 128; Brazil, 22, 76, 163; Chile, 3, 24, 25, 90, 101–4, 171; justification of, 129; ratio of prosecutions versus, 23, 212n3; Spain, 179–80. *See also* death penalty; death squads; dirty war; disappearances
Kirchheimer, Otto, 6, 34, 196
Kirchner, Nestor, 167
Kittrie, Nicholas, 33
Koch, H. W., 177
Kubitschek, Juscelino, 44, 67

Labor Association, 53
labor movement, 61; Argentina, 53, 120; Brazil, 67, 83–84; Chile, 49, 51, 95–96; Latin American, 214n6
Ladurie, Emmanuel Le Roy, 2
Lagos Osorio, Joaquín, 103

Lamarca, Carlos, 83, 218n24
land invasions, 95–96
Langer, Máximo, 39
Lanusse, Alejandro Agustin, 58, 121, 125, 138
law: Argentine violation of, 117–39; Brazil and, 43, 74–75; Chile and, 48, 94–98; secret, 101; state versus, 74–75. *See also* authoritarian legality; courts; legality; national security legality; rule of law
Law for the Permanent Defense of Democracy (Chile, 1948), 49–50
Law for the Restoration of the Professional Civil Service (Germany, 1933), 176
Law of National Security (*O direito da segurança nacional*) (Pessoa), 74, 164
Law of Political Responsibilities (Spain, 1939), 179
Law of Repression of Sabotage (Argentina, 1976), 133
Law of State Security (Chile, 1958), 50–51, 92, 97, 101, 106, 108, 126
lawyers. *See* defense lawyers
Lawyers' Committee on Human Rights, 137
Lefort, Claude, 2
legal culture, 11, 192
legal system. *See* authoritarian legality; courts; law; legality; national security legality
legality: conservative versus revolutionary, 32, 68–70, 100–101, 119; U.S. and post-9/11, 183–89. *See also* authoritarian legality; national security legality
legitimacy, political trials as affording, 33–34
Leigh, Gustavo, 113
Lenin, V. I., 34, 145, 150
Lesser, Jeffrey, 86
Letelier, Orlando, 24, 108
Levingston, Roberto M., 58
Lewis, Paul H., 130
ley maldita, 49–50
Lichbach, Mark Irving, 27
Lindh, John Walker, 188
Linz, Juan, 6, 16, 104, 132, 225n40, 232n19
Loewenstein, Karl, 43
Lopes Machado, José, 46
López Rega, José, 25
Lorscheider, Ivo, 86
Loveman, Brian, 38, 50
Lula da Silva, Luiz Inácio, 163

Magalhães, Antonio Carlos, 87
Malamud-Goti, Jaime, 131
Malbran, Carlos, 224n23
Manilla, Eduardo, 126
Mann, Michael, 193
Marchak, Patricia, 222n2

Martins, Nestor, 123
Mazzilli, Pascoal Ranieri, 45, 65–66
McCarthy, Joseph, 70
McSherry, J. Patrice, 55
Medeiros, Carlos, 66
Médici, Emílio Garrastazu, 66
Mein Kampf (Hitler), 177
membership, crimes of, 76
Menem, Carlos, 167
Mercado, Antonio, 226n4
El Mercurio (newspaper), 96
methodological individualism, 31
Mignone, Emilio, 3, 223n17
Mignone, Monica, 3
military: Argentina, 40, 52–59, 120, 166–67;
 Brazil, 40, 42, 45, 47, 55, 67, 161–65; Brazil-
 ian-U.S. relations, 43–44; Chile, 40, 48–52,
 55, 97–100, 102–5, 169; conscription into, 42;
 guardian role of, 51, 133; judicial constraint
 of, 197–98; political involvement of, in
 interwar period, 40. *See also* judiciary-
 military relations; military courts; political
 repression
military court districts (Circunscrições Judiciárias Militares, CJMs), 75–85
military courts: Argentina, 124, 133; Brazil, 22,
 47, *64*, 75–85, 87, 89, 140–58, 162–63, 165
 (*see also* courts: hybrid military-civilian
 (Brazil)); Chile, 2–3, 4, 10–12, 25, 51–52, *91*,
 101, 102–3, 105–7, 169, 171; defense lawyers
 in, 140–58; peacetime versus wartime, 101,
 106; Portugal, 181–82; Spain, 178–81; U.S.
 military commissions, 184, 186–89
Military Public Ministry (Ministério Público
 Militar), 47, 75
military regimes: Brazil versus Chile, 92–94;
 definition of, 231n2
Miller, Richard Lawrence, 176
MIR. *See* Movement of the Revolutionary Left
 (Movimiento de Izquierda Revolucionario,
 MIR)
Miranda, Nilmário, 159
modes of transition, 30
Montoneros, 25
Morocco, 185
Morse, Richard, 39
Moscovici, Serge, 2
Mothers of the Plaza de Mayo (Madres de
 Plaza de Mayo), 137, 230n24
Mourão Filho, Olympio, 65
Moussaoui, Zacarias, 188
Movement of the Revolutionary Left (Movimi-
 ento de Izquierda Revolucionario, MIR),
 95–96
Müller, Ingo, 177

Nascimento, João do, 154
National Alliance for Renewal (Aliança Reno-
 vadora Nacional, ARENA), 162 226–27n20,
 229n9
National Commission on the Disappearance
 of Persons (Comisión Nacional sobre la
 Desaparición de Personas, CONADEP),
 134, 137
National Commission on Truth and Reconciliation, 169–70
National Executive Power (Poder Ejecutivo
 Nacional, PEN), 133–34
National Intelligence Directorate (Dirección
 Nacional de Inteligencia, DINA), 24, 102–3,
 113
National Intelligence Service (Serviço Nacional
 de Inteligência, SNI), 20
National Liberationist Action (Ação Libertadora Nacional, ALN), 76, 88
National Penal Court (Cámara en lo Penal de
 la Nación), 58, 121–27, 129–31, 137–38, 195,
 222–23nn6–7, 224nn20–21
national security: concept of, 18; external versus internal threats to, 39. *See also* national
 security legality
national security law (Brazil, 1953), 44, 126, 150
national security legality: Argentina, 74; Brazil,
 44, 73–75, 140–58; Chile, 74; comparative
 study of, 16–36; evolution of, 37–62; United
 States, 183–89. *See also* political trials
National Security Court (Tribunal de Segurança Nacional, TSN), 43, 59
nationalization, in Chile, 98
Navy Mechanics' School (ESMA), 128
Nazi Germany, 174–78
Neder, Antônio, 66
Neumann, Franz, 183
Nino, Carlos, 54
North, Douglass, 11, 29, 30, 31–32
Nunca más (Never Again) (Argentine National
 Commission on the Disappeared), *21*, 166

O'Donnell, Guillermo, 193, 210n14, 218n25
Oliveira Brandt, Vinicius, 1–2, 141
Oliveira Vianna, Francisco José de, 44
Onganía, Juan Carlos, 56, 58
Operation Clean-Up (Operação Limpeza), 67
Operation Condor, 24, 220n4
Operational Command for Internal Defense
 (Comando Operacional de Defesa Interna,
 CODI), 20
Organization of American States (OAS), 70,
 137
Ortega Peña, Rodolfo David, 124
Orúzar, Enrique, 100

Orwell, George, 132, 225n39
Oteiza, Eduardo, 54
Ovalle, Jorge, 100

Padilla, José, 189, 233n23
Panish, Neal P., 96
Paraguay, 24
pardons, in Argentina, 167
participation, crimes of, 76
La Patagonia trágica, 53
path dependency, 213n20
Patriotic League, 53, 54
Payne, Stanley, 179
PCB. *See* Brazilian Communist Party (Partido Comunista Brasileiro, PCB)
Peace and Justice Service (Servicio Paz y Justicia, SERPAJ), 137
Pellegrino, Helio, 146–47
PEN. *See* National Executive Power (Poder Ejecutivo Nacional, PEN)
People's Court (Volksgerichtshof, VGH), 175–78
Perez, Carlos, 2–3
Permanent Assembly for Human Rights (Asamblea Permanente por los Derechos Humanos, APDH), 137
Perón, Juan Domingo, 25, 40, 55–56, 99, 120, 125–26
Perón, María Estela Martínez de (Isabel or Isabelita), 25, 120, 126–27, 133
Peronism, 120
Perriaux, Jaime, 57
Pessoa, Mário, 73–75, 77, 164
Pinochet Ugarte, Augusto, 16, 24, 50, 101–3, 131, 168, 170, 171, 178
Pion-Berlin, David, 222n2
Piveta, Idebal, 2, 143, 152–54, 225n2, 226n4
Plan Z, 93
Plenary Criminal Courts (Tribunais Criminais Plenários, TCPs), 181
police: Brazil, 20, 155, 164; Chile, 49
Police for Political and Social Defense (Policia de Defesa Política e Social, PVDE), 181
Policzer, Pablo, 24, 103
political economy, and political repression, 27–28
political emergencies. *See* emergency powers
political justice, 18–19. *See also* political trials
political repression: Argentina, 4, 52–59; background to, 38–41; Brazil, 3–4, 20–23, 41–47, 67–68, 70–71; Chile, 4, 23–25, 48–52, 103–4; comparative study of, 9–14; comparisons of, 21; explanations of variation in, 27–32;

judicial repression and, 82; patterns in, 18–27; types of, 3–5, 5, 176. *See also* purges
political rights, deprivation of: Argentina, 57; Brazil, 2, 67
political trials: acquittal rates, 77–79, 79, 81, 81, 82–84, 83, 84, 107, 109, 110–11, 123, 143; actors in, 75; Argentina, 121–27, 133–34; authoritarian regimes and role of, 32–36, 192, 196; Brazil, 64, 75–88, 79, 80, 81, 83, 84, 85, 140–58; characteristics of, 36, 144; charges brought in, 76–77, 84, 84–85, 106, 145–55; Chile, 104–14; chronological variation in, 82; civil society and, 86–88; comparative study of, 13–14; conduct of, 106; contestation of, 86–88, 112–14; crimes of belief, 145–47; defense lawyers in, 140–58; defenses presented at, 141–42; definition of, 213n24; ideological justification of, 74–75; intimidation as purpose of, 19, 32, 33, 77; judges' role in, 144; Nazi Germany, 175–78; Portugal, 181–82; regional variation in, 78–79, 79, 80, 109, 110–11; sentencing in, 78–80, 80, 85, 85, 108, 110, 111–12, 112, 133, 143; Spain, 178–80; time served, 85; United States, 183–84; violent versus nonviolent crime, 77–78. *See also* authoritarian legality; courts; national security legality
Popular Unity (Unidad Popular, UP), 74, 93, 96–99, 107, 115
populism, 40, 55–56, 95, 214n6
Portugal, 174–75, 181–83
positivism, 42
Potash, Robert A., 53, 54
Poulantzas, Nicos, 2
Prats, Carlos, 24
Prestes, Luís Carlos, 145, 150
proceso (process of national reorganization), 135
progressive-regressive cycle, 160, 168
protection rackets, 35, 214n28
Protestant churches, 106
PRT. *See* Revolutionary Workers' Party (Partido Revolucionário dos Trabalhadores, PRT)
Prussianization of Chilean military, 12, 48–49
PT. *See* Workers' Party (Partido dos Trabalhadores, PT)
PTB. *See* Brazilian Labor Party (Partido Trabalhista Brasileiro, PTB)
purges: Argentina, 56, 58, 128, 160, 166, 167, 172; Brazil, 16, 22, 47, 67–70, 89; Nazi Germany, 175, 176, 177. *See also* political repression
PVDE. *See* Police for Political and Social Defense (Policia de Defesa Política e Social, PVDE)

Qaeda, al, 188, 233
Quadros, Jânio, 45, 67
Quiroga, Jorge, 126, 224n24

Radical Party, 165
Radicals, 54
Raimondi, Carlos, 131, 225n46
Ráo, Vicente, 42
Rasul v. Bush (2004), 189
rational choice model of political repression, 28–29
Rawls, John, 19
Rawson Prison, 125
Rehnquist, William, 235n49
Reid, Richard, 188
religious groups, in Argentine opposition, 137. *See also* Catholic Church; Protestant churches
Remmer, Karen, 6
reparations, in Argentina, 166
repression. *See* judicialization of repression; political repression
Rettig Commission, *21*, 169–70
Rettig, Raúl, 169–70
Revista militar (magazine), 130
Revolutionary People's Army (Ejército Revolucionário del Pueblo, ERP), 25
Revolutionary Workers' Party (Partido Revolucionário dos Trabalhadores, PRT), 1
Rocha, Alberto João, 152–54
Rodríguez Espada, Héctor, 130–31
Rodrigues, Nelson, 147
Rome, 193
Romeiro dos Santos, Teodomiro, 86–87, 113–14, 143
Roniger, Luís, 160
rule by law, 194
rule of law, 19, 194, 196; authoritarian legality and, 198–200; Chile and, 94–98; opposed to populism, 40
Rumsfeld, Donald, 185

Sabato, Ernesto, 166
Salazar, Antonio, 174, 181
Sales, Eugenio, 86
Sanchez de Bustamente, Tomas, 128
Sarney, José, 162
Saudi Arabia, 185
Schamis, Hector, 6
Schirmer, Jennifer, 19, 199
Second Institutional Act (Brazil, 1965), 47, 70–71
secret laws, 101
self-amnesty, 158, 166, 170
semana trágica, 53

September 11, 2001 attacks, 183–89
Serbin, Kenneth, 88
Silva, Eduardo, 98
Silveira, Enio, 155
Simas, Mario, 218n22, 226n4
slavery, 41–42
Smart, Jaime, 124
Smulovitz, Catalina, 129
SNI. *See* National Intelligence Service (Serviço Nacional de Inteligência, SNI)
Soares, Airton, 226n4
Sobral Pinto, Heráclito, 86
Socialist Party, in Chile, 23, 41
Sodré Bittencourt, Niomar Moniz, 148
soft-line group, 69
Solari Yrigoyen, Hipólito, 127
Sorbonne group, 69, 71
Soviet Union, 155
Spain, 171, 174, 178–81
Special Courts of Political Responsibilities, 179–80
SS (Schutzstaffel), 175, 178
Stanley, William, 35
states of siege. *See* emergency powers
status groups, 10, 211n24
Stenzel, Clóvis, 86
Stepan, Alfred, 6
STF. *See* Supreme Court: Brazil
Storni, Ernestina, 224n34
structuralist explanations of political repression, 27–28
subversion, crimes of, 149–55
succession, regime breakdown and political, 30, 31
Superior Military Court (Superior Tribunal Militar, STM), 2, 47, 75–78, 87–88, 114, 142–43, 145–46, 148–51, 153–55
Superior War College (Escola Superior de Guerra, ESG), 70
Supreme Court: Argentina, 54, 56, 58, 124, 128, 166–67; Brazil (STF), 2, 47, 66, 70, 75, 76, 87–88; Chile, 95–97, 99–100, 113, 115, 170, 171, 195; Portugal, 182; United States, 188
Supreme Military Command, 66
Sznajder, Mario, 160

TCPs. *See* Plenary Criminal Courts (Tribunais Criminais Plenários, TCPs)
tenentismo, 42, 60, 61
terrorism: Argentina and, 123; Brazil and, 72–73, 86; Nazi Germany and, 176; United States and, 183–89
TFR. *See* Federal Resources Court (Tribunal Federal de Recursos, TFR)

third-wave democracies, 200
Thompson, E. P., 199
torture, 171–72; Argentina, 119, 122, 134, 223n9; Brazil, 1, 47, 72, 75–76, 85, 88, 143, 229n17; Chile, 90; United States, 185
Torture Never Again (Tortura Nunca Mais), 229n17
totalitarianism, political offender treatment under, 33
Touraine, Alain, 2
trade unions. *See* labor movement
transitional justice, 159–72; Argentina, 165–68; Brazil, 161–65; Chile, 168–71; comparisons of, *160*; trials of perpetrators and, 160, 166; truth commissions and, 160, 163, 166, 169–70
treason, 177
trials of perpetrators, 160, 166
Tribe, Laurence, 187
Triple A. *See* Alianza Anticomunista Argentina (Triple A)
trustworthy courts, 190, 192, 198
truth commissions, 160, 163, 166, 169–70
TSN. *See* National Security Tribunal (Tribunal de Segurança Nacional, TSN)

UDN. *See* União Democrático Nacional
União Democrático Nacional (UDN), 147
unions. *See* labor movement
United Nations, 105, 134
United States: and Argentina, 129–30; Brazilian coup role of, 63, 65–66; Brazilian ties to military of, 43–44, 60; Chilean coup role of, 66, 92–93; Cold War role of, in Latin America, 61; consent and complicity of, 18;

judicial-military relations in, 15; Operation Condor and, 24; post-9/11 legality, 183–89
universities, purging of Argentine, 56
unlawful combatants, 184
Uriburu, José Félix, 54
Urrutia Manzano, Enrique, 96, 99
Uruguay, 16, 18, 24, 92
USA PATRIOT Act (United States, 2001), 185

Valadão, Roberto, 159
Valenzuela, Arturo, 48
Vannucchi Leme de Matos, Alexandre, 76, 88, 142
Vargas, Getúlio, 40, 42, 44, 45, 47
Verdugo, Patricia, 103, 171
Vergera, Esteban, 124
VGH. *See* People's Court (Volksgerichtshof, VGH)
Vicaría de la Solidaridad (Vicariate of Solidarity), 106–7, 112–13, 169, 201, 211n26
Vidal, Hernán, 51
Videla, Jorge Rafael, 130, 133, 135
Viegas, José, 165
Vietnam, 147
Viola, Roberto, 88

Wolfe, Alan, 187
Workers' Party (Partido dos Trabalhadores, PT), 161–62
The Working Class (newspaper), 155

"years of lead," 150

Zaverucha, Jorge, 162
Zuckerman, Alan S., 27